Legal Writing

Principles of Juriography

Myra A. Harris

PRENTICE HALL PARALEGAL SERIES

PRENTICE HALL
UPPER SADDLE RIVER, NJ 07458

Library of Congress Cataloging-in-Publication Data

Harris, Myra A.
    Legal writing / Myra A. Harris.
        p.   cm.
    Includes index.
    ISBN 0–13–238627–5
    1. Legal composition.   2. Law—United States—Language.
KF250.H37   1997
808'.06634—dc20
                                                96–5091
                                                CIP

Acquisitions Editor: Elizabeth Sugg
Director of Production and Manufacturing: Bruce Johnson
Managing Editor: Mary Carnis
Editorial/Production Supervision and
    Interior Design: Tally Morgan, WordCrafters Editorial Services, Inc.
Cover Design: Bruce Kenselaar
Manufacturing Buyer: Edward O'Dougherty

© 1997 by Prentice-Hall, Inc.
Upper Saddle River, New Jersey 07458

Printed in the United States of America

10   9   8   7   6   5   4   3   2

ISBN 0-13-238627-5

PRENTICE-HALL INTERNATIONAL (UK) LIMITED, *London*
PRENTICE-HALL OF AUSTRALIA PTY. LIMITED, *Sydney*
PRENTICE-HALL CANADA INC., *Toronto*
PRENTICE-HALL HISPANOAMERICANA, S.A., *Mexico*
PRENTICE-HALL OF INDIA PRIVATE LIMITED, *New Delhi*
PRENTICE-HALL OF JAPAN, INC., *Tokyo*
PRENTICE-HALL OF SOUTHEAST ASIA PTE. LTD., *Singapore*
EDITORIA PRENTICE-HALL DO BRASIL., LTDA., *Rio de Janeiro*

Contents

Preface

Legal Writing: Principles of Juriography is designed to present the fundamentals of the subject to the beginning paralegal or law student. The text emphasizes the rules of writing and provides opportunities for students to learn and practice these rules. It includes illustrations of various legal documents, so that students have a model for understanding the various principles. Legal writing must always reflect the particular problem that is addressed. As with all communication, the writing must be clear and easy to understand. *Legal Writing* stresses the need for clarity.

Thanks go to my husband, Bill, who helped with this production. (In many ways, it truly *seemed* like a production at the time!) I also thank my students at the American Institute, as well as Rodney Elkins, Betty Leavitt, Cindie Edlow, Alicia Bray, and Connie Niebling, who graciously allowed me to use their writings as model papers.

ACKNOWLEDGMENTS

The author wishes to express her gratitude to the editors at Prentice Hall and WordCrafters for their assistance in producing this book.

Copyrighted materials from the West Publishing Company are reprinted with their permission. Westlaw screens are published by permission of the West Publishing Company. Connie Niebling, Alicia Bray, Cindie Edlow, Betty Leavitt, and Rod Elkins all graciously allowed me to reprint their papers as samples.

1 *Introduction*

Like all writing, legal writing is a simple form of communication. When you engage in legal writing, you are explaining or informing others of your arguments, beliefs, claims, or conclusions in a manner they can readily understand. Unfortunately, for many, legal writing is more than an exercise in communication: Over the years, it has become a way to obfuscate information and confuse the reader. This is not your goal. Instead, your aim should be to tell others, clearly and effectively, what you know or believe is the law.

We do many kinds of legal writing. Mostly, our writing is either in an analytical or informative style, or in a persuasive manner. Our legal writing style will depend on whom our intended audience is. We write differently if we want to convince a judge of the rightness or believability of our claim than we do if we merely wish to inform our supervisors of the facts about or authority for a position we are considering advocating. We also write differently when we wish to emphasize our position than we do when we wish to detract from the claims of our adversaries. No matter which style we choose, however, we should be aware that we can influence the outcome by our choice of words.

Words are our most essential tools. In order to write effectively, we must become friends with the nouns and verbs that form the English language. We should also have more than a passing acquaintance with two major tools of writing: the dictionary and the thesaurus. These books are indispensable. Since we work with words all the time, we need to be familiar and comfortable with both publications. We will discuss how to use the dictionary and the thesaurus in the following pages. We also need to feel comfortable using legal research books and form books, since these will provide authority and guidance for our writing.

In this book, we will learn how to write letters, draft legal documents, brief cases, and write simple legal memoranda. However, at all times we must be aware that no matter what or how we write, we must follow simple rules of English composition. We will discuss some of these basic rules, as well as remind ourselves of the importance of correct grammar. Here, of course, I can almost feel a collective shudder from readers as we all recall the horrendous days of early grammar lessons. You may surprise yourself and learn that grammar is not, and does not have to be, boring. Boring English lessons result from boring sentences. Use interesting illustrations, and the boredom will lessen if not evaporate.

Finally, learn to play with language. English is a most interesting language. Modern-day English has its roots in Anglo-Saxon, Latin, and French. Each of these languages contributed to the richness of present-day English, so that you now have a range of choices when you are seeking words to express your thoughts. You should recognize, however, that this variety allows you to emphasize or lessen the impact of your ideas by your choice of words. Words that come from Anglo-Saxon roots are direct and emphatic. Words that originated with the French language are not usually as strong. Therefore, when you wish to emphasize a point, choose Anglo-Saxon words to describe the situation. When you wish to lessen the impact of a term, you should select a word derived from French.

Finally, remember that language is, and has always been, fun. When you were young, you first realized how much fun you could have with language when you played with puns and riddles. Language can still be fun. Indeed, some of our greatest literature is based on word games. *The Odyssey*, by Homer, illustrates this point. Odysseus, the hero of the tale, is trapped in a cave with Polyphemus, a one-eyed giant possessed of 20/20 vision. Rather than telling Polyphemus who he really was, Odysseus gave his name as *Outis*, which is Greek for "No Man." When Odysseus then attacked Polyphemus in order to escape from the cave, the giant called to his fellow monsters for help, crying "*Outis* (No Man) is killing me." His colleagues took him literally and made no attempt to aid Polyphemous, whom Odysseus subsequently slew. Polyphemus may have been the first victim of a literary pun. So, as you begin your career as a legal writer, remember that language is fun.

REVIEW QUESTIONS

1. List two styles of legal writing.
2. Differentiate between analytical and persuasive writing.
3. List two major tools of legal writing.
4. How can you lessen the boredom that often accompanies grammar lessons?
5. Which English roots carry the most impact?
6. What languages contribute to modern-day English?
7. Who may have been the first victim of a literary pun?

2 *English Grammar*

2.1
INTRODUCTION

English is a varied, wonderful, and expressive language. Using English properly allows the writer a great deal of latitude in expressing his or her thoughts. Unfortunately, most legal writers face each writing task with trepidation. Writing is, and should be, fun. It is your chance to express your views or summarize the law that you have read. Once you realize that English grammar is interesting and your choice of words a creative exercise, you should begin to enjoy your writing efforts.

The first problem facing a writer is fear. Hopefully, the lessons in this chapter will dispel some of the fear of English grammar that you may face as you write. Remember, all writing is only a matter of sentences, and we all write sentences one at a time. Therefore, you will never have to worry about more than one sentence at any time. Rather than thinking of each project as a myriad of complex points, think of your writing project as an organized collection of individual sentences. Remember also that every sentence is no more than an organized collection of words. In sum, then, you are only working with an organized collection of a few words at any one time. These small groups of words will ultimately form individual sentences. Thus, you will need to deal with grammar problems for only one sentence at a time.

The sentence is the building block of all writing. Each sentence is made of words. However, not all words are created equal. Different words in each sentence serve a distinct purpose. Some words form the subject of the sentence, while others form the predicate. To have a complete sentence, you must have both a subject and a predicate. Simply put, a subject is what the sentence is talking about. The predicate is the part of the sentence that says something about the subject. Sometimes we have a simple subject—one subject—in the sentence. At other times, we have a compound subject. When we have a compound subject, the sentence is about more than one thing. Compound subjects are joined by the words "and," "or," or "nor." Compound subjects share the same verb or are doing the same thing. Just as we have compound subjects, we also have compound predicates. These predicates, too, are joined by "and" or "or." In that case, all parts of the predicate describe the subject of the sentence.

This is a sentence with a simple subject:

> The complaint was poorly written.

The word "complaint" is the subject of the sentence.

This is a sentence with a compound subject:

> Neither the complaint nor the answer was filed in a timely fashion.

The words "complaint" and "answer" form the compound subject of the sentence.

This is a sentence with a simple predicate.

> The defendant answered the interrogatory.

The words "answered the interrogatory" form the simple predicate.

This is a sentence with a compound predicate:

> The court reversed and remanded the decision.

The words "reversed and remanded" belong to the same subject, court.

Now that you have seen the essential parts of a sentence, we can talk about the different grammatical forms that each word in the sentence may take. There are eight different types of words. The same word can be categorized more than one way because we categorize words according to the way they are used in a sentence. The eight types of words are *nouns, pronouns, verbs, adjectives, adverbs, prepositions, conjunctions,* and *interjections*.

2.2
NOUNS

A *noun* is a person, place, or thing, or an abstract idea or concept. Examples of persons are ballerinas, addicts, and policemen. Places can be parks, cities, and Paris. Things are marijuana, dolls, shampoo, and candy. Silence, death, pride, and fairness are abstractions. A compound noun is formed by more than one word. "Reasonable man" is an example of a compound noun.

We also categorize nouns as common or proper. A common noun refers to a member of a large class of objects, and not to one specific thing. "Case" is a common noun, since the specific case is not identified. In contrast, we have proper nouns, which name a specific person, place, or thing. *Roe v. Wade* is a proper noun, since it identifies a particular case. We also have a special name for common nouns that include a group of items, persons, or things. For example, "harem" would be a collective noun, since a harem consists of more than one individual. It is not a proper noun, because it does not identify any particular harem by name.

Nouns are abstract or concrete. An abstract noun refers to an idea or quality such as trouble, shame, ethics, or time. A concrete noun is readily identified by one of our five senses and includes words like blood, dancer, piano, and ticket.

Nouns and pronouns (see next section) can be used as the subject of a sentence, as the object in a sentence, or as the object of a preposition. The subject of a sentence is what is being talked about. It tells who or what did the action. It usually comes before the verb, but this is not a hard-and-fast rule. Sometimes the verb may come first.

Nouns can also be used as objects in a sentence. An object receives the action. If a noun is used as a direct object, you will identify the term as the answer to the question "What?" or "Whom?" First, identify the subject and verb. Then ask yourself the question "What?" or "Whom?" The noun or nouns that answer the question will be the direct objects of your sentence. If the noun in the sentence is used as an indirect object, you will be able to identify it as the word answering the question "To whom?" "For whom?" "To what?" or "For what?" Like nouns, pronouns can function as either direct or indirect objects.

2.3
PRONOUNS

A *pronoun* takes the place of a noun that has already been mentioned. The words "him," "her," "it," "them," "his," "hers," "its," and "theirs" are called personal pronouns. Pronouns are described by person and by case. There are three persons: first, second, and third. The first person is "I" and "we." The second person is "you." The third person is "he," "she," "it," and "they." The term "case" refers to whether the pronoun replaces the person speaking (nominative case), the person being spoken to (objective case), or the person being spoke of (possessive case). The personal pronouns just listed are in the nominative case. In the objective case, we would have "me" and "us" for the first person, "you" for the second person (both singular and plural), and "him," "her," "it," and "them" for the third person. The same terms in the possessive case are "my," "mine," "our," and "ours" for the first person, "your" and "yours" for the second person, and "his," "her," "hers," "its," "their," and "theirs" for the third person.

In addition to the personal pronouns, we have indefinite pronouns, interrogative pronouns, and relative pronouns. Indefinite pronouns include words such as "one," "someone," "anyone," "everyone," "no one," "nobody," "several," "each," "all," "neither," "either," "both," "many," "few," "any," and "some," which do not refer to particular people. Instead, they could refer to anyone. Interrogative pronouns, such as "who," "whom," "which," "what," and "whose," pose questions. The most commonly used relative pronouns are "who," "whose," "what," "which," and "that."

Other pronouns include demonstrative pronouns such as "this," "that," "these," and "those" and reciprocal pronouns such as "each other" or "one another." Reciprocal pronouns involve actions between two individuals. Reflexive pronouns include words that refer to the self, such as "myself," "yourself," "himself," "herself," and "itself" in the singular and "ourselves," "yourselves," and "themselves" in the plural.

2.4
ADJECTIVES

An *adjective* describes or limits a noun. The adjective may be descriptive, stating what kind of person, place, idea, or thing the noun really is. For example, we may find interesting ideas, archaic references, or difficult concepts. Other adjectives called possessive adjectives, interrogative adjectives, articles, demonstrative adjectives, and numerical adjectives give some idea of how much is discussed or describe the identity of something. Possessive adjectives are words such as "his," "her," "my," "your," "their," and "our." Interrogative adjectives are "which," "whose," and "what." Articles are "a," "an," and "the," and demonstrative adjectives are "this," "that," "these," and "those." Finally, either cardinal or ordinal numbers can be numerical adjectives. A cardinal number is the number one, two, three, etc. An ordinal number is first, second, or third. Adjectives most commonly come before nouns. However, they may follow the noun if they are linked to it with a verb such as a form of "to be" or the word "seems."

Adjectives come in three forms: positive, comparative, and superlative. The positive form simply modifies the noun. The comparative form compares an attribute of two things or actions, while the superlative compares three or more items.

Examples:

This is a good case.
This is the better of the two cases.
This is the best case.

2.5
VERBS

Verbs are the most important words in the English language. They give action and meaning to sentences. In fact, without verbs, our sentences would be no more than fragments of sentences. They would be hopelessly incomplete. Verbs are powerful words. They assert something about the subject of a sentence. Every sentence must have a subject as a companion to its verb. Even in one-word commands, such as "Go!" there is a subject, understood to be "you."

A verb may describe a state of being or an action. Most commonly, the verb "to be" is used to describe a state of being. We see this when a writer uses the word "is," "am," or "are." Other verbs are action words. In law, we often see the verb "hold" or "held" used to describe a ruling that a court has made. Sometimes our verbs are accompanied by other, auxiliary or helping, verbs. The most common helping verb is "have," which may take many forms. You will find sentences using "had been," "have been," "had," "have," and "will have" together with other verbs. For example, you may write (or read) that the court's jurisdiction had been invoked or that a particular rule should have been construed in accordance with a specific case.

We also find alternative uses for verbs. By changing the structure of a verb, we can turn it into another grammatical form. For example, by using the "ing" form of a verb, we can create a gerund, which functions like a noun:

Losing a case is difficult.

In this example, "losing" is used as the subject of the sentence. Gerunds may also be the objects of prepositions. If so, they will be linked to prepositions such as "in," "by," or "through," as, for example, in the sentence

> In holding that the earlier case should be overruled, the court discussed the public policy considerations of a finding of cruel and unusual punishment.

In this sentence, the gerund "holding" is the object of the preposition "in." "The court" is the subject of the sentence.

Whenever you work with verbs, you must consider their tense. Is the action occurring in the present, or did it occur in the past, or will it occur in the future? You must select the tense in which you wish to write. And remember to remain in your chosen tense. You usually indicate the past tense by using the "ed" form of the verb. To indicate the future tense, we use the helping verb form "will" together with the verb. Other tenses in addition to the present, past, and future are the present perfect, the past perfect, and the future perfect. The present perfect tense requires a helping verb. An example would be "have" or "has," together with the past tense of the verb:

> The court has held that the Fifth Amendment does not apply.

The past perfect tense uses the past tense of the main verb coupled with the past tense of the helping verb—in other words, the helping verb "had" plus the past tense of the main verb. An example would be

> The court had held that the Fifth Amendment applied, but later reviewed this decision.

Finally, the future perfect tense uses the "will have" form of the helping verb together with the past tense of the verb:

> The court will have ruled on the motion before the trial is set.

Remember, once you choose your tense, you should try to remain with it for at least several sentences. If you jump tenses, you will needlessly confuse your writing.

You must also ensure that your verb matches your subject. A plural subject requires a plural verb, whereas a singular subject needs a singular verb form. Count the number of the nouns, pronouns, and gerunds that form the subject of your sentence. Then match that number with the verb form.

In selecting verbs, you must also pay attention to the voice of the sentence. We have two voices: active and passive. The active voice is chosen when the subject of the sentence does the action. The passive voice is used when the object of the sentence does the action.

Examples:

> The EEOC published a final rule implementing the ADA. (Active)
> A final rule implementing the ADA was published by the EEOC. (Passive)

Note that the passive sentence has a helping verb: "was." The use of a form of the verb "to be" is one of the identifying features of a passive sentence. So is the use of the object of the sentence to do the action. Finally, we often find indefinite subjects as identifying hallmarks of the passive sentence. An example of an indefinite subject in a passive sentence is the well-known warning sign, "Trespassers will be prosecuted."

Legal writers generally choose the active voice because it is easier to use, is more understandable, and allows for stronger writing. Use the passive voice when you wish to divert attention away from your subject.

2.6
ADVERBS

Adverbs modify verbs, adjectives, and other adverbs. Frequently, adverbs end with the suffix "ly." Examples of these types of adverbs are "diligently," "speedily," and "rapidly." Not all adverbs are of this form, however; other adverbs are "very," "rather," "quite," "most," and "here." Adverbs tell how, where, when, or to what extent an action is done or a state of being exists. They may tell the time of an action, the manner in which the action was done, the place where the action occurred, or the degree of amount of the action.

2.7
PREPOSITIONS

Prepositions are used to relate words in a sentence. They are often part of a grammatical structure called a prepositional phrase. A prepositional phrase is made of a preposition, a noun or pronoun, and, occasionally, some modifiers of the noun or pronoun. Prepositions tell you where or how something may be accomplished. They include the words "on," "with," "by," "to," "from," "through," "into," and "of." Other prepositions you might use are "above," "across," "along," "after," "among," "around," "at," "before," "behind," "below," "beside," "besides," "between," "beyond," "but," "down," "during," "for," "in," "inside," "near," "off," "outside," "over," "past," "since," "till," "toward," "towards," "under," "until," "upon," "within," and "without."

Some prepositions are made of two or more words. These include "apart from," "as for," "as well as," "aside from," "because of," "by means of," "in front of," "in place of," "in spite of," "together with," "with regard to," and "instead of." Again, these are not the only prepositions, just some of the more common ones. You should feel free to use less common prepositions wherever appropriate.

2.8
CONJUNCTIONS

Words that join different ideas, words, phrases, or clauses are called conjunctions. The most common conjunctions are "and," "or," "if," "but," "neither," "nor," "for," "whereas," and "yet." Other conjunctions are "also," "besides," "consequently," "afterwards," "earlier," "furthermore," "however," "moreover," "nevertheless," "still," "since," "then," "thus," "therefore," "otherwise," "later," "accordingly," and "hence." Still other conjunctions are "until," "because," "before," "after," "although," "as if," "that," "so that," "unless," "while," "when," "where," and "even though."

2.9
INTERJECTIONS

The interjection has little meaning, but is used to express emotion. There is little occasion to use interjections in legal writing. They are, however, very common in spoken English and express immediate and powerful feelings. Words like "Wow!" "Oh!" "Dear Me!" or even an outdated exclamation such as "Great balls of fire!" are categorized as interjections.

2.10
BUILDING THOUGHTS

The parts of speech are like building blocks because you can combine them in many different ways to express your thoughts. Each time you combine words, you construct a different thought. Your skill in combining words determines how well you write. Practice is important. Even the few natural writers must practice if they wish to achieve their potential. In the sections that follow, we will look at some rules to help you express your thoughts.

Always begin with a thought. This is the first and most necessary step. Without a thought, you have nothing to write. So, think first. Then you will need to determine how best to state your idea clearly. You should consider beginning your writing with your subject. Your subject is the center of your writing universe. Let it shine.

Next, show the relationship between the subject and the rest of the sentence. You do this by choosing your verbs and making sure that the verbs agree with the subject. Agreement is a positive force. As in life, where agreement is preferred over conflict, agreement between the subject and verb in a sentence is always the correct and therefore better way to write.

Since the verb must always agree with the subject, a plural subject requires a plural verb form, while a singular subject must be paired with a singular verb. This is a simple rule, but it can be difficult to apply when you are faced with internal distractions. In some sentences it may be hard to determine just what that number of the subject is. Sometimes words that intervene between the subject and verb separate the verb from what should be its closely aligned subject. In checking for agreement, you should ignore these intervening words. They will only distract you from your task. Focus on just the subject and verb. Parenthetical expressions, which are enclosed by a pair of commas, are one such distraction.

Look at the last sentence in the preceding paragraph. The phrase "which are enclosed by a pair of commas" is an example of a parenthetical expression separating the subject from the verb. The subject of the sentence is "parenthetical expressions," and the verb is the word "are." Note that the subject is plural. Therefore, we must use a plural verb form. Parenthetical expressions are introduced by words such as "with," "like," "together with," "as well as," "including," "no less than," "in addition to," and "which."

When you use two or more subjects in a sentence and join the two subjects with the word "and," you have a plural subject, which requires a plural verb. The only exception is when the two subjects describe the same thing or when the subject is preceded by the term "each" or "every." When two terms describe the same thing, you may use a singular verb, as in the sentence

My best case and binding authority is. . . .

Here, the term "best case" and the term "binding authority" refer to the same document, so the verb is singular. You would fill in the name of the case. Similarly, whenever your subject includes the term "each" or the term "every," you also use a singular verb, since the words "each" and "every" are themselves singular.

You also use singular verb forms when your sentence has two independent subjects joined by the word "or," as in

Statute A or Statute B results in a criminal penalty.

You use a singular verb here because the subjects are alternatives. That is, the sentence could be read as

Statute A results in a criminal penalty, or Statute B results in a criminal penalty.

However, when the subjects are joined by "either . . . or," "neither . . . nor," "not only," "but not," or "but also," the verb must agree with the subject that is nearest to it.

Example:

Not only the statute, but the regulations, were construed.

Some words appear to be plural, but are really singular. These words, including the terms "physics," "mathematics," "ethics," "measles," "politics," "statistics," and "molasses," need singular verbs, as in the sentence

Legal ethics is difficult to understand.

There are exceptions to this rule. For example, words such as "scissors" and "trousers" use plural verbs even though they refer to only one item.

Still other exceptions exist. Titles, even when in the plural, use singular verbs. Collective words, referring to a group, use a singular or a plural verb. The key question is whether the collective noun is thought of as a unit itself or whether it is held to refer to each individual separately. Thus, the term "majority" uses a singular verb when the members of a majority are thought of as a unit. Note that the term "it" is always singular. Whenever "it" is the subject of a sentence, be prepared to use the singular verb form. Just as there is only one "Cousin It" in the Addams Family, "it" is a singular subject.

There are other special rules of agreement. Sums of money and measurements are always singular. Therefore, we say that 5 thousand dollars *is* due and owing. Similarly, we refer to a term of years in the singular. Thus, in sentencing a criminal defendant to a term of years in the state penal institution, a judge might say that 20 years *is* the maximum sentence for the crime.

2.11
PHRASES

Writing is more than words: It is a connected series of thoughts. To help express our thoughts in a more detailed manner, we use phrases. Note that the words "in a more detailed manner" in this last sentence are a phrase. There are several different types of phrases: prepositional phrases, infinitive phrases, participial phrases, gerund phrases, verb phrases, and absolute phrases.

A prepositional phrase may be used as a noun, an adjective, or an adverb. It is made of a preposition, an object of the preposition, and modifiers. Prepositional phrases are introduced by prepositions. Look for words such as "with," "in," "by," "over," "through," "beyond," and "beneath," as well as other prepositions. These are the hallmarks of a prepositional phrase.

An infinitive phrase is created when you combine an infinitive with an object. Like a prepositional phrase, an infinitive phrase may be used as an adjective, adverb, or noun and may be used as the subject or object in a sentence. Recall that an infinitive is a verb preceded by the word "to." "To dance," "to threaten," and "to execute" are all infinitives. When followed by an object, an infinitive forms an infinitive phrase, as in

He wanted to escape from jail.

In this sentence, the words "to escape from jail" form an infinitive phrase that is used as a direct object.

Participial phrases are used as adjectives. They always include either present or past participles. Present participles are verbs ending with "ing." Past participles are verbs ending with "d," "ed," "n," "en," or "t." Similar in format to participial phrases are gerund phrases. Like present participles, the words end with "ing." However, gerund phrases are used only as nouns, while participial phrases are used exclusively as adjectives.

Verb phrases never contain subjects. These phrases allow you to combine verbs in a sentence in a more interesting fashion, as, for example, in

His attorney has been invited to witness the execution.

An absolute phrase combines a noun or pronoun with a participle. Absolute phrases exist independently from the rest of the sentence.

Example:

The evidence having been admitted, he confessed.

In this example, the noun, "the evidence," is coupled with the present participle, "having."

2.12
CLAUSES

Like prepositions, clauses are groups of words. In each clause, you will find a subject as well as a predicate. Some clauses are independent, others are dependent. An independent clause has its own meaning; it does not rely on any other grammatical form to create meaning or understanding. An independent clause could be a separate short sentence. However, when combined with other word groups as part of a longer sentence, we call it an independent clause. Two or more independent clauses may be combined to make longer and more interesting sentences.

Example:

He offered her a contract, and he refused to accept any rejection.

In this sentence, each clause can stand on its own. "He offered her a contract" is a complete sentence. "He refused to accept any rejection" is also a complete thought. When the two are combined, we have a sentence with two independent clauses.

In contrast to the independent clause is the dependent clause. A dependent clause must always lean on another part of the sentence. It can never form a complete sentence on its own. Each dependent clause has its own subject and verb. However, a dependent clause relies on the remainder of the sentence to produce a complete thought. Dependent clauses are introduced by conjunctions, such as "if," "who," "before," "which," "that," "since," "where," "as if," and "because." When these introductory words are omitted, the result is often an independent clause. With the conjunctions, the clause is forever dependent.

Dependent clauses can be classified in a variety of ways. An adjective clause modifies a noun or pronoun and is often introduced with the word "who." The clause tells us more about the noun or pronoun it modifies. Sometimes the information it contains is essential to the meaning of the sentence. At other times the information, while interesting, is not essential to the meaning of the sentence. When you absolutely need the information to identify the noun and perhaps tell which noun is under discussion, you use a restrictive adjective clause. If the information is not needed to identify the noun and merely provides additional interesting information, the clause is a non-restrictive adjective clause.

Example:

> The lab assistant who actually performed the DNA test is present in court.

The words "who actually performed the DNA test" constitute a restrictive adjective clause, since they are integral to identifying the particular lab assistant who is in the courtroom.

Example:

> The lab assistant, who studies law, is present in the courtroom.

The words "who studies law" constitute a nonrestrictive adjective clause, since the fact that the lab assistant studies law is merely incidental to the meaning of the sentence. You can also tell the type of clause by whether it is set off by commas in the sentence. A restrictive adjective clause is incorporated into the sentence without any special punctuation marks separating the clause from the remainder of the sentence. A nonrestrictive adjective clause is offset from the rest of the sentence by a pair of commas. If you omit the commas and the words inside of them, you will still convey the essential meaning of the sentence.

A second major type of dependent clause is the adverb clause. An adverb clause is similar to an adverb and can identify a time or a place, or express a manner, in which an action occurs. It can also indicate purpose. Adverb clauses identifying a time are introduced with the words "after," "until," "when," or "before," while those identifying a place follow "where" or "wherever." Adverb clauses expressing a manner begin with "as" or "as if." Adverb clauses indicating a purpose are introduced by "because" or "since." Other adverbial clauses are used to show a comparison or a concession. Introductory words for these clauses are "if," "unless," "provided that," "in order that," "so," "so that," and "as."

Sentences are also classified by the number and kind of clauses they have. A simple sentence has a single independent clause. A compound sentence has two or more independent clauses. A complex sentence has at least one independent clause and one or more dependent clauses. Finally, a compound-complex sentence is a combination of a complex sentence and a compound sentence. It has at least two independent clauses, plus one or more dependent clauses.

2.13
GRAMMATICAL CAUTIONS

Perhaps the most common mistake writers make is using less than a complete sentence. An incomplete sentence, or sentence fragment, masquerades as a sentence because it ends with a period or question mark. In reality, however, it is nothing more than a dependent clause or phrase. Be wary: Fragments are the bane of all writers. Make sure that each sentence is complete before you end it.

A second writing sin is often committed when you use a comma splice instead of a period or semicolon to link two independent clauses. This is permitted only when the clauses are concise. Generally, you should use a period or semicolon when you have two or more independent clauses. Be especially careful when using the words "also," "afterwards," "hence," "accordingly," "besides," "consequently," "earlier," "however," "later," "nevertheless," "moreover," "otherwise," "therefore," "then," "thus," and "still." These words usually introduce independent clauses. Avoid commas immediately before them, and you will avoid the comma splice.

2.14
AT LAST, THE SENTENCE

The ultimate goal of writing is to construct the perfect sentence. In legal writing, perfect sentences express your ideas cogently. Short active sentences are preferred because they create power. Be careful, however, to avoid a choppy or simple-minded style when using a simple sentence. Vary the structure of your sentences. Remember, active sentences can be difficult to write. Even though their grammar is simple, short active sentences require that you fully understand what it is you are writing.

If and when you use the passive voice, use it because you have determined that it is appropriate. Do not use it out of habit. The passive voice is most often used when you have an indeterminate subject or you wish to deflect attention away from a concept. Use the active voice to emphasize your strong points. Write passively when you wish to de-emphasize an idea.

Strive for euphony in your writing. Euphony gives a rhythm to your writing. Rhythmic writing sings a song of its own. It is easy to read and understand. The rhythm of each sentence carries the reader along so that he or she is barely conscious of the sentence. Add variation to your writing by using synonyms, antonyms, and, occasionally, a metaphor. Create word pictures so that your readers will "see" your points and arguments. You can most effectively persuade your audience by selecting the appropriate words and coupling them with a varied grammatical structure. Whatever you do, remember that a well-written document will move your eyes along. You will easily go from the beginning to the end of the document. If your writing does not flow, and your eye movement stops partway along what you have written, look carefully at what you have written and see if you should change it.

Finally, you should consider the following admonitions: Avoid colloquialisms; they can make your writing trite. Never use a double negative. Your limit is one negative word per sentence or idea. A second or double negative does not emphasize the negativity. Indeed, it is not negative at all; instead, it creates the opposite effect, and the sentence is actually a positive statement. Words like "hardly," "barely," and "scarcely" are negative. They should never be used with "not."

Do not use the phrase "whether or not." The correct form is to use "whether" by itself, since the "or not" meaning is implied by using the term "whether."

Couple your adverbs with the verbs they modify. Similarly, locate clauses and phrases near the words they modify.

Keep your tenses consistent. If you are writing in the past tense, all of your sentences should be in the past tense. If you are using the present tense, use it throughout. Readers find it disquieting when they have to switch from the past to the present to the future in a single sentence or paragraph. Similarly, make sure that your subject remains in the singular or in the plural (but not both) as you write about it. If you begin with a plural subject, you should use plural pronouns. If you write about a single subject, use singular pronouns. Lastly, do not shift voices in the same sentence. If you begin a sentence in the active voice, remain in that voice. If you choose to write a sentence in the passive voice, continue in that voice for the entire sentence.

2.15
WORD USAGE

Good legal writing should not sound like it was written by lawyers. Plain English is most effective. You will not be paid by the word. Avoid verbosity.

Select your words carefully. English is a rich language, and similar words often have different connotations. Be sure that you are familiar with the fine shades of meaning for the words you choose. For example, "child-like" has a positive meaning, whereas "childish" is negative. Similarly, "trip" or "travel" is more serious than "junket." A house is not always a home. "House" connotes a physical structure, while the word "home" makes a word picture that may include the family around the fireplace with popcorn popping. Either word may be appropriate. You will need to select the word that fits the particular situation. Your thesaurus and dictionary can be invaluable tools in helping you to locate the precise word. Use them.

2.16
PROBLEM WORDS

Words are your tools. As with other tools, you need to select the correct one for the job. The following list gives some words that create problems for legal writers because they are often misused:[1]

1. *Alternative.* Use this word only when there are two choices. If there are more than two, use "choice" or "option."

2. *Case.* This is a specialized term that refers to a judicial opinion or to a litigation problem. Do not use the term in its more generalized English meaning, e.g., "in many cases," "in any case," "that is not the case," or "in the case of both men and women." Instead, use the following locutions: "often" or "frequently," "from any point of view," "that is not so," and "both men and women."

3. *Disinterested.* "Disinterested" means "impartial." Do not confuse the term with "uninterested." Judges should be disinterested, but, hopefully, never uninterested.

4. *Due to.* This term is overused in legal writing. Substitute "by" or "as a result of."

5. *Fact.* A fact is something that has happened or has been done. It is not an opinion, theory, question, or truth. Facts are not abstract and are demonstrated by some form of evidence. A fact, in law, is an actual occurrence. Therefore, you should avoid the following phrases: "the fact to be determined is," "with the exception of the fact that," "in view of the fact that," and "notwithstanding the fact that." Substitute "since," "although," possessives, or other phrases. Also, never say "The facts are inaccurate"; facts can never be inaccurate.

6. *Finding* v. *holding.* A finding is a determination of a fact. A holding is the court's determination of a point of law.

---

[1]This list is by no means complete; other words can be as much of a problem. For this reason, you must always look carefully at the words you use. Synonyms or substitute words must also be carefully selected. Although words may be synonymous, they sometimes become, through long use or use in specialized fields, quite different in meaning. Always be alert to exceptions to "rules," since little in English is set in concrete.

7. *Literally* v. *figuratively.* "Literally" indicates that the writer means exactly what he or she has written. "Figuratively" illustrates an emotion or an "as if" condition. If you write that someone literally died of embarrassment, the reader would be justified in searching for a corpse.

8. *Rule* or *ruling.* A rule or ruling is the court's direction. A judge rules on points of evidence or on motions.

9. *Said.* "Said" means "mentioned before" and is often synonymous with "this," as in "the said document." "Said" is one of the most overused words in legal writing. It makes the writing stilted. The term was often used in the 19th century. It is an anachronism in modern legal writing.

10. *Shall.* "Shall" is mandatory language and means that the act it refers to is required. "May" indicates that something is permissible.

11. *State.* "To state" means to express something clearly or fully. "Say" is synonymous with "state" and may be a good substitute for it.

12. *To wit.* This is an example of archaic legal jargon. Replace the term with "namely," or omit it altogether.

13. *While.* "While" means "during the time that an action occurred." It does not mean "although."

Avoid using archaic legal jargon. Words that "sound as if they came from a lawyer" are jargon. You may think that words such as "moreover," "insofar as," "hereinafter," "aforementioned," "therein," "same," and "thereto" are legal terms. They are not. These words were often used during the first half of this century and are a carryover from writing styles popular in other centuries. They have no place in modern legal writing. Remember that your goal is understanding: If your readers do not understand what you are writing, you communicate nothing. Omit anything that detracts from this understanding.

REVIEW QUESTIONS AND EXERCISES

Review Questions

1. What is the first problem facing a writer?

2. When writing, how much must you write at one time?

3. What is the building block of all writing?

4. What two basic parts constitute a sentence?
5. What is the subject of the sentence?
6. What is the predicate?
7. How do you join compound subjects in a sentence?
8. What do compound subjects share?
9. List the eight types of words.
10. What is a noun?
11. What is a compound noun?
12. What is the difference between a common noun and a proper noun?
13. What is a collective noun?
14. What is a concrete noun?
15. What is an abstract noun?
16. How can you determine the direct object in a sentence?
17. How can you determine the indirect object in a sentence?
18. What is a pronoun?
19. List the personal pronouns.
20. List the three cases.
21. Distinguish between the nominative case, the objective case, and the possessive case.
22. List the words for the first person in the possessive case.
23. List the words for the third person in the objective case.
24. What is an indefinite pronoun?
25. What are the relative pronouns?
26. What are the interrogative pronouns?
27. List other kinds of pronouns.
28. What is an adjective?
29. What is an article?
30. What purpose do adjectives serve?
31. What is the difference between a cardinal and an ordinal number?
32. Where are adjectives usually placed?
33. What is the difference between the positive, the comparative, and the superlative forms of adjectives?
34. What are the most important words in the English language?
35. What is the most common helping verb?

36. What is the verb "to be"?
37. What is a gerund?
38. Why should you select a tense and keep writing in that tense?
39. How do you write the present perfect or past perfect tense of a verb?
40. Must your verbs match your subject?
41. Which voice is stronger and is the voice of choice for legal writers?
42. What is an adverb?
43. How are prepositions used?
44. What is a conjunction?
45. What is an interjection?
46. What is a parenthetical expression?
47. How do you select the verb form to use when your subject is joined by the phrase "either . . . or"?
48. List three exceptions to the normal rules of agreement.
49. List three types of phrases.
50. What is an infinitive?
51. What is an independent clause?
52. How does an independent clause differ from a dependent clause?
53. List four words that can be used to introduce a dependent clause.
54. How does a restrictive adjective clause differ from a nonrestrictive adjective clause?
55. List four words that introduce an adverb clause.
56. What is the most common mistake in writing?
57. When should you use the passive voice?
58. What is euphony?
59. How can you add variety to your writing?
60. Should your writing sound "legal"?
61. What is the difference between the terms "uninterested" and "disinterested"?
62. What is a fact?
63. Differentiate between the term "holding" and the term "finding."
64. What is the meaning of "figuratively"?
65. When should you use the term "said"?
66. What does the term "said" mean in legal writing?

67. List five "lawyerisms" that you should avoid.

68. What is the meaning of "shall" when used in legal writing?

Exercises

1. Read *In re Rosenkrans*, 84 N.J. Eq. 232, 94 A. 42 (1915). See Appendix A. Rewrite the case using short active sentences.

2. Review the story of Little Red Riding Hood. Assuming that you represent the wolf, write one sentence that is a statement of your position.

3. Assume that you represent the hunter. Write one sentence that is a statement of your position.

4. List three fairy tales. Write the story of each in no more than five paragraphs, using the active voice. Next, rewrite the story, using the passive voice. Which version do you prefer?

5. Rewrite the following paragraph, avoiding the sins of writing discussed in this chapter:

It is a plain fact that defendant was deprived of his Constitutional right when the officer investigating the narcotics charges, hereinafter referred to as police officer, failed to advice him or warn him of the consequences of admitting his guilt. This fact, standing alone, compels the conclusion that there was a deprivation of defendant's Constitutional rights and resulted in defendant's agreement to talk with same before mentioned officer. Such conversation was detrimental to defendant's rights.

6. Rewrite the following sentences. The sentences all refer to a portly Vietnamese potbellied pig, Aunt Rupert, who was removed from her home because of her weight problem. Her owner, Ms. Feedem, would like the authorities to return Aunt Rupert.

a. The question addressed here is whether our client was in violation of the law.

b. The fact that our clients "pet pig" was overweight and in no apparent danger.

c. Even so, they should have taken the proper procedure to legally remove animal from premises the issues or point we can pursue is the fact that the animal was removed illegally and therefore violated our client's "Constitutional Rights" which would supercede the opponents (Animal control) right to remove animal even if they had proper authority (not the right) to take animal.

d. A person must be aware of the fact that they are being cruel.

e. It is a government ran protection for animals in cruel or abusive homes.

f. Unnecessarily fails to provide proper food, drink, air, light, space, shelter, or protection from weather.

g. Deprives the owner of property which has been earned.

h. The idea of a person's pet becoming property and the seizure of the property without compensation.

i. Case law established in *United States v. State Marine Lines*, 334 F. Supp. 84 (S.D. N.Y. 1971).

j. The statute in which Ms. Feedem was charged in violating is vague in its construction and application to the actions of Ms. Feedem.

k. If a person is happy being fat, regardless of their doctor's warning, they continue to do so.

l. Cruelty defines issues that are intentional and brutal.

m. Food is a symbol of love, never intending to harm the animal, and cruelty to animals is unjustifiable infliction or pain with the act of having some malevolent or mischievous motive there must be something willful or wanton about it.

n. In *People v. Brian*, an animal owner was found guilty of not caring for his animals as required by section 597(b) of the California animal law, but the judge disagreed holding that conviction of this code requires proof of criminal negligence which means that the defendants conduct must amount to a reckless, gross or culpable departure from the ordinary standard of due care; it must be such a departure from what would be the conduct from an ordinary prudent person under the same circumstances as to be incompatible with a proper regard to (animal) life.

3 *Writing Letters*

3.1
INTRODUCTION

Law office letters are similar to other types of business correspondence. Although you may write many different kinds of letters, all of your letters share common characteristics. You should strive to answer all letters within 24 hours. Even when you cannot, you should be prompt. If it will take some time for you to answer, you should send a short letter telling your correspondent that the answer will be forthcoming and informing the person as to approximately when he or she can expect a response. Always send something, even if the something is only a simple acknowledgment of a request.

The next basic rule is to organize your thoughts. You should know the purpose of the letter before you begin writing it. Try and limit the letter to that purpose. You should have a single goal for each letter. If you must discuss several concepts or ideas, you may wish to send several letters. More than one central idea in a letter distracts the reader. If you must write about a number of ideas, *be sure to organize your thoughts carefully*. Remember that the more ideas you present in a letter, the less impact each idea will have.

Letters are usually addressed to a single reader. You are writing to a specific person. Try to visualize the person who will receive your letter when you write. Begin the letter carefully and clearly, since the beginning will set the tone for the entire letter. It is generally best to begin your letter with a direct statement that introduces its subject. Alternatively, you might wish to focus on the reader or make a request. State the reason(s) for writing the letter, and include information that the reader might need. Conclude your letter by telling the reader how you want him or her to respond to it.

3.2
THE STRUCTURE OF A LETTER

The body of every letter includes detailed information that tells the reader the reason for the letter. You should be clear, so that the reader cannot misunderstand what you want. Avoid pomposity; say what you are planning to do. Remember that no one understands what "giving my immediate attention to the problem" means. Say exactly what you are doing, will do, or have done. If you have written, telephoned, or filed something, say so. If you have not taken any concrete action, your reader may believe that your "immediate action" means nothing.

The first paragraph of your letter should be no more than five lines long. Remember that short paragraphs and short sentences are easier to read and more effective than long ones. You may have a paragraph as short as a sentence or two. Each sentence should have only one idea. Each sentence should be short. Similarly, each paragraph should be short. Finally, the entire letter should be short.

Your letter must be "letter perfect." Typographical and grammatical mistakes make a letter sloppy. Sloppy letters discredit the entire office.[1] Make sure that you read the letter before you send it.

Before beginning the letter, decide whether it will be informal or formal. You need to decide this first so that you can set the tone. Letters to clients may be more informal than letters to adversaries or to the court.[2]

3.2.1   Letterheads

Like most government offices, most law firms use letterhead or special stationery that identifies them and gives the office address, fax number, telephone number, and a list of all attorneys in the firm. Letterhead is used only for the first page of a letter. Later pages match the first page in color and texture, but are not imprinted.

---

[1]The advent of word processors and computers has changed the standard for all written documents. Erasures and corrections are unacceptable.

[2]You make letters informal by including personal pronouns.

3.2.2   *Openings and Closings*

The standard opening for a letter is the salutation, "Dear." If you are responding to an inquiry, the name that follows the salutation is obvious: You respond to the person who first wrote to you. Address the letter using the same name and/or title that the addressee first used. However, if you initiate the letter, you will need to pay more attention to the form of address. Use "Mr." for men and "Ms." for women. If you do not know the identity of the recipient or whether the addressee is male or female, you might consider omitting the salutation. Avoid cutesy closings; "Very truly yours" and "Sincerely" are appropriate closings.

You will need to add a signature block. Remember that when someone responds to your letter, he or she will refer to your signature to determine how to address the letter. The usual signature includes a first name, middle initial, and last name. Add any title to the signature line, immediately below the signature. Your signature block should match the way you would like to be addressed in return.

3.2.3   *Date*

Every letter must have a date. Usually, you place the date at the beginning of the letter, below the letterhead and centered. The date should be the date the letter is mailed.[3] Do not use the date of a draft. Remember that the date of correspondence may be important in litigation, particularly when the number of days required to respond to a request is at issue.

3.2.4   *Mailing Notations*

You may need a special mailing notation if your letter will be sent other than by first-class mail. If you send the letter by fax, by registered mail, or by hand, you should so indicate on the first page of the letter. You should indicate this immediately after the date and before the salutation. Alternatively, you can indicate the fax notation at the end of the letter, by using an "enclosure" notation.

3.2.5   *Re*

The term "re" means "regarding." It tells the reader what topic the letter refers to. The notation "re" may include the title of a case, the topic of the letter, a client identification number, or anything else that will help identify the subject of the letter.

---

[3]Always check the date before you print the final draft of the letter.

3.2.6   *Enclosures and Copies to Others*

You will sometimes include copies of other correspondence, documents, or photocopies of records or laws or other items. When you do, remember to indicate in the letter that you have enclosures and then enclose the listed item. You use the abbreviation "encl." to indicate enclosures.[4]

If you will be sending a copy of a letter to another person in addition to the recipient named in the salutation, indicate this in the text of the original letter. The letters "cc" mean "carbon copy" and indicate that a copy of the letter will be sent to someone else. Today, carbon copies are replaced by photocopies. Nonetheless, the abbreviation "cc" is used to indicate that copies have been or will be sent to others.

3.2.7   *Letter Formats and Writer Identification*

You will usually include a reference to whoever wrote and typed each letter. Writers and secretaries are indicated by using their initials. If Theodore E. Beare wrote a letter that was typed by Edward G. Crane, you would see the initials "TEB" (in capital letters) and the initials "egc" (in lowercase letters). The two sets of initials would be separated either by a colon or by a slash.

> **Examples:**
>
> TEB/egc
> TEB:egc

Letters are usually single spaced. Double or additional spacing indicates the different components of a letter. Expect double spacing between the date and the inside address and again between the inside address and the reference notation. You will also find double spacing between each paragraph of the letter.

Some people indent the first sentence of each paragraph. You would usually use five spaces for indenting. Alternatively, you may prefer a block style, which uses no indentation. Your left-hand margin should be justified, which means that each line begins or ends at the same distance from the edge of the paper. Sometimes you may write a letter that is right justified. When

---

[4]At times, you may need to specify exactly what is enclosed. Remember that litigation may be expected in some cases if you cannot later specifically identify what was actually enclosed with a letter. Items listed as enclosed will often be assumed to have been enclosed only if the letter identified what should be there. In this way, the recipient has a chance to object should the enclosure be missing. If no enclosures are listed and identified, and some documents or records are missing, the recipient may not be aware that the documents have not been received and may later object that they were not enclosed at all.

you justify the right margin of a letter, you must also justify the left margin. Every line in the letter will be even, and the letter will have a block appearance. You usually see right justification in books. Although it presents a pleasing appearance, letters written in this format may be difficult to read. Right justification causes every line to end at the same point. In order to do this, a word processor or computer rearranges the spacing between and within words. This sometimes results in reading problems because many readers are accustomed to reading words with a fixed amount of space between the letters. Justification eliminates the traditional spacing within the word and for each character and may either expand or contract the spacing that the word is allowed.[5]

3.3
OPINION LETTERS

The opinion letter is, perhaps, the most complex and difficult type of letter to draft. An opinion letter is used to give advice to clients. When a client wants to know the legal consequence of an act or of the failure to act, a law office may respond either orally or through an opinion letter. Although paralegals rarely sign opinion letters, they may have significant input into their content.

In any opinion letter, you must answer the client's questions in terms that the client can understand. Here you must use clear and concise English so that clients know the legal answers to their questions. Simple declarative sentences are best. If the opinion is unfavorable, you must tell the client about alternatives or substitutes. Clients do not like to be told that they cannot do what they want to do. Clients do like to be reassured. You may be in the position to provide this support. Often, however, you will need to prepare your clients for disappointment as they learn that they cannot do what they want to do or that they must do what they do not want to do. Here, again, you must be completely clear so that your clients can easily understand the legal advice. Legal opinions can haunt you. Make sure that your research is thorough before you begin to write.

You should also caution your clients that the law is always changing and that the opinion expressed in the letter is accurate only until the law

---

[5]Fixed spacing may expand the space used in a word so that a line will end at the correct point. Proportional spacing allows different amounts of space for each character or letter in a word. Some letters take more space to print. For example, the letter "l" needs less space than the letter "m." In fixed spacing, the printer may allow the same space for an "l" as for an "m" so that the line will end at the appropriate place. In proportional spacing, used when you do not justify, each character or letter is allowed the space needed for the shape of that particular letter.

changes. Clients need to be reminded of the constantly changing law, as they tend to share letters or refer to older letters. You must also remind clients that even a small change in the facts can result in a different legal result. Clients may believe that the opinions expressed in an opinion letter are always valid. This is wrong, and clients must be cautioned about it. In order to protect yourself, your firm, and your client, you must restrict your opinion letter to the specific facts and law discussed in the letter. Warn your clients that they should not rely on the opinion for any other situation or at a later time or place, as it may not be valid in those circumstances. Be clear that you are offering an opinion based on the current facts and law and not stating any unchanging rules or law. The law is not immutable; it is always changing. Your clients need to appreciate this. Remember that if your letter leaves room for your client to interpret what you mean, the letter is probably not well drafted. You can leave your client with a choice as to what to do; however, you must not leave the client confused as to what you meant.

A supervising attorney retains the final responsibility for all opinion letters. You must ensure that all legal research is accurate and that the facts are correctly developed. Your supervising attorney must read and approve any opinion letters before they are sent.

You need to organize your letter. Your client is most interested in the conclusion, which, after all, provides the answer that the client has asked for. Place the conclusion at the beginning of the letter if this seems appropriate.[6] There are no hard-and-fast rules. Some lawyers favor placing the conclusion at the beginning because that is the most important part from the client's viewpoint. If you need to advise your client of any limitations or conditions, you should discuss them at the beginning of the letter. You must alert your client to these limitations or conditions because the client may not always read your entire letter. You run a risk that your client will ignore your preliminary instructions if you do not tell him or her how important it is to read the complete document.

In some situations you may want to "hedge your bets." The law is not carved in stone, and clients must be warned that slight factual changes can affect the advice they are given. Some areas of the law are uncertain. Warn your clients specifically of those areas.

Like other letters, legal opinions are usually dated, addressed to a particular person or group, and signed by the person giving the advice. The opinion is meant for the addressee. If there is any possibility that others might rely on the opinion, you might want to qualify the letter.

---

[6]If you place the conclusion first, make sure that it refers to the rest of the letter. You want the client to read the entire document and not just the beginning paragraph(s).

Most opinion letters include the reason for the opinion and a description of the subject of the letter. Terms of art should be defined so that the reader can understand what they signify. Particular laws should be specified. You may also wish to include photocopies of relevant laws. You should also indicate the extent of any investigations performed. If specific documents or records were used to help formulate the opinion, you should discuss this as well.

3.4
COLLECTION LETTERS

Collection letters are used in-house for collecting the law firm's unpaid bills and out of house to collect for a client. Collection letters are usually written in a series of three. Each letter is progressively more demanding.

The first collection letter is often written to remind the recipient to pay a bill that is 30 days past due.[7] You usually include a copy of the bill and a simple reminder. You may want to stamp the bill with the words "Past Due. Please Remit" and include a self-addressed stamped envelope. Alternatively, you may wish to write a simple request informing the recipient that the bill is overdue and requesting prompt payment. Be courteous: Whenever you ask someone for money, even if the money has already been earned, you want to be polite. Courtesy results in faster payment.

Sometimes, no matter how polite the request, the recipient continues to ignore his or her obligation. You will then need to send a more forceful second reminder. If this letter is to a client, it should be a personal letter which shows that the firm is aware of the client and of any problems the client may have. The attorney who will sign the letter (even if you draft it) should ask the client to respond by a specified date and explain any reasons for nonpayment. The language should be polite and suggest that the lawyer believes that there must be a good reason for any delay of payment. If the case is still open, the writer might indicate that further payment is necessary for additional work to take place on the case.[8] This letter should also mention concern for the client's welfare. Close the letter with a request for a definite response. If you still do not believe that the client is likely to pay, you may wish to include a statement telling the client what will happen if payment is not forthcoming. However, do not make any threats, and do not suggest that

---

[7]Assuming bills are sent on a monthly basis.

[8]Be sure to check your *Rules of Professional Responsibility* before suggesting that you will cease work on a case. In some instances you cannot do so.

you will take action unless you are prepared to do so. You can make a general statement of intent such as "take appropriate legal action" or provide similar information if you are writing to someone who is not a client of yours.

If the client still does not respond, and no payment is forthcoming, you will need to send a third letter. A lawyer cannot threaten to withdraw from a case because of nonpayment.[9] However, the lawyer can inform the client that it is difficult to successfully pursue a case without payment. Never make a threat that you (or your firm) are not prepared to carry out. If you cannot get a response from a client, the firm can always sue for nonpayment or breach of contract, depending on the law of your state and the terms of the fee agreement.[10] If you are writing to someone other than a client and seeking payment on behalf of your client, you can, once again, inform the recipient that you will be taking legal action where this is appropriate.

You may need to respond to collection letters and demands. After you review the facts of each demand, determine the steps that your client would like to take.[11] Your first and most necessary step is to respond to the letter. If your firm is representing the client, you should explain this. Next, determine whether you are responding to a second or third collection letter. If so, you should begin with a short apology for not responding in a timely manner. Then you would briefly explain why the client has ignored the demands. You may need to offer a compromise or negotiate terms that your client can meet. In many instances, the main reason for not responding is financial difficulties. Explain this to the creditor. Many creditors will respond favorably to a payment plan that is offered, since the alternative is often no payment. When offering a payment plan, be sure that your client can meet all of the terms agreed to. Be definite: Explain the payment amount and suggested payment dates. If you can, and if it is appropriate, include an initial payment with the letter. Sometimes, however, it is better to indicate that the funds to make the first payment are in trust and will be forthcoming when an agreement is reached.[12] End by thanking the creditor for his or her patience.

---

[9]Here, too, you must check your *Rules of Professional Responsibility*. Different states have different standards.

[10]Use caution when threatening a client with legal action. An irate client may respond by filing a complaint with your State Bar. This will always cause problems for a lawyer or law firm. Even when the complaints are spurious, the lawyer must respond to the complaint, which will take time and cause stress.

[11]Remember that if you are a legal assistant, your attorney is responsible for this decision. Do not usurp the attorney's role: A legal assistant or paralegal may not give legal advice.

[12]Never say that the money is in trust unless it is actually in a trust account.

3.5
LITIGATION LETTERS

Most litigation letters are general responses to requests for information, the requests themselves, and informative letters telling clients about suggested offers. These letters may also tell clients about the status of a lawsuit or about the place and time of any deposition or hearing. Letters may also serve to confirm an agreement or the receipt of documents or other things.

Litigation letters are often short. They follow the standards for all business letters and include the date, the address of the addressee, and a "re" notation. Each letter must be signed by the author. As with all other legal writing, you should remember to write clearly and concisely.

Always send a confirmatory letter to opposing counsel to confirm the details of an offer or the date, place, and time of a deposition. Send one also to confirm an extension of time. Agreements must always be confirmed. You should send frequent letters to clients informing them of the status of their litigation. Remember that one of the most common reasons for complaints to bar organizations stems from lack of contact. Clients need to feel that their attorneys are interested in their cases. You bolster this feeling of confidence when you keep in contact with your client. You will also need to inform clients of upcoming depositions, trials, and hearings. Be specific: Tell the client where to meet. Tell your client whether to meet at the law office first or go to the location of the hearing, deposition, or trial on his or her own. You should also give the client any specific instructions that you want him or her to remember. When giving directions, be detailed.[13]

3.6
COMPLAINT LETTERS

Complaint letters always require a great deal of thought and preparation. First, determine what your goal is. Know the action you would like the recipient to take before you begin your letter. Are you writing to complain about goods or services? Do you or does your client want to be reimbursed for money already spent, or do you (on behalf of your client) wish to disaffirm a

---

[13]Always remember that in every lawsuit at least one person is unhappy. Thus, your status letters may have to form the basis for a defense to either a Bar complaint or an E & O (errors and omissions) complaint. Frequent and very clear and concise status letters may become your best defense against an unhappy former client. Clients and former clients can make claims against their lawyers. Even winning a case is no guarantee that the client or former client will be satisfied. Protect yourself against these potential claims by keeping your clients fully informed.

contract? Knowing what you want will help determine the style of your letter, as well as the identity of the addressee. In some instances, the complaint should be addressed to someone other than the person with whom you or your client initially had direct dealings. You may wish to address the letter to more than one person. Sometimes you may wish to send other administrators, corporate officers, or interested parties copies of the letter. You will almost always wish to send a copy of the letter to your client.

Consider the tone of the letter carefully before you write the letter. Remain professional at all times, even when you feel that you or your client has been treated badly. Your best approach is to state the problem, the reason for the complaint, and your suggested solution. Professional courtesy is better than threats, which will only engender angry responses.[14] Your goal is not to vent your feelings, but to resolve the problem.

Begin your letter with a short introduction which tells the reader that your law firm is representing the client. Explain the relevant facts surrounding the client's complaint. If you need supporting documents, be sure to include copies of these documents and note that they are enclosed. Feel free to discuss the enclosed items. As stated earlier, list and specifically identify each item that you enclose. Indicate the dates and check numbers of payments. List invoice numbers where pertinent. You might wish to highlight relevant portions of documents so that the addressee can easily identify the problem(s) about which you are writing. Next, tell the recipient how you would like him or her to resolve the problem. This is the goal that you formulated before you began to write. Set a deadline for fixing the problem, as well as for the action you would like the recipient to take. If necessary, explain acceptable alternative actions. If you expect to take alternative steps should your addressee fail to respond, you may wish to indicate those steps. Alternatively, you may not wish to tie yourself down to a particular response. Consider your legal options before suggesting your next course of action, since you do not want to write that you plan to take a particular action and then fail to take that action. Should you fail to act, you will lose credibility with the recipient. Finally, remember to include your address and phone number so that the addressee can respond to you. Remember that the address and phone number should be those of the attorney and not of the client.

You may need to respond to a complaint letter at some point. If you or your client has received a complaint letter, you should consider the merits of

---

[14]Threats also pose another problem. If you threaten to do something, but do not do it, your credibility will suffer. Further, should you want to negotiate after a threat, you may find that you have limited your options. Threats are almost never beneficial.

the complaint and the appropriate response before you begin your letter. Be sure that your client fully agrees with this response before you begin the letter. You may wish to confirm the client's agreement in writing before you respond to the complaint.[15] Next, you should determine whether the complaint has merit. However, whether it has is important only to the substantive portion of your letter; the facts of the claim themselves will determine your response. You should, however, use a conciliatory tone in responding to most complaints. This is because most complaints lend themselves to negotiation, and you will lose a negotiating advantage if your letter sounds rude. The complaint may be justified. If so, apologize for the inconvenience, and tell the complainant how you will resolve the situation. If the complaint has no basis, you will need to reject it. Do so in as positive a way as possible. Tact is advisable, particularly when dealing with irate and unhappy people.[16]

You may need to respond to a complaint about the amount of a legal fee. These letters always require tact. Unhappy clients often file bar complaints and/or lawsuits when they feel that they have been overcharged. Refer to the terms of the fee agreement when answering these letters. Explain, in detail, the fee and how the charge was determined. You may need to provide supporting documentation. Often, clients simply want to understand why they receive a bill that is larger than anticipated. Be prepared to provide time sheets and itemized lists of costs with your letter. Suggest to your client that you will meet with them to explain the fees and costs in more detail if they so wish. When you do so, be sure that the client understands that he or she will not be charged for this conference.

3.7
REPRESENTATION
AND NONREPRESENTATION LETTERS

All clients are entitled to know whether the law firm will accept their case or cases. You should respond to every client and potential client within two or

---

[15]As a general rule, fully informing your client protects both the client and your law firm. If time allows, use this opportunity to be sure that there are no misunderstandings between you and your client.

[16]Remember that the person who wrote the complaint almost certainly thought that it had merit when he or she made it. A poor response can impede communication. If you want to resolve the complaint, communication is essential.

three days after the initial meeting and tell the client whether your firm plans to provide legal representation for him or her. If your firm has accepted the case, you should outline the proposed representation and summarize the terms of the fee agreement for the client. Include a copy of the fee agreement, and list its enclosure in the letter. Provide a space for your client to accept your offer of representation, and have the client sign the letter, indicating that the client wishes your firm to represent him or her if this is appropriate. Be clear and concise when listing the terms of the representation. You do not want a client to claim later that he or she did not understand the terms of the representation. Write in simple English.

Nonrepresentation letters are as important as representation letters. In a nonrepresentation letter, you explicitly, firmly, and without equivocation reject your potential client's offer of employment. Rejection is hard; clients do not like to feel rejected and may be angered or depressed by your firm's failure to accept their case. Be as tactful as possible. You want the client to realize that you are rejecting a case and not the client. If you are considerate, the client may return with a different problem at a later date and may refer others to you. If you are discourteous, be assured that the potential client will tell everyone in sight about another "awful" attorney. Make absolutely sure that there is no misunderstanding about the nonrepresentation.

When writing a nonrepresentation letter, you should always warn the potential client about any impending statutes of limitations. Problems with statutes of limitations will cause you grief if the potential client is unaware of these limits to a lawsuit. You do not want a client to misunderstand that you are *not* taking the case and rely on the hope that you will reconsider. Tell the client when the statute of limitations will expire, and provide a copy of the applicable statute with your nonrepresentation letter. Note the enclosure in your letter.

Suggest that the client promptly seek legal representation from someone else. If you know of other law firms, you can include the names and addresses of several that the client might wish to consider. Avoid listing only one firm: If the client approaches the firm you suggest and is not happy with the results, the client might blame you for the referral. Therefore, suggest several firms, so that the choice belongs to the potential client. If you are not aware of other law firms dealing with the particular legal problem, you should suggest that the potential client contact one of the local lawyer referral sources in your area. Provide the telephone number, fax number, and address of the source. Finally, you might suggest that the potential client contact you should he or she have other (different) legal problems. In this way, you can reject a particular case without rejecting the client.

3.8
SETTLEMENT LETTER

The settlement letter is one of the most complex and difficult letters to write. In many settlement letters—particularly when you are asking for money—you are telling the recipient why he or she should pay you some money. No one likes to pay money. Therefore, your recipient will not be pleased to receive your letter. Accordingly, you must write more persuasively than with any other type of letter. Settlement letters are similar to opinion letters in that you will need to summarize the facts, as well as provide some legal basis for your conclusion. Before beginning your letter, you must prepare both factually and legally. Be sure that you have all of the facts necessary for your claim. Refer to specific factual support and include supporting documents. Here, again, list the particular documents that you enclose, so that you have a record of which documents you send with your letter. You will often include the facts of the incident, as well as a statement of the damage that your client now has. Treatment costs, as well as projections for future treatment, should be listed. Summarize the reports of experts that your client has consulted. Costs for other damages should be presented. You may wish to include copies of medical bills, as well as of the medical records. Remember to include a paragraph or two detailing the costs of lost wages and of pain and suffering where appropriate. Tell your reader of any limitations your client now has. You will sometimes describe a day in the life of your client if the client has a major impairment. Make sure that you can support whatever you say.

After you summarize the facts, tell the reader what you would like him or her to do. Include legal support for your claim. You will need to first research the law and then demonstrate how the law applies to the particular facts for your claim. Be realistic: You will achieve nothing by overinflating or overstating your case. Remember that the recipient, often an insurance adjuster, is almost always familiar with the applicable law and will have independently investigated the basis for the claim. You may wish to include information on potential jury verdicts. Here you would first need to do some jury verdict research for your local area, as well as researching verdicts on similar injuries elsewhere where appropriate.[17] Present this information to the adjustor. Remember that adjusters are familiar with the risk and cost that are part of litigation. You should then include the actual settlement demand or offer. Finally, remind your reader that the settlement offer is for purposes of settling the case and is neither a complete analysis of all of the client's in-

---

[17]Not all injuries will have been litigated locally. If you need to use jury verdicts from other areas, be sure to show their local applicability.

juries and damages nor an admission of facts. Instead, it is an offer to reach a mutually acceptable settlement.[18]

3.9
DOCTOR LETTER

When you work in the area of insurance, social security, personal injury, or workmen's compensation, you will often need to request medical information from a doctor.[19] Remember that you will need an information release from your client if you wish a doctor to release medical information. Include a copy of the signed release with your letter. If you want a doctor to examine a client, you will often send some medical records to the doctor[20] and request that he or she examine the client and provide a written report to your office. You will frequently summarize the facts leading to or causing the medical condition that you need to have checked or substantiated. Be specific: Tell the doctor what you need him or her to do and the type of report the doctor must write.[21] Never tell the doctor what conclusion to reach.

3.10
GET OFF THE TREADMILL

Many legal letters follow a standard form. You are writing to communicate specific information. However, you should try to avoid sounding as if every letter was ground out of a machine. Do not begin each response by referring the addressee to the date and content of his or her letter. Such an approach is not only formalistic, but boring. Refer the addressee to his or her prior correspondence only if you really believe that the recipient will need to be reminded of it. If the recipient will not know why you are responding, you might consider referencing their letter. Otherwise, begin your letter with some content.

---

[18]Case law in your state may dictate how this is to be done and may indicate the specific language you should (or must) include.

[19]This may also be true for other administrative areas.

[20]Here, too, remember to identify and list all records that you send.

[21]Check to see whether the agency or administrative law judge wants or does not allow certain things. Since the letter may come to the agency's attention, an error here might seriously compromise your client's claim.

You should also avoid pomposity. The law is known for its verbiage and verbosity. The last sentence is an overly pompous way of saying that lawyers and legal writers often use too many words to get their ideas across. We love big words as well. Effective letter writing uses simple English. If you are using or have used some of the following pompous phrases, plan to eliminate them now. Do not use the verb "advise," "inform," or "state" if you can use the word "tell" or "say." Do not say "attached please find" when you can substitute "attached is." Avoid the phrase "meets with our approval" when you could more simply say "we approve." Use "send" instead of "transmit" and "in closing" rather than "in conclusion." You should also omit useless phrases such as "please be advised," "I should further point out," and "take this opportunity to." If you wish to point something out, do so. And indeed, take the opportunity, but do not bore your reader with the preliminary phrase. Write simply, and your reader will understand. Understanding is the first step to achieving your goal.

3.11
CONCLUSION

Finally, remember that you are writing a letter to say something to someone. When you have finished a draft of your letter, read what you have written. Did you say what you wanted to say? Is your letter clear? Is the letter written in the tone you wanted? Does it go clearly from beginning to end, or does it cause your attention and direction to wander. Finally, is this letter one you would like to receive?

If you read your letter and it passes these tests, it is probably a good letter. Feel free to polish it if necessary, and let it go its way. Should the letter fail any of the tests, think carefully before you send it. A letter that does not pass these simple tests should probably be rewritten. Remember that it is generally much easier to fix a poor letter before it goes out than to fix the extra problems later that the letter may cause.

3.12
SAMPLE LETTERS

Letterhead

June 14, 1994

Theodore E. Beare, Esq.
Attorney at Law
1402 E. HunneyPot Lane
Madison, Wisconsin

Re: Francis Lille Putian

Dear Mr. Beare:

I have received your request to furnish a medical report on my patient, Ms. Francis Lille Putian. You stated that you wanted copies of all of my medical records about Ms. Putian, as well as a report on her current status and her projected recovery period. She has signed a medical release giving me authorization to release these documents to you.

I originally treated Ms. Putian on January 3, 1994, for injuries she sustained in an automobile accident. She was discharged from my care as of May 19, 1994, when her symptoms were controlled and she had resumed almost all of her normal activities. I am including with this letter a copy of my treatment notes, my medical records, and my medical report. I hope that this will answer your questions about Ms. Putian's medical status.

Very truly yours,

George M. Jungel, M.D.

GMJ:rtt
Enclosures:
Medical report
Medical treatment notes
Medical records

FIGURE 3–1 Letter from a doctor to an attorney in response to a request for medical information

Letterhead

January 17, 1994

David G. Copperfield, Esq.
476 Workhouse Road
New York, New York

Re: Oliver Twiste

Dear David,

I am sending you the Joint Pretrial statement for the Twiste case. Please read and edit it, and return it as soon as possible so that we can file it. Thank you for your cooperation.

Very truly yours,

Ebeneezer Skruge
For Skruge & Skruge, P.C.

EJS:lm
Enclosure
Joint Pretrial Statement

FIGURE 3–2 Letter from an attorney to opposing counsel in a lawsuit

Letterhead

June 2, 1992

Ms. Lucy P. Legal
233 Research Drive
Citytown, Arizona 85280

Re: Herman Houseplant, Inc. v. Palm Tree U.

Dear Lucy,

I hope that you can help me with a research project. I represent a local nursery called Herman Houseplant, Inc. Herman began a lawsuit against Palm Tree U., an Arizona corporation, on November 15, 1990, for breach of contract. Palm Tree U. was in the business of importing and exporting palm trees. Palm Tree filed its answer in January, 1991. We filed a Motion for Summary Judgment against Palm Tree U. in April of 1991, and judgment was granted in our favor in August 1991. Formal written judgment was entered in November 1991.

Palm Tree U. has no assets. In February 1991, Palm Tree U. gave all of its assets to WEE PLANTEM, a Nebraska corporation. A debtor's exam has shown that:

1. Palm Tree assigned all of its assets.
2. Palm Tree claimed that it owed WEE PLANTEM money in excess of the value of the assets it assigned.
3. A Mr. Geoffrey Gardenia was a principal shareholder, officer, and director in both corporations.
4. Palm Tree U. had few assets in Arizona other than its receivables. All of the receivables were given to WEE PLANTEM.

I would like to get a judgment against WEE PLANTEM under the Uniform Fraudulent Conveyance Act. I am enclosing copies of the assignment between Palm Tree and WEE PLANTEM, as well as the summary judgment, complaint, and answer in our lawsuit. Please prepare a memorandum of law on the issues of liability. Thank you for your anticipated help.

Very truly yours,

Theodore E. Beare
Theodore E. Beare, P.C.

TEB:pd
Enclosure

FIGURE 3–3 Letter to an independent paralegal about contract research

REVIEW QUESTIONS AND EXERCISES

Review Questions

1. How long can you wait before answering a letter?
2. How should you begin a letter?
3. What is wrong with telling your correspondent that you will give the matter your immediate attention?
4. How long should your paragraphs be?
5. Why should each letter be dated?
6. What is the purpose of the "Re" heading?
7. Why should you specifically list each enclosure?
8. What spacing rules are usually used with letters?
9. What is the difference between fixed and proportional spacing?
10. Why should you justify a letter?
11. What is an opinion letter?
12. What cautions must you include in an opinion letter?
13. Why are opinion letters fact specific?
14. Who is responsible for the opinion letter?
15. Why should you write a collection letter?
16. How many collection letters should you write to a client before initiating litigation?
17. How should you structure a collection letter?
18. Should you include a statement of what might happen if payment is not forthcoming? Why?
19. Why must you be cautious in threatening a client with legal action?
20. How do litigation letters differ from opinion letters?
21. Why should you send a confirming letter to opposing counsel?
22. What is a status letter?
23. How often should you write a status letter?
24. What types of threats should you make in a complaint letter?
25. What tone should you use in responding to a complaint?
26. How should you respond to a complaint about the size of a legal fee?
27. Why are nonrepresentation letters as important as representation letters?
28. What should you include in a representation letter?

29. What warning(s) must you give potential clients when you reject a case?

30. What is a settlement letter?

31. What types of facts should you summarize in a settlement letter?

32. What information must you include in a letter to a doctor?

Exercises

1. Your attorney represents a newspaper consortium, the *Daily World News*.[22] Recently, Seldon S. contacted the paper and reported that he was able to receive pornographic materials depicting children over the information superhighway via his computer. He asked the newspaper to investigate the matter, as he was concerned that this material was so readily available. The newspaper reporter assigned to the investigation photographed the computer and the materials that were received via the modem. The action was reported to the Prosecutor's office. The county attorney has now requested all copies of the photographed materials and has threatened to institute criminal charges against the newspaper and its employees if all copies of these materials are not turned over to the government. The newspaper is planning a series on child pornography and does not wish to be compelled to turn over all copies of the materials. It has asked your attorney to provide a legal opinion on its right to keep a copy of these materials despite a state statute prohibiting possession of child pornography. Draft an opinion letter for your client.

2. Draft a letter to the County Attorney claiming First Amendment privilege and refusing to release the documents on behalf of your client.

3. Draft a letter to the newspaper informing it of the status of the case and advising that a letter has been sent to the County Attorney claiming First Amendment privilege.

4. Draft a letter to the client informing him that the county attorney has rejected the First Amendment privilege claim and enclosing the county attorney's letter.

5. Recently, a client came to your office asking to sue a doctor for medical malpractice. The client suggested that the doctor was responsible for the death of the client's sister. The sister had been diagnosed with bone cancer and had refused chemotherapy. The deceased sister did not believe in treatment for what she thought was a terminal condition and main-

---

[22]The name is fictitious and does not have any relationship to an actual newspaper.

tained that she did not want to experience the pain often associated with chemotherapy and radiation. Several months after consulting the doctor, she died from her cancer. The client believes that the doctor had a duty to force her sister to undergo medical treatment and that, had the doctor been adamant about the treatment, her sister would still be alive. Draft a letter to the client refusing representation.

6. Your attorney represents an automobile-leasing company. The Statlers purchased a car in 1996 on a lease-purchase option. They were to pay $313.98 per month for the automobile. They made all payments in a timely fashion until six months ago, when they stopped making payments. Draft a demand letter on behalf of the client asking for payment and instructing the Statlers that unless payment is made within five days, your firm will take legal action.

7. Your client, Barbara Variety, was injured in an automobile accident. She sustained a broken hip, numerous contusions, and a broken wrist. The driver of the other car is insured by AutoIns. Co. Your client has been unable to work for five months. Barbara is a paralegal for a medium-sized law firm and earns an annual salary of $28,000.00 She was in traction for six weeks and has had to relearn how to walk. She suffered a complication following the broken hip. She developed a blood fungus and needed additional treatment and hospitalization. Her medical bills totaled $35,567.67. During the past five months, Barbara has been unable to participate in her aerobics class. She has also been unable to care for her children and has had to rely on a succession of baby-sitters and housekeepers. The children are five and seven years of age. Draft a demand letter on Barbara's behalf.

8. You work for Skruge and Skruge. One of your clients, J. Dombey, has asked you to file a lien against some real property. J. Dombey is a general contractor working primarily on large office buildings. Mr. Dombey has not been paid for his work on the Salem Towers and would like to place a lien against this property. Draft a letter telling Mr. Dombey that the lien was filed last week.

9. The owner of Salem Towers, Mr. Ichabod Prynne, has now filed an action to clear the title on his property, the Salem Towers. He has noticed a deposition for your client, Mr. Dombey. Draft a letter telling Mr. Dombey that he must appear at the deposition in two weeks. Indicate the date, time, and location of the deposition. Since Mr. Dombey has never been involved in any litigation, include some general instructions and information on the deposition process, and tell him what he will be expected to do at a deposition.

10. After successfully settling Mr. Dombey's claim, your firm sent him his first bill last month, but has not yet received payment from him. Draft a letter requesting payment and including a copy of the bill.

11. Three months have gone by. Your firm has not heard from Mr. Dombey since the lawsuit ended. Draft a reminder letter to Mr. Dombey.

4 *Legal Citation*

Citing legal references correctly, commonly referred to as "cite checking," is one of the banes of the paralegal's existence. You have two distinct tasks when cite checking. First, you must determine whether the authorities cited are still good law. This means that the case must still be effective authority. Any case that has been reversed, vacated, or overruled is no longer good law and should not be used. The only exceptions are where a case is only partly vacated, partly overruled, or partly reversed or where you wish to reargue the position that was overruled, vacated, or reversed. In these instances you may elect to use the case, but must tell your reader that it is no longer good law or has been partly reversed, partly overruled, or partly vacated. You must then cite the case that has overruled, vacated, or reversed the case you wish to use. The second part of your cite-checking task is to make sure that the citations you give are in the correct form. You must comply with a number of rules to assure the accuracy of your citations.

4.1
THE UNIFORM SYSTEM OF CITATION

Harvard University publishes the best known guide to the format of citations: the *Uniform System of Citation*, also known as the Bluebook. The University of Chicago publishes a competing authority called the *Chicago Manual of Legal Citation,* or the Maroon Book. You must become familiar with these publications; do not depend on citations from other legal references. Many legal books and guides use improper citations. For example, many West publications give you the unofficial citation of a case before the official citation. This is not correct according to Bluebook format. Always rely on the Bluebook for the authority, even when other books tell you how to cite the authority. You may experience problems with the Bluebook because the citations featured in it are for use in law review articles. This form of citation differs slightly from the form commonly accepted in court.

Much of your work may be directed to producing documents for court. You will then need to convert the citation format given for law reviews into the format used in court. The Bluebook has a special section called the "Practitioners' Notes" that will help you perform the conversion. This section is printed on light blue paper and is at the beginning of the volume, following the introductory section.

The Bluebook also includes specific sections on the laws of each state. The states are alphabetically arranged, and for each one, the Bluebook includes the names of the official and unofficial reporter volumes, references to the statutory compilations, information on how to cite the session laws, and a reference to administrative codes or compilations. The Bluebook also includes references to foreign jurisdictions. You will find a summary of the standard format for citations inside the covers of the book. The inside of the front cover of the current (15th) edition of the Bluebook summarizes how to cite materials for law review articles. The inside of the back cover of the book is a quick reference guide for use with court documents and legal memoranda. Access these sections for a summary of the information in the Bluebook.

Your next job will be to familiarize yourself with the myriad rules for correct citations. You will also need to learn certain word signals which tell the reader that the authority has already been (or will be) cited. The following paragraphs give a more in-depth explanation of Bluebook rules. Remember to consult the Bluebook for further illustrations, since it is the authority.

The Bluebook is divided into five main sections: the introduction, the "Practitioners' Notes," "General Rules of Citation and Style," "Tables and Abbreviations," and an index. The introduction discusses the use of citations and the structure of the Bluebook and analyzes a typical legal citation for a case, statute, rule, regulation, book, or periodical. The "Practitioners' Notes," printed on blue paper, indicates the typeface conventions used on court documents. This section reminds the writer to use both official and unofficial reporter names when citing state cases. Tax materials use special citations. If the document or memorandum discusses only the current version of federal tax laws, you may omit the publisher and year from the citation of the Internal Revenue Code. Similarly, citations of treasury regulations may omit the year.

The third section of the Bluebook has the general rules of citation. This section gives an overview of the rules for correct citation, as well as introductory signals to use when listing authorities. The section includes rules for citing cases, statutes, and constitutions, as well as for citing secondary authorities such as encyclopedias, books, and periodicals.

The fourth section, printed on blue paper, contains tables indicating the reporter names for each state and the abbreviations for foreign jurisdictions. This section also gives the correct format for citing international materials by the United Nations, the League of Nations, and the Inter-American Commission on Human Rights.

The final section is an alphabetically arranged index, located at the back of the book. The index refers you to the correct page rather than to a section number. As with most indexes, this one is organized by descriptive words.

In your legal research classes, you have learned (or will learn) of the importance of supporting each of your assertions with a reference to a legal authority. You cannot simply state a rule of law when you write; you must support your statement with a reference to a legal authority. These authorities are the items that we both cite and cite check. For ease in reading, all citations must follow an established format. This gives consistency to legal writing. Consistency in legal citation allows all attorneys, judges, and legal writers to easily find the authorities in support of a given statement.

4.2
CASE CITATIONS

Cases are among the most frequently used sources of primary law. Each case must be correctly cited. A case citation must include the following information:

1. The name of the case.
2. The volume number, name of the official reporter, and the page on which the case begins.
3. An indication of the court which decided the case, unless that is already apparent in the citation.
4. The year the case was decided.
5. Any subsequent history about the case.

In this section, we will explore the different rules associated with writing the case correctly. Before beginning a citation, you introduce the case authority to the reader, using certain words which signal that the authority is being introduced. Among these words are the terms "see," "see, e.g.," and "compare."

4.2.1 Underlining

You either italicize or underline the name of the case. Underlining is more common. Underline the entire name, including the "v." Also, underline any other procedural terms that are part of the name of the case, such as the words "in re" or "ex parte." Underline the introductory signals "see," "see, e.g.," and "compare" when they accompany a citation and together, the signal and the citation form the complete sentence. Underline terms indicating the prior or subsequent history of a case. These terms are abbreviations for "affirmed" or "reversed" and are written "aff'd" or "rev'd." Finally, always underline terms that refer to a more complete citation elsewhere in your document. These terms are "supra," "infra," and "id."

In citing cases, remember to use only the last names of individuals. The one exception is where the name of the party is in a foreign language in which the surname is given first—for example, Chinese or Korean. In such circumstances, you would use the entire name. However, if the name is a combination of an English name and a foreign name, use only the surname.

If the case involved several parties, use just one representative name for the appellant and one for the appellee. However, when citing a corporation or partnership, use the complete partnership or corporate name, even if it includes first names or more than one name. Similarly, if one of the parties has a particular title, you may need to include the title. Do not use terms such as "et al." to indicate other parties to the action. The appellant's name is usually listed first, to the left of the "v." However, this general rule changes when we are citing criminal cases. In criminal cases, the appeal is usually brought by the convicted felon. Despite this, the case name will be listed as "State v. Appellant," where the word "Appellant" substitutes for the actual surname of the felon.

You do not indicate the name of the state in the citation when you are referring to a state court decision. If the case was later appealed to the United States Supreme Court, you would substitute the name of the state and omit the word "state." Thus, the "Miranda" case began with the case name of "State v. Miranda," and this name is used when referring to the state court case. If you wish to cite the later U.S. Supreme Court decision, the case is referred to as "Arizona v. Miranda." Although state court decisions do not actually include the name of the state in which the action occurred, the reader will know the correct jurisdiction. You provide this information either through the name of the reporter or the name of the court that will be a subsequent part of the citation. At the federal level, you use the name "United States," which you never shorten or abbreviate. Similarly, you never add the words "of America" to the name "United States."

If your case deals with property, you will usually list only the first type of property in the name of the case. These cases are often known as "in re" cases, meaning "in regard to" and are used for cases dealing specifically with property. You would thus list a case dealing with an automobile and a weapon as "In re automobile" and omit the weapon from the name. No particular type of property is preferred in selecting the property to be named. Instead, you select whatever property is listed first.

You may use abbreviations. "Ex rel" is the correct abbreviation for phrases such as "on the relation of," "on behalf of," or "for the use of." Use the phrase "in re" to mean "in the matter of," "application of," or "petition of." You may also use other abbreviations, as, for example, the following:

And	&
Association	Ass'n
Brothers	Bros.
Company	Co.
Corporation	Corp.
Incorporated	Inc.
Limited	Ltd.
Number	No.

Still other abbreviations are listed in Table T6 of the Bluebook. The general rule is that a word of eight or more letters may be abbreviated if the abbreviation is unambiguous and will save a substantial amount of space. Note that you usually omit the word "the" from a case name, unless you are referring to "The King" or "The Queen" or to an established popular name. When using initials to represent an organization, omit the periods between the letters. Thus, you would write "SEC" rather than "S.E.C." You may also abbreviate the names of countries or states. The Bluebook lists appropriate state and country abbreviations in Table T10.

Once you complete the name portion of your citation, you must tell the reader where to locate the case. You will need to cite to the correct reporter volume(s). Here, again, the Bluebook provides guidance about the various reporter names. Table T1 indicates which reporters to cite for most court decisions. Many state court cases are published in two or more sources. Whenever a case is reported in more than one publication, we call the multiple sources *parallel citations*. When writing court documents, you always refer to parallel citations for state cases. When writing other legal documents, such as legal memoranda or law reviews, you need only cite the regional reporter. If you use only a regional reporter citation, remember to include the name of the state and the level of the court in parentheses following the citation. Thus, when citing a case in a court document, your citation would be, for example,

> *Bisaillon v. Casares*, 165 Ariz. 359, 798 P.2d 1368 (App. 1990)

When citing the same case in a legal memorandum, you could simply write

> *Bisaillon v. Casares*, 798 P.2d 1368 (Ariz. App. 1990)

Whenever you use parallel citations, the order of the citations is important. You always use the official citation before the unofficial, regional one. An official citation comes from a reporter volume that is published by the government. Official state reporters are usually easily identified, as they carry the name of the jurisdiction. Thus, the *Arizona Reports* and the *Wisconsin Reports* would be official reporters.

In addition to the official reporters, many cases appear in reporter volumes published by private companies, such as the West Publishing Company. West publishes state court cases in reporters that collect state cases from geographic regions. West has divided the United States into seven different regions, each covering several states. The seven regions are the Atlantic, Pacific, Northeastern, Northwestern, Southern, Southeastern, and Southwestern regions. The text of the case in the official reports does not differ from the text of the case in the unofficial regional reporters. However, the regional reporter reprints of a case will contain editorial features to help you understand the decision. West Publishing Company publishes summaries of each case, as well as headnotes.* The summary, or synopsis, gives an overview of the case, together with its disposition. The headnotes tell you the terms under which the case has been indexed in the West Digest System. In addition, the headnotes pinpoint the exact portion of the case that is summarized and give summaries of each legal point covered in the case. These summaries are called *headnote paragraphs,* while headnote numbers pinpoint the actual section of the reported decision. Each headnote number corresponds to a number in brackets in the case. If you are interested in a particular concept from a case, you can easily determine whether the concept appears in the case and then locate the court's language about it. If the official reporter

---

*For further information, consult a legal research text such as Harris, *Legal Research* (Prentice Hall, 1997).

for your state is printed by the West Publishing Company, it will also include these helpful hints. If West does not publish the official reporter, you may not find either the synopsis or the headnotes in the official source. Remember that neither the synopsis nor the headnotes has been written by a judge. They are not part of the opinion and have no legal force or effect. Never quote these segments.

You may find that your case is not printed in one of the common unofficial reporters. Some cases are not reported at all in the regional reporters, while others are only reported in specialty reporters or on the Westlaw or Lexis systems. You should cite an unofficial reporter, a service such as CCH, a computer data base, a slip opinion, or a newspaper, in that order. When citing a service such as CCH, remember to give the paragraph number as well as the name of the court and the complete date (day, month, and year) in parentheses. If you are citing either Lexis or Westlaw, be sure to include the complete citation: Lexis and Westlaw citations always include a four-digit year plus the name of the computer company as part of the citation, in addition to an actual retrieval number. Citations to newspaper articles contain the name of the newspaper, the day, month, and year, and the number of the page on which the case is printed. Include the court name and the date of the decision in parentheses.

You may sometimes encounter unusual names for some reported cases. Early American reporters were often named after their editors rather than the jurisdiction, as is common today. The first 90 volumes of the *United States Reports* follow this pattern, as do many of the early state reporters. You may use both citations when citing these early volumes. If the page number is the same in both the jurisdictionally named reporter and the original reporter (carrying the name of the editor), you can include the name of the original reporter in parentheses. This parallel name will appear between the name of the jurisdictional reporter and the number of the page on which you find the case, as, for example, in

Green v. Biddle, 21 U.S. (8 Wheat) 1 (1823)

If the pages differ, write the two citations as parallel citations with the original reporter (carrying the name of the editor) second.

Every citation must include an indication of the court that decided the case. Sometimes we name the court explicitly. At other times, the name of the reporter volume will be enough, since that reporter would report cases from only one court. United States Supreme Court cases are the only cases reported in the *United States Reports*, the *Supreme Court Reporter*, and the *United States Supreme Court Reports, Lawyers' Edition* and *Lawyers' Edition, 2d*. Therefore, you do not need to indicate the court that decided the case when you cite any of these reporters. On the other hand, the *Federal Reporter* prints cases from all of the circuit courts. You will therefore need to indicate which circuit court decided the case whenever you cite this source. Similarly, the *Federal Supplement* reports cases from all of the federal district courts, so you must do the same when you cite it. Your court indication will appear in parentheses, together with the date when the case was decided. To indicate a numbered circuit, write the ordinal number plus the abbreviation "Cir." Thus, a second-circuit decision is abbreviated as "2nd Cir." You may sometimes find the abbreviation "CA2" in some sources. This is not correct.

Abbreviate district courts with the letter "D" plus an indication of where they are located. You only need to indicate a particular district court; you do not need to include the division of that court.

You will also have to indicate the names of state courts. If the name of the reporter is the same as the name of the jurisdiction, you will need to indicate only the names of the lower and intermediate courts. The reporter name will indicate the jurisdiction, and the absence of a court name means that the highest court in the jurisdiction decided the case. Of course, if the name of the jurisdiction is not conveyed (as when you cite only a regional reporter), you must indicate which court decided the case.

You will only need to indicate the year the case was decided when citing reported cases. However, if you are citing slip opinions, periodicals, electronic data bases, or looseleaf services, you will need to give the exact date (day, month, and year). The date follows the court.

Once you have given a complete citation, you may use a short form each time you cite the same source in your document. Be sure to indicate clearly that the complete citation may be found elsewhere in the document. Your reader should also be easily able to determine what you are referencing. Your short citation does not include the entire case name; usually, only the name of one of the parties is listed. The first page of the case and the court and date are also omitted. Instead, the short citation lists the name of one of the parties, the volume number and reporter name, and the word "at" indicating the page on which specific materials appear. Sometimes the entire case name will be omitted. If the previous citation includes the name, you may be able to omit the name as well. Instead, you will substitute the word "*id.*"[1] Remember to underline the term (including the period). Capitalize "id." only when it begins a sentence or stands alone. If you wish to refer your reader to the identical source (including the same page) as in the previous citation, you can use the term "id." without any page references at all. *Supra* and *infra* are Latin terms meaning "above" and "below." Traditionally, they

---

[1]"*Id.*" is an abbreviation for the Latin term *Ibidem,* which means "in the same place."

were used to refer to earlier citations. Now, however, a short form of citation is preferred, so these two terms are commonly replaced by "id."

You may occasionally have a source that is difficult to identify by the short form of citation. In such instances, you can create your own short form of citation and introduce it by the signal word "hereinafter." Cite the source completely, and follow it with the term "hereinafter" plus the shortened form of citation. You should include both the signal word ("hereinafter") and the citation in square brackets.

4.2.2   *Order of Citations*

You may wish to give more than one source for a particular legal point. Using several sources at one time is called *string citing*. This is usually not favored. Instead, you should select the best source for your legal point and cite it rather than adding numerous citations, all of which say the same thing. The practice of using many citations for each legal point is cumbersome. The numerous citations not only take up space (remember that your local court rules may limit the number of pages you may write), but also detract from the flow of your writing. Unlike scholarly papers, in which the aim is to impress readers with the quantity of research performed, court documents support legal arguments. Judges do not want to be impressed; rather, they want to understand the focus of your argument and know what legal authority(ies) support your claim. Any additional citations distract them from their task.

If, for some reason, you are committed to using several citations for a particular legal point, you should separate each one from the next with a semicolon. You should also consider the order of the citations. If one particular authority is more helpful than another, it should be placed first. Otherwise, relevant constitutions should be the first source listed, with the U.S. Constitution preceding any state constitution. If you plan to cite to more than one state constitution, list them in alphabetical order. Foreign constitutions and international charters are next in the order of precedence. Statutes should follow any constitutional references. List the federal statutes before any state statutes. If more than the federal statute will support your point, list the federal statutes according to their title and section number in numerical sequence. If you plan to refer to any federal statutes that are not part of the United States Code,[2] you should list these statutes by date, with the most recent statute first and the older statutes later. Any rules of evidence or procedure follow your federal statutory citations. Then come the state statutes. Here, again, as with federal statutes, you list multiple state statutes by their

---

[2]Or U.S.C.A. or U.S.C.S.

title and section (codification) numbers. When citing laws from several states, list the states in alphabetical order, and include all statutes from a particular state according to their statutory designation. Follow each state statute with references to applicable state rules of evidence and procedure. International agreements follow statutory material.

Next in the order of importance are cases. Begin your case listings with decisions from the U.S. Supreme Court. These cases are followed by decisions from the circuit courts of appeal and then by decisions from the federal district courts. Federal agency decisions come next. State court decisions are listed after the federal cases, alphabetically by state. Within each state, higher court cases precede decisions from lower courts. State agency decisions are then listed. Foreign court decisions follow state decisions. Finally, list decisions by international courts, such as the International Court of Justice.

Include other primary sources after these main classes of documents. References to pending legislation follow case law. Administrative and executive materials are listed after pending legislation, followed by intergovernmental sources and secondary materials. Secondary sources are also ranked.

Restatements and model codes are the most authoritative of the secondary materials and are therefore listed as the first of the secondary sources. Books by a single author are next. These are followed by references to law reviews or law journal articles. The complete ranking of citations is given in rule 1.4 in the Bluebook. A quick review of the order of citations shows that the various documents are listed in order of importance. Constitutions are the most important source and are listed first. Statutes are next in a generic ranking order and appear as the second group of citations. Cases follow statutes in importance and are listed after applicable statutes, while agency rules and regulations are the least important of the primary sources and are therefore listed last. Note that primary law outranks secondary law. Therefore, list all primary sources before referencing any secondary materials. Of course, you will not use all of these documents to support a given point. However, should you need to reference two or more types of authority, the general classification pattern just presented shows which to list first.

4.3
CONSTITUTIONS AND STATUTES

Whenever you cite a constitution, you must include the name of the jurisdiction as well as the abbreviation CONST. You then include the reference to the particular article, amendment, or preamble. A citation to the U.S. Constitution would be written as

U.S. CONST. Art. 1 S8, c1. 18

or

U.S. CONST. amend. 2

If the constitutional provision is currently in force, you do not need to include a date with this citation. If the particular provision has been repealed or amended, you would indicate this fact and the date of the amendment or repeal in parentheses. Alternatively, you may cite the repealing or amending provision—for example,

U.S. CONST. amend. XVIII (repealed 1933)

or

U.S. CONST. amend. XVIII, repealed by U.S. CONST. amend. XXI

Do not use a short citation form with a constitutional provision, except for "id."

You may cite statutes by either the official or the unofficial code. The correct citation form for the codes and session laws of the federal government, each state, federal territories, and the Navajo nation are listed in Table T1 of the Bluebook. The United States Code (U.S.C.) is the official federal code. Unofficial federal codes are the United States Code Annotated (U.S.C.A.) and the United States Code Service (U.S.C.S.). Each state has its own codes, listed in the alphabetical state sections in Table T1 of the Bluebook.

All statutory citations contain the name of the code, the title and section number (or paragraph or article number), and the year of the code. The year of the code is on the spine of the volume or on the title page, or else it is the latest copyright date. When citing federal laws, place the title number before the name of the code. The form of state code citations varies; consult Table T1 in the Bluebook for the statutory form used by the various states. If a code is identified by the title of its subject matter, as with a family code or a vehicular code, include the title as part of the citation. Sometimes you will find your citation only in a pocket part, or supplement. If so, indicate this in parentheses after the citation. If the citation appears in both the hardcover and the pocket part or supplement, cite the year shown in the hardcover and an indication of the supplement plus its copyright date in parentheses following the citation.

Not all statutes are codified at the time you wish to refer to them. When citing laws that have not been codified, cite the session law. Always give the name of the statute and the public law or chapter number. You may give a popular name as well as a chapter name. Give the volume number and the abbreviated name of the session law. When citing state session laws, always include the name of the state, even if the name is not part of the official title. If you are citing an entire act, you should give the page of the session law on which the act begins. If you are citing only a part of the act, you will need to give the page on which the act begins, as well as the actual page on which the relevant section is found.

Rules of evidence and procedure are cited without any date. Use the name of the rule and indicate the number. When citing a uniform act that is the law of a particular state, cite the uniform law as a state statute. When you are not citing the law of a particular state, cite the uniform law by its name, and give the title and section number. Always include the year of the act as part of the citation.

4.4
SECONDARY AUTHORITIES

Model codes and restatements require the section or rule number in addition to the name of the source. You must also give the year the code, restatement, or standard was adopted. Standard abbreviations for codes, restatements, and standards appear in Table T6 of the Bluebook. If you are citing a proposed draft or tentative draft, you should indicate that in parentheses following the citation. Include the year of the draft in the parentheses. Note that you omit references to uniform laws proposed by the National Conference of Commissioners on Uniform State Laws. However, if the standard or model rule was authored by a different group, you would abbreviate the name of the group in parentheses.

Citations of books and pamphlets include the name of the author or editor, the title, the volume or serial number (if any), the page, the section or paragraph number, the publisher, and the date. You would refer to a particular edition if there is more than one. Always give the author's full name the first time you cite the work.

Dictionaries and encyclopedias demand special forms of citation. Give the name of the dictionary and the page on which the definition you are quoting is found. Include the edition number and date in parentheses. For example, we would have

BLACK'S LAW DICTIONARY 684 (6th ed. 1990)

Encyclopedias require a reference to the volume number, the name of encyclopedia, the topic, the section number, and the copyright date. As with other citations, the date is placed at the end of the citation in parentheses.

4.4.1   *Law Journals*

Include the complete name of the author of a law journal article, as well as the title, the volume number, the name of the journal, and the first page of the material you are citing. Enclose the date in parentheses. Rules 16.1 through 16.3 of the Bluebook give the specifics of this form of citation. If there is no particular volume number, use the year of publication as the volume number.

4.4.2   *Annotations*

Some selective case reporters include annotations as well as cases. To cite these annotations correctly, you should include the author's full name followed by the word "Annotation." Next, include the title of the annotation, the volume number, the name of book, the page, and the date. As is usual with legal citations, enclose the date in parentheses.

4.5
COURT DOCUMENTS

You may need to cite court documents or court filings. Usually, you abbreviate the title of the court document, cite a particular paragraph or page number, and enclose the citation in parentheses. If the citation forms a complete sentence, use a period at the end of the paragraph inside the parentheses. You string multiple citations together using semicolons. Be sure that you identify each court citation completely, so that a reader can easily determine specifically to which document you are referring. You may also wish to use signal words in your citation.

4.6
CITE CHECKING

You need to remember the citation rules so that you can expedite your cite checking. You will usually cite check in order to ensure the accuracy of all citations that you present to a court or your attorney. Your first task will be to assure that the authority actually represents the legal point you want to make. You next need to assure that the citation is correctly written and that the volume and page number are accurate. Check the Bluebook format. If you are using a signal word, make sure that the word is correctly used and underlined. Finally, remember to cite check all sources for accuracy.

REVIEW QUESTIONS AND EXERCISES

Review Questions

1. What two tasks must a paralegal perform when cite checking?
2. What must you do if you cite check and locate a citation that has been overruled in part, yet you still wish to use the citation?
3. List the two authorities on the format of citations.
4. How is the Bluebook arranged?
5. Which section(s) of the Bluebook will be most helpful when preparing documents for court?
6. What is an introductory signal?
7. What is the meaning of the abbreviation "v.," and where do you most commonly use this abbreviation?
8. In addition to underlining the names of the parties to a legal dispute, what other terms or words are underlined in a case citation?
9. In case citations, you usually only use the last names of individuals. What is the exception to this rule?
10. Which party is usually listed first in a case citation?
11. How do you cite the name for the federal government?
12. When do you use the term "in re"?
13. What is the meaning of the phrase "ex rel"?
14. What is the general rule concerning abbreviations?
15. How do you correctly cite the name of a federal agency?
16. What is a parallel citation?
17. When must you use parallel citations?
18. Why would you want to include parallel citations?
19. What is an official reporter?
20. What is a regional reporter?

21. List the names of the seven regional reporters.

22. What is a headnote number, and how can you use it to help you in your reading of cases?

23. How should you cite an unpublished case that appears in either Lexis or Westlaw?

24. What should you include in a citation to a newspaper article?

25. How are early reporters often cited?

26. Why must you include a court designation with the federal reporters?

27. How should you indicate a numbered circuit court?

28. Why must you indicate a state court name when your only citation is to a regional reporter?

29. When and why must you give an exact date?

30. What is a short citation?

31. What is meant by the term "id."?

32. Differentiate between the terms "supra" and "infra."

33. When should you string cite? Why?

34. When using more than one citation, which citation should be placed first?

35. Correctly cite the Fourteenth Amendment.

36. Do you need to include the date with a citation to the First Amendment?

37. Which code is the official federal code?

38. Where can you find a listing of the state statutory sets?

39. How do you cite laws that have not yet been codified?

40. Must you give the year a rule of evidence or procedure was enacted?

41. Must you give the year a model code or restatement was adopted?

42. How should you cite a legal dictionary?

43. How does the citation of a legal dictionary differ from the way in which you cite a book or pamphlet?

44. How should you cite an annotation?

45. When citing multiple court documents, how can you string multiple citations?

Exercises

1. Correct the following fictitious citations:

   a. Doit v. Mesage; 913 F. Supp. 2d 54 (2nd Cir. 1995)

    b. Nabre versus Nabry. 786 P.2d 312 (Colo. App. 1989)

    c. Nichols v. Neare: 456 U.S. 312, 687 A.2d 43 (1992)

    d. Sethie v. Shrine, 233 A.2d 563 (N.J.1976)

    e. Montie v. Illinois: 455 U.S. 2, 106 S. Ct. 32 (1981)

    f. Ronin v. Kai; 312 S.E.2d, 43, 22 N.C. App.461 (1977)

    g. N.M. CONST. art.V S 2

    h. U.S. Const. AMEND. 14

    i. 17 U.S.C.S. 101

    j. 1993 Westlaw 23897

2. Correctly cite the following:

    a. Restatement (Second) of Torts section 16

    b. House Resolution 234 from the 101st Congress. Second session.

    c. A Second Circuit Court decision involving Honeypot and Cinnamon. The mythical case was decided in 1994. Create a possible citation, and use the correct reporter name for the case.

    d. Refer to section 43 from the topic of schools in the *Corpus Juris Secundum* encyclopedia.

    e. Refer to section 57 from the topic of constitutional law in the second edition of the *American Jurisprudence* encyclopedia.

    f. Cite *Black's Law Dictionary*. Select a word of your choice.

    g. Cite the Bible.

5 Cases and Case Briefing

5.1
INTRODUCTION

Cases form the backbone of the common law; therefore, reading and briefing (summarizing) cases is an important skill. Before we can brief a case, we must first learn how to read one and then examine the reasons why we summarize case law. This chapter explores both of these ideas.

Although published cases often have many segments to them, it is the judge's opinion that forms the heart of the case.[1] Each published case has a name or title segment and a listing of attorneys who were involved in the litigation. You will also find the date the case was decided and the name or names of the judge or judges who authored the opinion. In addition, many publishing companies add segments designed to help a researcher locate and understand the case. These segments are called the *synopsis* and the *headnotes*. The synopsis is an editorial summary of the entire case. The headnotes are

---

[1]For purposes of this chapter, a case means a judge's written opinion. Most written opinions are published in reporter volumes. Some, however, are never published, while others are available only in looseleaf reporters or on computer research services such as Lexis or Westlaw. Judges usually write opinions at the end of an appellate argument. The federal courts and a few state courts also write opinions at the trial court level.

summaries of individual legal points from the case. The headnotes and synopsis are not part of the opinion proper; they are not part of the case as written by a judge and have no legal effect in any jurisdiction. Rather, the headnotes and synopsis are a crutch that may help a reader to understand a case. Do not rely on these editorial helps: The more you rely on a crutch, the longer it will take you to learn to walk (or brief) independently.[2] If you have a case with a published synopsis and headnotes, you will probably never have to brief the case. However, you may read cases that are so new that no one has yet added these editorial features. Similarly, you may read cases that are not otherwise reported and for which no synopsis or headnotes will ever be written. In these instances, you will need to have the skill of case briefing. Furthermore, you should not rely on an editorial summary over the actual writings of the judge or judges, for it is the latter's writing that creates the law.

5.2
ANATOMY OF A CASE

To understand a case, you must first identify the facts of the case. A case may have both substantive and procedural facts. These facts tell the story of the case. The substantive facts tell you what happened to the parties of the ligitation and why they litigating. The procedural facts tell you about the different steps and stages of the litigation—that is, how a case proceeded through the legal system. A case may include discussions of the procedural as well as the substantive facts. In some instances a case may be decided on procedural facts, even though the substantive facts suggest that a different result is appropriate. You will sometimes want to summarize these two different kinds of facts. Other times, you will summarize just one or the other of them. To determine whether you need to include both kinds of facts, you will need to identify the issue or issues in the case.

The term "issue" refers to the question before the court. The issue is always the pivot or crux of any case because it is the problem the judge(s) must resolve. Some cases have only a single issue; other cases contain multiple legal and factual questions. You must locate the supporting or explanatory facts that illustrate or provide the dimensions of each issue in the case. In sum, then, you will first read the case and then determine what the issue or issues are. Once you find the issue(s), you look at the facts of the case and select those which relate to each issue. These are the facts that you must include in any case brief.

---

[2]Headnotes and synopses are accurate most, but not all, of the time.

Finding the issues of a case may be easy or difficult. In more modern opinions, judges tend to list the issues before the court at the beginning of the opinion. These cases are easy to brief because the authoring judge or judges have done most of the work for you. In other cases, the judge or judges seem to begin in the middle of the case and then include the issues and supporting facts later on. These cases are more difficult to understand and to brief. Of course, the more familiar you are with the area of law that you are reading, the easier it will be for you to read, understand, and brief the opinion.

Once you find the issues in a particular opinion, you should list them. Remember that issues are really the questions before the court or problems that the judicial panel must resolve. You write the case issues as questions when you brief a case.

Questions deserve answers. The court's answer to each question is called the *holding*. For each issue, there will be a holding. Holdings are the rulings that the judge or judges make after hearing the arguments in each case. Holdings create law. When you hear legal researchers or writers refer to judge-created law, they are really talking about the holdings of a number of cases. This is the essence of the common law. You will write the holdings as statements in your case brief.

Judges usually provide authority to support their holdings. This authority is usually legal authority—statutes, constitutions, or case law. It may, however, be public policy arguments. The authority or public policy provides support for the newly created law. The authority explains the reasons, or rationale, the judges used to arrive at the new opinion.

Every case brief must include the four basic categories that we have already discussed: facts, issues, holdings, and rationale. You must also include a correct and complete citation so that others can easily find the case.

When briefing a case, you should remember your purpose. Many firms request paralegals to brief new cases. These cases do not have a synopsis or headnotes, as they are often too new. At other times, paralegals are asked to brief cases that have been cited in appellate documents or in memoranda of points and authorities. The purpose here is to remind the attorney of the case should the attorney be questioned about a cited authority during oral argument.

5.3
READING THE COURT CASE

You may encounter several problems as you begin reading cases. These problems are neither unique nor insurmountable. However, as you read the cases, you may suddenly find that you feel "stupid." Remember that you are learning to read all over again. Case law reading is a deceptive exercise. Cases look somewhat familiar, as they appear to be written in English. However, this is not true: Cases are written in a separate language—the language of the law. When you begin to read a case, you may feel confused because you think that you are reading in English and that you should know the words. But you are not, and often you do not. You are reading law, a language in which familiar words and terms may have different or new meanings.[3] You should always have a good legal dictionary within easy reach when you begin to read case law.[4] Judges do not always define the terms that they use. Instead, they write as if readers were totally familiar with legal language. Furthermore, judges often pepper their writing with allusions to legal terms. Each time you meet an unfamiliar term, you should look it up in your legal dictionary. Just as you learned in elementary school, learn each new term as you encounter it. If you do, you will develop speed for future case readings. Unfortunately, however, legal dictionaries are not a panacea for language problems when one reads cases: Judges may not always use a word as it is used in the dictionary you consult. Accordingly, the dictionary will only be a guide to the meaning of an unfamiliar term. A legal dictionary is indeed a useful tool, but it will not always resolve case-reading difficulties.[5]

Legal reading is beset with problems other than unfamiliar language: Judges do not always write well. Good English prose is not a job requirement for a judicial position. Many case opinions are poorly organized, rambling, and inconsistent. Judges may stray from their assigned task and include writings that are not necessarily germane to the topic. Indeed, straying from the topic at hand is so common that lawyers have a term to describe this activity: *dicta.* The word (Latin for "words" or "remarks") refers to a judge writing about a peripheral issue. A poorly constructed opinion is difficult to understand. Nonetheless, you cannot simply disregard it; you will just need to spend more time reading these cases and avoid the tendency to merely quote portions of them. The essence of good case reading is understanding. You may need to actually translate some of these opinions, sentence by sentence or phrase by phrase. This is tedious, but necessary. In general, you should not go on to the next phrase or sentence unless and until you fully understand the preceding one.[6]

---

[3]You may need to define legal terms, terms of art, and Latin phrases.

[4]If a word does not seem to fit or make sense, consult your legal dictionary. You may have to translate from English to "legalese" so that you can understand the meaning of a phrase or sentence.

[5]You may also wish to consult a legal encyclopedia, such as *Corpus Juris Secundum, American Jurisprudence,* 2d., or *Words and Phrases.*

[6]You will, however, find times when the meaning of the sentence is not clear until you have read the entire section.

Case reading can be slow, difficult, and ponderous. However, remember that you are not reading for enjoyment; rather, you are reading to locate and understand the law, and this may require effort. Go slowly. Even when case opinions are well written, the cases may be difficult to understand. Many cases deal with complex legal concepts, and you often learn these concepts from the cases as you read them. If you are reading in an unfamiliar area, be prepared to spend additional time with the opinion. Your speed will increase as you learn the area of the law and as you practice your case reading. As with other areas, practice often helps.

Once you read a case, you must determine whether you actually understand all of its major points.[7] As stated earlier, these major points are the issues the court must resolve. You will know that you really understand a case if you can explain it in simple language. Ideally, you should be able to restate the principles of a case so that a child could understand them. If you can teach this case to someone who is unfamiliar with law, you probably understand the case's concepts or lessons. If you find that you are only quoting from the judge's opinion and cannot tell others what the case means in simple English, you probably do not really understand the case.

To fully understand a case, you must be able to identify what it is about. You should first identify the people or parties to the litigation. Law is about people—their likes, dislikes, plans, organizations, and activities. In some opinions, the parties are easy to identify. In others, you may need to translate the names used so that you can identify who or what is involved in the litigation.[8] If the case involves a large number of people or groups, you may want to diagram the relationships between them and between their property or items. You may wish to diagram a complex situation or chart a number of actions over time. Judges often tend to use the generic names "plaintiff," "defendant," "appellant," "appellee," "claimant," and "counterclaimant." Be sure that you know who the judge means when the judge uses any of these terms. Also, remember that the plaintiff at an earlier stage may now be the appellee. You must know whom the judge is writing about if the case opinion is to make any sense.

You can often identify the parties from the caption. At times, the main party is described in the first few paragraphs of the case opinion. Be sure that you determine how the parties are related to each other. Why or how did these people come into conflict with each other? Sometimes you can identify the parties by their relationships with each other—for example, husband and

---

[7]You may need to consult some of the cited authorities to help you clarify a difficult-to-understand legal concept.

[8]Some cases may deal only with property (e.g., civil forfeiture cases). These cases carry titles indicating that they are about pool tables, guns, or other forms of property.

wife, buyer and seller, landlord and tenant, parent and child, or neighbors. Other relationships may be between the government and the accused, a driver or tort-feasor and his or her victim, and an employer or employee. Understanding these relationships will help you understand the parties to the litigation.

You should also discover the role each party has in each stage of litigation. When you read a case, you are reading about a particular stage of litigation. It is as if you were seeing one act of a play with several acts. The players had earlier scenes and will often have later ones. You are seeing only one stage in the play. Similarly, when you read a case, you are reading about only one stage of the dispute. There were earlier stages, i.e., pretrial and often trial stages. There may be later stages—for example, later appeals or a remand to a lower court. A particular party may have a different role at each of these stages. You need to identify the role the party currently has, the role he or she may have had earlier, and a future role the person may yet play. The terms or names given to these roles may change as the individuals go through the litigation process. Following are some of the names encountered:

Plaintiff: The party who begins the litigation, usually by filing a complaint.

Defendant: The party who must respond to the litigation and against whom the plaintiff initiated the action.

Appellant: The party bringing the appeal. This name usually signifies that the party lost at a lower level.

Appellee: The party who must respond to the appeal. This is the winner at the lower court level. Some courts use the term "respondent" in place of "appellee."

Petitioner: The party who makes a request to a court.

Movant: The party who makes or made a motion which is a request that the lower court take some action in accordance with the court's rules of procedure.

Parties may often have different, even contrary, roles. Thus, a particular person may be both a plaintiff and an appellee. This would signify that the person brought the original lawsuit and won and is now responding to an appeal that the original defendant is bringing. Similarly, a party might be both a plaintiff and an appellant, which means that the person who initiated the original lawsuit lost and is now asking the court to correct a problem so that he or she can win. Courts sometimes distinguish the different stages of litigation by using the term "here," which refers to the court writing the opinion at the current stage. Courts also use the word "below" to refer to a lower court proceeding. When you brief a case, you may wish to refer to the parties by their current status or else by their original roles. Whichever it is, be consistent. If you begin by identifying a party as the plaintiff, do not suddenly change and refer to him or her as the appellee halfway through your writing. Determine which role best describes the person, and use that term throughout. Similarly, do not begin by referring to a party as a landlord and suddenly switch and call the same party the appellee (even though he or she is).

Once you identify the parties, you must concentrate on the reason for the litigation. What is this cause of action about? Ask what the parties were fighting over and what each party wanted. You need to identify this to yourself so that you can understand the rest of the case opinion. You will not be able to understand the facts of the case unless and until you know what the parties want and why they believe they are entitled to receive it.

Most often the plaintiff wishes to have the defendant do or provide something or, alternatively, to stop the defendant from doing or providing something. Occasionally, each party may have dual objectives in the same litigation. This means that the plaintiff may wish to have the defendant do something which the defendant wishes to prevent, while at the same time the defendant also wishes to have the plaintiff do something which the plaintiff does not want to do. In these cases the parties have more than one objective and may take on dual roles, such as defendant and counterclaimant. You can sometimes determine these objectives from the nature of the relationship the parties have. You merely need to ask why the parties became involved in the litigation. Once you identify the reason for the litigation, you will understand the objectives and be able to focus on the meaning of the case.

Your next job will be to identify the obstacles that prevented the unsuccessful litigant from reaching his or her goal. You also need to understand why the other party was successful in the litigation. Both of these pieces of knowledge will help you understand the issues at a specific stage of the litigation. With regard to the unsuccessful litigant, you will be looking for frustrations—the immediate problems that stopped a party from achieving his, her, or its goal. Some of these frustrations will be procedural—i.e., problems the party encountered in using the rules of litigation. Among these problems may be which evidence can or should be admitted, what pretrial steps a party is forced to take, and whether a new trial should be granted. Remember that procedural problems are seldom the reason for litigation, but they may be the reason for a particular judicial opinion. Here we are concentrating not on summarizing a case, but rather, on the ways you go about understanding the case.

Once you determine the reason for the litigation, you will need to translate it into legal terminology. It is not enough to find what each party wants: You must also identify the legal reason why each party should or could be successful. In law, we call this a *cause of action*. Each time a plaintiff files or makes a complaint against someone, the plaintiff must have a legally acceptable cause of action. Similarly, each time a defendant asserts a claim against the plaintiff, the defendant must have a legally acceptable cause of action. That is, the party responding to the claim must be able to assert a defense which is a legally acceptable reason why the other should not and cannot win. A defense blocks the other party's claim. Note that the cause of action and the defense may be factual or something set by law. Whether raising a cause of action or a defense, the reasons given for winning must be based on the prevailing standard of law in the jurisdiction. This standard may be a statute, a constitutional provision, or a common-law doctrine. The defense may be a denial of the other's cause of action or a denial that the facts support the asserted claim. The skills learned in legal research become invaluable in making this determination, since it is by using those skills that you can learn which circumstances and events can lead to a cause of action or a valid defense.

You can usually identify a valid cause of action or defense from the beginning of a case. The court will often detail the cause of action by using introductory phrases such as "This action involves" or "The present action" or "We are asked to decide." These statements usually precede the Court's discussion of the legal causes that are central to the case.

You will next need to determine the issue that was before the court that wrote the opinion and what events occurred earlier in the litigation. Courts will often provide you with the background of the entire litigation. At times, this background material can be confusing, as it may be difficult to separate what happened early on from the problems the court is now facing. Courts usually use the phrase "prior proceedings" to identify what happened at a lower level or earlier time and include the word "here" to refer to issues currently before the court.

The key facts of each case are the facts of the present litigation that will explain the controversy currently before the court. Focus on the facts associated with the problem the court must now solve. This problem may or may not relate to the ultimate objectives of the parties.

The current controversy may be either procedural or substantive. In either case, you must identify the facts that explain the legal situation. Facts are crucial in law: You cannot understand legal issues in a vacuum. You can find the necessary facts throughout the case opinion. Some modern cases attempt to provide readers with the facts at the beginning of the opinion. However, you should never depend on this to locate all the relevant facts, because judges have a tendency to insert additional facts later in the opinion. Earlier cases (usually written prior to 1960) do not use headings, so you must read these cases carefully if you are to locate the necessary facts. Remember that a fact provides information about a person, place, thing, or occurrence that someone can discuss or testify to. Facts are closely related to the senses and what they can perceive. Usually, facts can be learned from answers to the "who, what, when, where, and how" type of question.

Each case is replete with facts. Some of these facts set the stage for the litigation and help the reader understand the underlying conflict between the parties and the prior stages of litigation. Other facts describe the current status of the litigation. Not all facts are created equal: Some are far more important than others at a particular time or at a particular stage of the litigation. You must identify which facts from all of those presented were most important to understanding the questions before the court that decided the case. Note that you are not to determine how you would litigate the case if you were to present or advocate the entire claim for a party. Instead, you emphasize those facts which are crucial to understanding the court's opinion. To identify these facts, ask yourself as you read whether each fact, if changed, would have affected the court's opinion. If, for any given fact, you answer this question affirmatively, that fact is key.

You may have problems identifying key facts. Indeed, legal scholars often differ as to the importance of certain facts. Were this not so, we would never find judges disagreeing. However, you will often be able to determine which facts are pivotal by weighing their relevance to the court's decision. Remember to weigh each fact in relation to its importance to a particular opinion written at a particular stage of litigation, and not the relevance of each fact to the parties' ultimate goals. You will also find facts that are important, but not critical, since facts run the complete spectrum from the irrelevant to the crucial. Each fact and opinion must be evaluated on its own merits. The more important a fact is to the conclusion that the judges reach, the more you will want to emphasize that fact. You often need to look at *all* of the facts in the case to determine which are the crucial ones, since it may be a combination of certain facts that is key.[9]

When looking for crucial facts, be sure to examine only the facts relevant to the litigation before the court. Courts sometimes illustrate legal points by referring to precedent and by discussing the facts of the case in which the precedent was set. Do not confuse the facts from the illustrated cases with the facts of the litigation before the court.

Once you understand the factual background of a case, you will need to determine the issue or issues before the court. The issues are the core of every opinion, the legal questions the court must resolve. The facts you have identified earlier provide the basis for the legal issues and aid in understanding the parameters of each issue. Recall that in litigation you will encounter two

---

[9]Remember that if you are reading a case as a part of research for your firm, a fact that is not critical in the case you are reading could be critical to your research. Read these cases in light of what you are trying to accomplish.

kinds of issues: factual and legal. A factual issue, or question of fact, is a question about what happened. Courts at the appellate level are not concerned with factual issues, since these are usually left to the trier of fact, jury, or the trial judge.[10] Questions of fact are answered by the jury's verdict or the judicial finding and do not form the legal issues that appellate courts must answer. Legal questions (legal issues), on the other hand, deal with rules of law and how these rules apply to the facts of a particular situation. A rule of law can be a constitutional provision, a rule or regulation, a statute, or a common-law doctrine. The court will need to determine whether the rule was correctly applied to the given facts of the situation, whether the rule can be interpreted in more than one way, or whether the rule used was the correct rule for the facts of the case. The court may need to establish definitions for ambiguous terms in statutes, rules, regulations, or constitutional provisions. Thus, in some instances, the court will need to determine whether a lower court correctly interpreted a rule based on the listed facts or whether a particular legal rule should have been used with the listed facts. Courts also need to ensure that rules of law are applied equally to all persons and that different legal rules do not conflict when applied to the case at hand. An appellate court may need to consider whether one legal rule is consistent with another.

You will need to identify each issue in a case. Refer to the rule of law and to the relevant facts that illustrate the rule's application in the case when you phrase your issue. Determine whether the court is addressing a substantive or a procedural issue. Be sure to determine the relevant facts for each type of issue. Finally, remember that the issues are best determined by looking for disagreements between the parties.

Questions demand answers. The court's answer to a legal issue is called the *holding*. You will have one holding for each issue the court decides.[11] The holding results from a court applying one or more legal rules to the facts of the litigation. A correctly stated holding should include the rule of law, as well as those facts which are necessary to understand how the rule of law applies to the situation of the litigation. The holding is written as a statement.

The last essential component of a brief is the rationale or explanation for the court's holding. Courts often refer to legal authority in formulating a rationale. The court may cite a constitutional provision, a statute, a rule, a regu-

---

[10]This is not true in all situations although it is a good guiding principle. One notable exception to the principle that appellate courts never deal with fact questions is where the appellate court is the court of original jurisdiction.

[11]Sometimes a court will decide a case on one issue and ignore the other issues that the party raised. When this occurs, only the issues that have been decided have value as precedent.

lation, or a case opinion. Courts also create their own explanations for actions that the judges determine to be just. These explanations are called *references to public policy,* which means that the court is deciding the issue because of what the judges believe to be fair, just, or correct. In forming the explanation, the court may create new law by defining or redefining terms that have been used before, but are now the subject of controversy. Judges may also determine the reason or legislative intent behind a particular statute. In so doing, the judges, after consulting the legislative history, will give the statutory language either a broad or a narrow interpretation. In part, these definitions will reflect the study of the legislative history that the judges make.

Courts will frequently decide a case in accordance with decisions made by other jurisdictions or in older cases. Here the court is using precedent. Lawyers for the litigants often present this precedent to the court. At other times, the judges, their clerks, or other legal staff will research an issue, looking for precedent.[12] Courts will then compare the facts of the current litigation with the facts of the cases that set the precedent. Each set of facts is compared with the rule of law the court is discussing. The precedent will be the measure or reference that the court will use. The court will compare the rule of law and the facts in the case that set the precedent with the rule of law and facts in the present case. Where the critical or essential facts are similar, the court will apply the rule of law to the new situation. Where the factual basis differs greatly, the court will either fashion a new legal standard or determine that the existing legal rule is accurate, but inapplicable to the current situation. In the first instance, the precedent will be analogous to the new situation; in the second situation, the court will hold that the rule of law is not analogous and cannot be used. In either instance, the court will usually explain why the offered precedent should or should not be applied.

Once you have identified the facts, the issues, the holding, and the rationale of a case, you are prepared to write a simple brief. Include a complete citation, plus entries for each of these four main categories, in your brief. You should write the fact component as a paragraph or series of short paragraphs. Issues are questions and should be phrased as such. The holding is the court's statement. Accordingly, write it as such, using a complete sentence. Finally, you should write the rationale or explanation of the case as a complete paragraph.

Cases contain additional segments. From time to time, a judge will stray from his or her assigned judicial task and write additional remarks that are not necessary to the issues at hand. These additional remarks or comments

---

[12]Consult your legal research text such as *Legal Research* (Harris, Prentice Hall, 1997) for a more complete explanation of how to find this kind of legal support.

are called *dicta*.[13] Whenever a judge offers a gratuitous remark, the comment has little value as a precedent. Case holdings create law in the common-law system because they are judicial responses to a litigated battle in which opposing sides advocate differing positions. Without this advocacy the issue may not be fully prepared and any gratuitous comments may be discounted.[14]

Cases also contain a *disposition,* which is the action the court must take as a result of the holding. The holding creates law; the disposition tells you the next step that the parties to the litigation must take. In some instances, the disposition will be to remand or send the case back to the lower court. In other instances, the appellate court will affirm or approve of the lower court's decision. Alternatively, the appellate court may elect to reverse the lower court's action. Other dispositions include approving or denying a particular request or petition. Some cases have a combined disposition, where the appellate court affirms a particular issue and reverses a different issue in the same case.

Not all of the justices or judges on a panel have to agree with the decision. A valid decision requires either a plurality or a majority of the judges to agree. Most judicial panels are made of an odd number of judges. Half or more of them must agree with an opinion for the opinion to create law. Sometimes several judges will agree, but for different reasons. These judges are said to *concur* in the case opinion. In rare instances in which there is no clear majority, the appellate courts will issue a plurality decision. In a plurality, more than half of the judges can agree as to who should prevail. However, they reach their conclusions for different legal reasons. When a judge agrees only with the ultimate decision, but does not agree with how the decision was reached, the judge may simply state that he or she concurs, or the judge may write a concurring opinion. Those judges who disagree with the entire opinion are called *dissenting* judges. A dissenting judge may simply dissent or may elect to write a dissenting opinion expressing his or her views.

[13]*Dictum* is the singular form of the word. *Dicta* is the plural form and is used as an abbreviation for the phrase *obiter dictum,* which means an unnecessary remark.

[14]Dicta are never part of a case holding, but are not usually ignored. The legal principles enunciated in dicta are still good legal principles. However, the case stands not for these principles, but for the legal standards that are stated in the holding.

5.4
SAMPLE CASE BRIEF

Lasley v. Shrake's Country Club Pharmacy, Inc., 880 P.2d 1129 (Ariz. App. 1994)

George LASLEY and Velma Lasley, husband and wife,
and individually, Plaintiffs–Appellants,

Rebecca Lasley Dunning; Mark Lasley and Meredith Lasley,
Plaintiffs/Intervenors–Appellents,

v.

SHRAKE'S COUNTRY CLUB PHARMACY, INC., an Arizona Corporation;
Mary I. Shrake; John Doe Shrake and Jane Doe Shrake,
husband and wife, Defendants–Appellees.

No. 1 CA–CV 92–0216.

Court of Appeals of Arizona,
Division 1, Department E.

April 5, 1994.

Review Denied Oct. 4, 1994.*

Customer sued pharmacist for damages allegedly arising out of filling of prescriptions for addictive drugs. The Superior Court, Maricopa County, Cause No. CV 91–08279, William P. Sargeant, III, J., entered summary judgment for pharmacist and appeal was taken. The Court of Appeals, McGregor, Acting P.J., held that material issues of fact existed as to whether pharmacist breached applicable standard of care by filling prescriptions for drugs known to have addictive properties.

Reversed and remanded.

1. Negligence ☛ 136(14)
   In determining whether negligence duty of care exists, trial court decides question as matter of law.

2. Negligence ☛ 2
   Specific details of conduct subsumed within standard of care do not determine whether duty exists in particular case, but instead bears on whether defendant who owed duty to plaintiff breached applicable standard of care.

3. Drugs and Narcotics ☛ 19
   Pharmacist owed duty to customer, to comply with applicable standard of care in dispensing of potentially addictive drugs.

4. Negligence ☛ 136(14)

Although in most cases question whether defendant's conduct met applicable standard of care is question for trier of fact, in some instances court may decide as matter of law that defendant did not breach applicable standard and thus was not negligent.

5. Physicians and Surgeons ☛ 14(1), 18.-80(8)

In cases involving alleged negligence of health care providers, standard of care is based on usual conduct of other members of profession in similar circumstances, and plaintiff must present evidence of accepted professional conduct so that jury may measure defendant's conduct against applicable standards. A.R.S. § 12–563.

6. Drugs and Narcotics ☛19

Standard of care imposed upon health care providers applies to pharmacists.

7. Judgment ☛ 185.3(21)

Material issues of fact, precluding summary judgment on behalf of pharmacist, existed as to whether pharmacist had breached standard of care owed to customer in filling prescriptions; there was evidence that pharmacist had filled prescriptions for Doriden (Glutethimide) and codeine, over ten-year period, without advising patient of highly addictive nature of drugs or advising prescribing doctor that patient was taking them in quantities inconsistent with manufacturer's recommended dosage guidelines.

Broening Oberg & Woods, P.C. by James R. Broening, Cynthia V. Cheney, Daniel A. Zanon, Phoenix, for plaintiffs-appellants.

Roush, McCracken & Guerrero by Charles D. Roush, Robert D. McCracken, Phoenix, for plaintiffs/intervenors-appellants.

Gallagher & Kennedy, P.A. by Stephen H. Scott, Barry D. Mitchell, Phoenix, for defendants-appellees.

OPINION

McGREGOR, Acting Presiding Judge.

The various plaintiffs and intervenors (appellants) appeal from the trial court's grant of a motion to dismiss in favor of Shrake's Country Club Pharmacy, Inc. (Shrake's). The trial court held that a pharmacy has no duty to warn either the customer or his physician that prolonged use of a prescription drug dispensed by the pharmacy or use of the drug in combination with another prescribed drug may lead to addiction or adverse side-effects. We hold that the pharmacy owed the customer a duty of reasonable care and that the trial court therefore erred in holding as a matter of law that Shrake's had no duty to warn.

I.

In an appeal from the grant of a motion to dismiss for failure to state a claim upon which relief can be granted, we assume the truth of all the complaint's material allegations and accord the appellants the benefit of all inferences reasonably supported by the complaint. *See Sun World Corp. v. Pennysaver, Inc.,* 130 Ariz. 585, 586, 637 P.2d 1088, 1089 (App.1981). In this case, however, both sides presented matters outside the pleadings to the court when it considered the motion to dismiss, including an expert's affidavit, documentation regarding standards of practice for the pharmacy profession, information about the drugs prescribed to Lasley, and answers to interrogatories. We therefore treat the motion as a motion for summary judgment. *See* Ariz.R.Civ.P. 12(b); *Howland v. State,* 169 Ariz. 293, 297, 818 P.2d 1169, 1173 (App.1991). Summary judgment is appropriate when no genuine dispute as to any material fact exists, only one reasonable inference can be drawn from the facts, and based upon the facts the moving party is entitled to judgment as a matter of law. *Orme School v. Reeves,* 166 Ariz. 301, 309, 802 P.2d 1000, 1008 (1990).

II.

From 1960 to 1990, William K. Helms, M.D. (Helms) treated appellant George Lasley (Lasley). Helms prescribed Doriden and codeine, which Lasley alleges are potent and addicting drugs. Lasley filled most of the prescriptions from Helms at Shrake's. For approximately ten years, Shrake's mailed one or more of the allegedly addictive drugs to Lasley at his residence in another state.

Allegedly as a result of taking Doriden and codeine for an extended period of time and in combination, Lasley required in-patient hospitalization for Doriden detoxification and psychiatric treatment for addiction. He suffered from a major clinical depression and related disorders.

In March 1991, appellants filed their complaint against Helms and Shrake's.[1] Appellants alleged that Shrake's had breached a duty to Lasley "to exercise that degree of care, skill and learning expected of reasonable prudent pharmacies and pharmacists in the profession." Shrake's filed a motion to dismiss for failure to state a claim upon which relief could be granted. It argued that, as a matter of law, a pharmacist has neither a duty to warn of a prescribed drug's dangerous propensities nor a duty to control or keep track of a customer's reliance on drugs prescribed by a licensed treating physician.

In response, appellants argued that Shrake's owed a duty of reasonable care to Lasley and that whether it had breached the standard of care applicable to that duty was a question for the trier of fact. They presented to the trial court an affidavit from an expert and portions of the American Pharmaceutical Association Standards of Practice for the Profession of Pharmacy. Those documents indicated that the standard of care for a pharmacist includes obligations to advise a customer of the highly addictive nature of a prescribed drug and of the hazards of ingesting two or more drugs that adversely interact with one another. Appellants' evidence further stated that a pharmacist should advise the prescribing doctor if it appears that the patient is taking an addictive drug in quantities inconsistent with the manufacturer's recommended dosage guidelines.

The trial court granted the motion to dismiss. It found that Shrake's owed no duty to appellants to warn of addiction or to refuse prescriptions written by Helms. Following denial of appellants' motion for reconsideration, the trial court entered judgment dismissing the complaint against Shrake's with prejudice. Appellants timely appealed from the judgment.

---

[1]Helms is not party to this appeal.

III.

A.

[1] Because this is a negligence action, we first determine whether Shrake's had "a duty to conform to a particular standard of conduct to protect [Lasley] against unreasonable risks of harm." *Alhambra School Dist. v. Maricopa County Superior Court,* 165 Ariz. 38, 41, 796 P.2d 470, 473 (1990). In other words, we must consider, as did the trial court, whether the relationship between Shrake's and Lasley required Shrake's to use care to avoid or prevent injury to Lasley. *Markowitz v. Arizona Parks Bd.,* 146 Ariz. 352, 356, 706 P.2d 364, 368 (1985); *Bellezzo v. State,* 174 Ariz. 548, 550, 851, P.2d 847, 849 (App.1992). The trial court generally decides the question of duty as a matter of law. *Alhambra,* 165 Ariz. at 41, 796 P.2d at 473.

[2,3] Shrake's contends that the trial court correctly ruled that Shrake's had no duty to warn Lasley or his physician of the potentially addictive nature of drugs legitimately prescribed for Lasley. We believe, however, that the trial court's ruling confuses the concept of duty with that of standard of care.

In *Markowitz,* the Arizona Supreme Court cautioned against confusing the existence of a duty with details of the standard of conduct. 146 Ariz. at 355, 706 P.2d at 367; *see also Coburn v. City of Tucson,* 143 Ariz. 50, 51, 52, 691 P.2d 1078, 1079–1080 (1984). Specific details of conduct do not determine whether a duty exists, but instead bear on whether a defendant who owed a duty to the plaintiff breached the applicable standard of care. *Markowitz,* 146 Ariz. at 355, 706 P.2d at 367. In explaining the concept, the *Coburn* court quoted from Prosser and Keeton.

It is better to reserve "duty" for the problem of the relation between individuals which imposes upon one a legal obligation for the benefit of the other, and to deal with particular conduct in terms of a legal standard of what is required to meet the obligation. In other words, "duty" is a question of whether the defendant is under any obligation for the benefit of the particular plaintiff, and in negligence cases, the duty (if it exists) is always the same—to conform to the legal standard of reasonable conduct in the light of the apparent risk. What the defendant must do, or must not do, is a question of the standard of conduct required to satisfy the duty. 143 Ariz. at 52, 691 P.2d at 1080 (quoting W. Page Keeton et al., *Prosser and Keeton on the Law of Torts* §53, at 356 (5th ed. 1984).

In its answer, Shrake's admitted that it owed a duty to Lasley to comply with the applicable standard of care. We agree. Thus, the anwer to the threshold question in this appeal is that Shrake's did owe a duty of reasonable care to Lasley. The trial court therefore erred in finding, as a matter of law, that Shrake's owed no duty to Lasley.

B.

[4] Once the court determines that a duty exists, the next question is whether the defendant breached the standard of care established pursuant to the duty. *Markowitz,* 146 Ariz. at 356, 706 P.2d at 368. In most cases, whether the defendant's conduct met the standard of care is a question for the trier of fact. *Bellezzo,* 174 Ariz. at 551; 851 P.2d at 850. In some instances, however, the court may decide as a matter of law that the defendant did not breach the applicable standard of conduct and thus was not negligent. *Id.* (citing *Markowitz,* 146

Ariz. at 357, 706 P.2d at 369); *see also Coburn,* 143 Ariz. at 53, 691 P.2d at 1081 (city's failure to remove bush adjacent to intersection did not fall below its standard of care); *Rogers v. Retrum,* 170 Ariz. 399, 404, 825 P.2d 20, 25 (App. 1991) (failure of high school and teacher to restrict students to campus did not create unreasonable risk of vehicular harm to students). Thus, even though the trial court incorrectly granted summary judgment based on duty, if we can say as a matter of law that Shrake's did not breach its standard of care, we may affirm the trial court's judgment in favor of Shrake's. See *Gary Outdoor Advertising Co. v. Sun Lodge, Inc.,* 133 Ariz. 240, 242, 650 P.2d, 1222, 1224 (1982).

[5,6] In an ordinary negligence action, the standard of care imposed is that of the conduct of a reasonably prudent person under the circumstances. *Bell v. Maricopa Medical Ctr.,* 157 Ariz. 192, 194, 755 P.2d 1180, 1182 (App. 1988). Health care providers and other professionals, however, are held to a higher standard of care than that of the ordinary prudent person when the alleged negligence involves the defendant's area of expertise, *Id.* In these cases, the standard is based on "the usual conduct of other members of the defendant's profession in similar circumstances [and] the plaintiff must present evidence of the accepted professional conduct" so that the jury can measure the defendant's conduct against the applicable standard, *Id.* The plaintiff then must show that the defendant's conduct did not adhere to the standard, *Id.; see also* Ariz. Rev. Stat. Ann. § 12-563 (1992) (to establish liability, plaintiff must prove that "health care provider failed to exercise that degree of care, skill and learning expected of a reasonable, prudent health care provider in the profession or class to which he belongs within the state acting in the same or similar circumstances"). We impose this higher standard of care upon pharmacists because they are professionals in the health care area.

[7] Arizona courts have not yet considered whether the scope of a pharmacist's duty of reasonable care includes an obligation to warn customers of possible adverse effects of prescribed medications. Other jurisdictions, however, have resolved this question, and we look to their decisions for guidance. See *Bellezzo,* 174 Ariz. at 551-52, 851 P.2d at 850-51. Two distinct approaches have emerged for considering whether pharmacists have a duty to warn their customers.

As Shrake's asserts, the majority of jurisdictions that have considered the scope of a pharmacist's duty to warn customers have concluded, in various factual settings, that no such duty exists. Some courts, considering whether a pharmacist has a duty to warn the customer of possible adverse side effects of prescribed medications, have held no such duty exists.[2] In these cases, the courts

---

[2]See *Ramirez v. Richardson-Merrell, Inc.* 628 F. Supp. 85 (E.D.Pa. 1986) (alleging that pharmacy negligently failed to warn pregnant plaintiff that Benedectin could cause birth defects); *Leesley v. West,* 165 Ill.App. 3d 135;116 Ill.Dec. 136, 518 N.E.2d 758, *appeal denied;* 119 Ill. 2d 558, 119 Ill.Dec. 387, 522 N.E.2d 1246 (1988) (alleging that pharmacy negligently failed to warn of known but infrequent adverse side effects of Feldene): *Ingram v. Hook's Drugs, Inc.,* 476 N.E.2d 881 (Ind.App.1985) (alleging that pharmacy's failure to warn of possible side effects of Valium proximately caused injuries customer suffered in fall from ladder), *Nichols v. Central Merchandise, Inc.,* 16 Kan.App.2d 65, 817 P.2d 1131 (1991) (alleging that pharmacy negligently dispensed to pregnant plaintiff prescription that caused bone abnormalities in subsequently born child); *Stebbins v. Concord Wrigley's Drugs, Inc.,* 164 Mich.App.204, 416 N.W.2d 381 (1987) (alleging that pharmacy negligently failed to warn customer of side effects of Tofranil and that he should not drive after taking the drug).

generally reason that imposing a duty to warn on the pharmacist would place the pharmacist between the physician, who knows the patient's physical condition, and the patient, and that recognizing such a duty could lead to harmful interference in the patient-physician relationship.[3]

Other courts, considering the duty to warn in a factual situation similar to that before us, have concluded that pharmacists have no legal duty to warn the patient or physician when the physician prescribes excessive doses of a drug.[4] Those courts conclude that the physician, not the pharmacist, has the duty to prescribe drugs properly and to warn the patient of any dangers from taking the medication. Imposing a duty to warn on pharmacists would compel them to second-guess every precription physicians write if the pharmacists wished to escape liability.[5]

We reject the analysis relied upon in these decisions for the reasons stated in *Markowitz*. The decisions do precisely what the *Markowitz* court cautioned against; they use details of the standard of conduct to determine whether a duty exists.

Other jurisdictions, applying the same distinction between duty and standard of conduct as that explained in Markowitz, have concluded that whether a failure to warn violates the applicable standard of conduct in a particular situation generally presents a question of fact for the jury. In *Dooley v. Everett*, 805 S.W.2d 380 (Tenn.App.1990), the plaintiff alleged that the pharmacy had a duty to warn a customer or the customer's physician or both of the potential adverse interaction between two drugs prescribed by the same physician on different days and filled by the same pharmacist on different days. The pharmacy moved

[3]*See Ramirez,* 628 F.Supp. at 88; *Nichols,* 817 P.2d at 1133.

[4]*See Jones v. Irvin,* 602 F.Supp. 399 (S.D.Ill. 1985) (considering whether pharmacist is negligent for failing to warn customer or notify physician that drug is being prescribed in dangerous amounts, that customer is being over-medicated or that various prescribed drugs in combination with others could cause adverse reactions); *Pysz v. Henry's Drug Store,* 457 So.2d 561 (Fla.Dist.Ct.App.1984) (alleging that pharmacy negligently failed to warn customer of addictive propensities of Quaaludes while filling Quaalude prescription for more than nine years and negligently failed to inform physician of customer's known addiction); *Fakhouri v. Taylor,* 248 Ill.App.3d 328, 187 Ill.Dec. 927, 618 N.E.2d 518, *appeal denied,* 152 Ill.2d 557, 190 Ill.Dec. 887, 622 N.E. 2d 1204. (1993) (alleging that pharmacy negligently filled prescriptions for quantities of Imipramine beyond those normally prescribed and negligently failed to warn physician or customer of excessive and unsafe quantities); *Eldridge v. Eli Lilly & Co.,* 138 Ill. App.3d 124, 92 Ill.Dec. 740, 485 N.E.2d 551 (1985) (alleging that pharmacy negligently filled prescriptions for quantities of Darvon and other drugs beyond those normally prescribed and negligently failed to warn physician that prescriptions were for an excessive quantity). *Adkins v. Mong,* 168 Mich.App. 726, 425 N.W.2d 151 (1988) (alleging that pharmacy negligently supplied plaintiff with excessive amounts of prescribed controlled substances for six years); *Kampe v. Howard Stark Professional Pharmacy, Inc.,* 841 S.W.2d 223 (Mo.App. 1992) (alleging that pharmacy failed to monitor or evaluate plaintiff's use of prescribed drugs during the two and a half years it filled the prescriptions). *McKee v. American Home Prod. Corp.,* 113 Wash.2d 701, 782 P.2d 1045 (1989) (alleging that pharmacists who filled plaintiff's drug prescriptions for ten years had duty to warn her of adverse side effects of long-term administration of drug).

[5]*See Jones,* 602 F. Supp. at 402; *Pysz,* 457 So.2d at 562; *Fakhouri,* 248 Ill.App. 3d 328, 187 Ill.Dec. at 930, 618 N.E.2d at 521, *McKee,* 782 P.2d at 1050, 1051, 1053.

for summary judgment, arguing that as a matter of law the pharmacist owes no duty to his customer to warn of potential drug interactions. In opposition to the motion, the plaintiff filed an expert's affidavit that set forth various standards of care that the pharmacy allegedly had violated.

The *Dooley* court first noted the distinction between duty and standard of care and determined that the pharmacy owed its customer a duty to use due care under the attendant circumstances. 805 S.W.2d at 384. The court then considered whether the scope of the duty the pharmacist owed the customer included an obligation to warn. The court concluded that, because the plaintiffs had introduced expert testimony to dispute the pharmacy's argument that warning of potential drug interactions was not part of its duty, the disputed issue of fact prevented the granting of summary judgment. *Id.* at 386.

Similarly, in *Hand v. Krakowski,* 89 A.D.2d 650, 453 N.Y.S.2d 121 (1982), the court reversed summary judgment in favor of a pharmacy, finding that a jury question existed when the pharmacist knew that the customer was an alcoholic and knew or should have known that the prescribed drugs were contraindicated with the use of alcohol. Under those circumstances, the court believed that the pharmacist may have had a duty to warn the customer of the danger involved and to inquire of the prescribing doctor whether the drugs should be discontinued. 453 N.Y.S.2d at 123. In *Riff v. Morgan Pharmacy,* the court affirmed a jury verdict that found the pharmacy jointly liable for injuries sustained from a potentially toxic drug prescribed without a warning describing side effects that could result from exceeding the maximum safe dosage. 353 Pa.Super. 21, 508 A.2d 1247 (1986), *appeal denied,* 514 Pa. 648, 524, A.2d 494 (1987). The court held that "the pharmacy had a legal duty to exercise due care and diligence in the performance of its professional duties." 508 A.2d at 1251–52. The court concluded the plaintiff had presented sufficient credible evidence to establish that the pharmacy breached its duty by failing to warn the patient or notify the physician of inadequacies on the face of the prescription that "created a substantial risk of serious harm to the plaintiff." *Riff,* 508 A.2d at 1252.

In response to Shrake's motion to dismiss, appellants presented an affidavit from an expert stating that the standard of care applicable to a pharmacist includes a responsibility to advise a customer of the addictive nature of a drug, to warn of the hazards of ingesting two or more drugs that adversely interact with one another, and to discuss with the physician the addictive nature of a prescribed drug and the dangers of long-term prescription of the drug. Appellants also presented excerpts from the American Pharmaceutical Association Standards of Practice for the Profession of Pharmacy that described similar standards. On this record, we cannot say as a matter of law that Shrake's did not breach the standard of care for the duty it owed to Lasley.

IV.

For the reasons explained above, we reverse the trial court's grant of summary judgment in favor of Shrake's and remand to the trial court for further proceedings.

JOHN FOREMAN**, Superior Court Judge, Maricopa County, and WILLIAM J. O'NEIL,** Superior Court Judge, Pinal County, concur.

5.5
SAMPLE CASE BRIEF

Lasley v. Shrake's Pharmacy, 179 Ariz. 583, 880 P.2d 1129 (App 1994)

Facts: The plaintiff had been prescribed the addictive drugs Doriden and codeine for approximately 30 years. During this time, Shrake's pharmacy usually filled the prescriptions. The plaintiff became addicted to the drugs and required hospitalization, as well as psychiatric treatment. The plaintiff brought a tort suit against the pharmacy alleging that the pharmacy had a duty to warn him about the dangerous propensities of these drugs. The drugstore filed a motion to dismiss the case, which the trial court granted. The plaintiff appealed from the judgment dismissing the complaint with prejudice.

Issue: Did the trial court correctly rule that the pharmacist had no duty either to warn a customer of a prescribed drug's dangerous propensities or to keep track of the customer's drug usage?

Holding: The court ruled that the pharmacist had a duty to advise a customer of the addictive nature of a drug and to warn the customer about the danger of taking two drugs together.

Rationale: The court examined precedent from around the nation to determine whether pharmacists owed their customers a duty of care. The majority of jurisdictions found no such duty. Nonetheless, the Arizona court ruled that the pharmacy had a legal duty to exercise due care in carrying out its professional duties. The court relied in part on expert testimony holding that the standard of care for a pharmacist includes the responsibility to advise a customer of the addictive nature of a drug. In so doing, the court also relied on the American Pharmaceutical Association's "Standards of Practice for the Profession of Pharmacy."

Disposition: The court reversed the trial court's holding and remanded the case for further proceedings.

5.6
CONCLUSION

Briefing cases is a skill you acquire through practice. Reading and briefing 1, 2, or 3 cases will not provide you with enough practice to do more than learn the parts of a brief. Instead, you should begin with at least 75 cases. At first this number may sound daunting, particularly if you are currently spending several hours to read a single case. However, as with many other training devices, practice improves speed. Unfortunately, practice does not necessarily make perfect, despite the homily. Only perfect practice makes perfect. But practice does improve your speed and will help you to master the difficult skill of case analysis, a skill you will need in order to begin writing legal memoranda.

REVIEW QUESTIONS AND EXERCISES

Review Questions

1. What is the most important part of a brief?
2. What is a synopsis?
3. What is the purpose of a synopsis?
4. What are the facts of a case?
5. Are all facts in a case equally relevant?
6. What are procedural facts?
7. What are substantive facts?
8. What is the most important part of a case to identify?
9. In a case, why must you find the issue before you can determine which facts are important?
10. What is the holding of a case?
11. How does a holding compare with judge-created law?
12. What kind of authority does a judge usually cite to support his or her conclusions?
13. How does public policy support a judge's position?
14. What is the purpose of briefing a case?
15. List several sources you can use to find the legal definitions of words.
16. What is dicta, and why do judges write dicta?
17. Why should you not simply quote from the judge's opinion when briefing a case?
18. What is the difference between a plaintiff and an appellant?
19. What is the similarity between a plaintiff and an appellant?
20. What is the difference between a defendant and an appellee?
21. What is the similarity between a defendant and an appellee?
22. What is the meaning of the terms "below" and "here"?
23. What is a cause of action?
24. What is a defense?
25. What are key facts?
26. Why are facts so important in a case?

27. How can you identify a key fact of a case?
28. What is a factual issue?
29. What is a legal issue?
30. What is a holding?
31. How should you state a holding?
32. What is the rationale?
33. What is a precedential case?
34. What is the disposition of a case?
35. How does the disposition of a case differ from the rationale for the case?
36. How many judges must agree with the legal conclusion and decision to create law?
37. What is a concurring opinion?
38. What is a dissenting opinion?

Exercises

1. Read *Fisher v. Lowe*, 333 N.W.2d 67 (Mich. App. 1983). Brief the case. Why do you suppose the court wrote the opinion in rhyme?
2. Read *Helton v. State*, 311 So.2d 381 (Fla. App. 1975). Brief this case.
3. Read *Commonwealth v. Maritime Underwater Surveys, Inc.*, 531 N.E.2d 549 (Mass. 1988). List the key facts of the case. List the precedent the judge used to support his conclusion. Why did the court use a literary analogy?
4. Read *Roe v. Rampton*, 535 F.2d 1219 (10th Cir. 1976). Brief the case.
5. Read *Carroll v. Lordy*, 431 N.E.2d 118 (Ind. App. 1982). Why did the court include the recipe for elephant ears? Brief the case.
6. Brief *Cardozo v. True*, 342 S.2d 1053 (Fla. App. 1977).
7. Why did the court quote from Benjamin Franklin's commentary on the benefits of saving a penny in *Citibank v. Warner*, 449 N.Y.S. 822 (1981)? Brief this case.
8. Read *Schumer v. Schumer*, 129 N.Y.S.2d 119 (1954). The judge uses some colorful language. List the phrases that you believe add color to the opinion. How does this language contribute to the opinion? Does it make the ruling easier to understand? Does it help the reader to understand the judge's opinion? Brief this case.
9. *United States v. Satan and His Staff*, 54 F.R.D. 282 (W.D. Pa. 1971) is a procedurally interesting case. What is the issue in this case? Which facts are needed to understand the opinion? Do you need to know about the particular obstacles that the plaintiff faced? Why or why not? Brief this case.

6 *Legal Memoranda*

6.1
INTRODUCTION

A legal memorandum is the main way in which you communicate the result of legal research to a reader. Sometimes the reader is an attorney or other employee of the law firm. Legal memoranda directed to these people are called *internal* or *in-house* legal memoranda. At other times, you may be writing to an outsider. These types of memoranda are called *external* legal memoranda. Typically, external legal memoranda are written to judges in support of motions or requests. Such memoranda are often called *memoranda of law* or *memoranda of points and authorities*. These two types of memoranda share similarities in their approach; they differ in terms of format and writing style.

The first job you have in preparing legal memoranda is to perform thorough research on both the facts and the law you are writing about. You must know your facts. As mentioned in the preceding chapter, law does not exist in a vacuum: It has life only when it relates to a legal situation. Be sure you know your facts before you do anything further.

6.2
PREPARATION OF FACTS

You will most often learn your facts from the client's file. Normally, the file contains notes pertaining to client interviews, the complaint, the answer, pretrial disclosures, admissions, documents, interrogatories, and deposition transcripts.[1] You may also have reports from expert witnesses, statements by witnesses to the events, or other documentation that supports your client's claim. Your first task will be to organize these factual materials so that you can learn what actually occurred and gave rise to the legal situation. Once you have these materials organized, you will select those statements and facts which best support your client's claim. Remember to keep in mind any factual materials that detract from your client's claim as well: You would not like to be surprised by any detrimental materials at a later time, so be prepared to deal with negative facts, in addition to those facts which favor your position. Note any gaps in the facts. If you find that there are missing bits of information, you should be prepared to contact your client[2] so that you can fill in these omissions. Next, list the facts necessary to support your claim, and note where and how you found support for each of these facts. Even if you do not include the source for your facts in the writing you submit, you should be able to pinpoint the source for each fact if asked to. Keeping a listing of your factual sources as you prepare the facts will save you time later on.

6.3
LEGAL RESEARCH

Next, accumulate your necessary legal precedents. Remember to check relevant constitutional provisions, statutes, rules, regulations, and case law.[3] Prefer binding over persuasive law at all times, as long as the authority deals directly with your problem. In this regard, your first task is to locate law that in fact does deal with your legal problem. Collect law that supports your client. You should also seek law that will support your adversary. Depending on

---

[1]This listing is by no means complete; search your file for all of the relevant facts concerning your case or research problem.

[2]If allowed by your supervising attorney; always report these gaps to your supervisor before discussing them with the client.

[3]Refer to a legal research text such as *Legal Research: FUN-damental Principles* for details.

the type of legal memoranda you plan to write, you may or may not wish to cite law supporting your adversary. However, you should always have these contradicting references available so that you can quickly locate them. You always want to be prepared. If you know the weapons your adversary can use, you are in a better position to defuse them with your writing. Remember that after you collect your reference sources, you must always read and update these authorities. Do not neglect to read them: You cannot analyze a legal source you have not carefully read. Ignore the tendency to accept the headnotes or synopsis as the law. Headnote research may be fast, but it is not accurate. Shepardize and instacite or autocite your law.[4]

6.4
LEGAL ANALYSIS

Once you have collected your legal sources, you are ready to analyze these materials. You must determine how you plan to use each case that you have.[5] While you are reading each one, you should make notes indicating language that you might like to quote or paraphrase. You should also indicate how the case you are reading parallels your client's legal situation or how the case authority differs from your client's legal problem. Write down these similarities and differences. Note any significant gaps between the factual situation in the legal authority and your client's facts. You may want to "grade" your authority. Some case law is quite similar to a client's problem. If the court in that case resolves the difficulty in a way that would favor your client, you should note this on your copy of the case.[6] These notations will save time later on when you actually begin to draft your memorandum. You should also indicate whether the case law favors your client or your adversary. Again, while in the planning and researching stages, you should not discount or ignore any materials that might be relevant to your problem, whether the authority is positive or negative from your client's standpoint.

[4]This assumes that you have access to Westlaw for instaciting or Lexis/NEXUS for autociting.

[5]You may decide to use only some of your cases. This is acceptable. You usually find more authority than you need for your memo.

[6]Legal researchers often photocopy cases so that the case law is readily available for reference when preparing legal memoranda.

Statutes and constitutional provisions are the best sources of legal authority; take advantage of them. First, make sure that the statute or constitutional provision is on point (relevant to the client's case) and specifically resolves your legal problem. Next, ensure that you fully understand all of the terms in the statute or constitutional provision. Be sure that the statute was meant to handle the situation that involves your client. Determine whether you will be advocating the plain meaning of the statute (what it says is what it means) or its legislative intent. Find case law that discusses the constitutional provision or statute, and be prepared to locate legal support for both sides of the issue. Remember that your adversary will be arguing against your position. The more you know about your adversary's claim, the better able you will be to counter the claim in your writing.

You can defuse potentially negative sources by your choice of words when you write. Ethically, you cannot ignore law that directly contravenes your position. Much as you may like to pretend that these sources do not exist, you must contend with them. They simply will not go away. Furthermore, you cannot ignore relevant law that is directly on point from your jurisdiction just because the law does not say what you like. If you are writing to a court, you have an ethical obligation not to misstate the law. If you are writing an internal memorandum, you must apprise the other members of the firm of potential problems they may encounter. You should be prepared to deal with these sources honestly, but in a way that does not unduly emphasize their effect. You do not need to advocate your opponent's position; that is for your adversary to do. To best accomplish your goal of apprising your reader of negative law (law that does not advance your client's position), remember that your choice of verbs and voice will directly affect how the reader will regard this law. Recall that, to emphasize a point, you should use the active voice and strong verbs. To de-emphasize something, use the passive voice and weak verbs.

Next, organize your various legal authorities so that they will provide a logical progression. You may wish to go either from the most recent to the least recent or from the earliest to the latest to show the development of a legal trend. You may wish to go from a general pronouncement of a legal position to more specific illustrations of how the legal position is carried out. Another approach would be to create a plan of activity for your client and develop legal support for each stage of the plan. Still another approach is to list all of the law supporting a particular position and then give the law that challenges the position. There are no rules about which organizational scheme is best. Your best organization will directly relate to your particular problem. What is important is that you remember to develop your legal strategy for approaching your memorandum before you begin to write.

6.5
ORGANIZATION OF THE INTERNAL
LEGAL MEMORANDUM

Most internal legal memoranda follow similar organizational patterns. First, check whether your law firm has a standard form for you to follow. If so, use it. Most in-house legal memoranda contain certain basic information. Typically, the heading of the memo includes the name of the person writing the memo, the person to whom the memo is addressed, the date the memo was written, and an indication of the client's name, the billing number, and the subject of the memo. This information is often stated as a heading using the terms "to," "from," "re," and "date." The word "to" indicates the recipient of the memo, while "from" tells the reader who wrote the memo. Do not omit these terms because you feel that the attorney who assigned the task to you will automatically know who wrote the memo. You have no assurance that the person reading the memo is the same person who assigned the work.

Many law firms maintain memo files in which legal research on previous cases is indexed for later reference. The memo file is a valuable asset that allows attorneys to use research for more than one client. If a legal question has already been researched for a previous client or case, a lawyer can save a great deal of time by using the earlier research and updating it. When doing this, remember that the research was not done for the current client, so the case law may need to be evaluated and updated in light of the new client and new problem. Readers may have questions when they read the memo, and the "to" and "from" headings will tell these later readers whom to check with if they have any problems. The information pertaining to the date is crucial. Legal memoranda may be written in advance of the time when the law is actually needed. The date segment of the memo tells readers when the memo was written in the event that the reader needs to update or cite check the memo. If the date segment is available, future readers will need to update the memo only from its original date.[7] Note that when you access a legal memo originally drafted for a client other than your current client, the date segment will tell you how much updating will be required to complete the new research project. The "re" segment informs readers who the client is, for whom the research is done, and gives a quick indication of the topic of the research.

---

[7]When updating a memo, consider using a beginning date that is approximately three to six months prior to the actual original date of the memo. Choosing a somewhat earlier date as the point from which you update will help ensure that you do not miss any recent law. Remember that unless you do your legal research on a computerized system such as Westlaw or Lexis, the research may be three to six months out of date because of the lag in publishing court opinions.

The memo proper often begins with a statement of the parameters of the research. You may call this the *statement of assignment.* If you have limits on your research pertaining, for example, to a particular jurisdiction or period of time, or if you have only a limited amount of research time, you might expressly state this in your statement of assignment. As with the other segments of a legal memo, you should use the segment name, "Statement of Assignment," to head the section. Note that when you do not have limits on your research, you may not wish a statement of assignment.

The "Question Presented" or "Issue" segment is one of the most important sections in the memo. It tells the reader about the legal issue. Be specific in formulating your issue, and make sure that it relates to the case. Remember that, as with cases that have been decided, legal questions do not exist in a vacuum. Thus, you cannot simply ask whether the Eighth Amendment prohibits cruel and unusual punishment; instead, you must ask whether a particular kind of sentence violates cruel and unusual punishment standards and describe the sentence as part of the "issue" segment of the memo. Observe that this segment is a query and should be phrased as such. You may find it helpful to think of your issue as the answer to a sentence that begins "This is the story of. . . ." This sentence should help you to focus on the theme or central point of the memo. Your legal memo is not just a discussion of an interesting legal question; rather, you are writing about how a law or set of standards applies to someone's conduct.

Usually the "Question Presented" segment is followed by the Conclusion of the memo. The conclusion is a short summary of the results of your research. You may find it easier to write the conclusion at the end of the memo. If so, you can move the conclusion to the front of the paper once you complete the memo. You should not begin analyzing the issue with a preconceived conclusion. However, once you reach the writing stage,[8] you may find that you can make your point more forcefully if you begin with the conclusion, which then acts as a guidepost for the remainder of the paper. Many attorneys prefer a short answer to the legal question immediately after it is posed, so that they know the substance of the longer discussion.

The discussion is the heart of the paper. It includes a summary of the facts and legal principles that relate to the issue. You begin by describing the important or relevant facts. Be specific and avoid generalities. It is easy to fall into the trap of making conclusions in your facts. Facts should be factual. Do not simply use adjectives to describe a situation, as adjectives are often im-

---

[8]Remember that the analysis portion of any writing precedes the writing itself. Your analysis or thinking stage is separate and independent from the writing stage. By the time you begin writing, you should have already formulated the conclusion that results from your research and the application of the law to your facts.

precise. For example, if you say that a box is heavy, does anyone really know what you mean? In order to understand the meaning of "heavy" in this context, the reader would need to know how strong the person describing the situation is. What is heavy to a 10-year-old child is not heavy to a weight lifter. Instead, if you were to write that the box weighed 30 pounds, the reader would know exactly what you mean.

In the discussion segment of the memo, you also present those authorities which illustrate the legal principles that form the foundation for your conclusion. You analyze case law as well as statutes. In some ways, this legal analysis replicates the type of legal analysis you do in briefing a case. When you discuss a legal principle, give a complete citation for your legal authority. For each case you mention, include a short discussion of how the case applies to the facts of your litigation. Tell how your client's situation is similar to or different from the situation of your illustrative case. Suggest that the court follow or ignore this precedent if appropriate. If you do make a suggestion, be sure that your reasons are clearly and concisely expressed.

Remember that with an internal legal memo, your purpose is to explain and not to convince. Therefore, use an expository style and explain the law descriptively. Just as a judge would in writing an opinion, present both sides of the issue and discuss the strengths and weaknesses of the case. When you discuss the weaknesses, be alert so that you can locate or determine ways to distinguish these cases from your factual situation. When discussing the strengths, compare your researched cases with the factual situation. Be realistic: If the law goes against your position, you should state this. Omit personal opinions from your legal discussion; however, you may include public policy arguments in your memo. When the legal authorities conflict or when there is little law in the area, you may elect to discuss policy considerations.

Quotations from relevant case law are sometimes helpful. Quotations should be short and correctly cited to the specific page in the case. Do not use too many quotations. Similarly, do not use very long quotations, because they can distract your reader from the point of your discussion. Finally, be sure that each quotation you use is accurate.

The last section of an internal legal memorandum is reserved for recommendations. Recommendations can be tricky: Senior attorneys often do not take kindly to them when they are suggested by juniors. Consequently, when you make a recommendation, make sure that you actually have something substantive to recommend. Never suggest that a case will definitely have a successful outcome. Even when the law supports your position, you cannot be sure of success. If you predict in writing that a case will be successful, and your client should lose, your written prediction can be used in a malpractice action against your firm. Any recommendation or suggestion you make should be for a specific type of action that you feel the firm should take.

6.6
THE EXTERNAL LEGAL MEMORANDUM

An external legal memorandum is directed to someone outside of the law firm. Most of these legal memos go to courts in support of motions or to resolve a question of law in response to a judge's request. External legal memoranda differ in style from internal legal memoranda, since their purpose is not just to explain, but to also convince. Accordingly, they use a persuasive writing style. Because they often deal with more than one topic, use headings to separate different topics. Since your goal is to convince the judge, your headings should be phrased persuasively. You should also emphasize the strengths of your client's case, as well as the weaknesses of your opponent's position. In this type of legal memorandum, you will primarily refer to law that supports your client. Your adversary will apprise the court of contradictory information. You cannot misstate the law, and you must tell the court of any controlling authority that directly supports your opponent. However, you do not need to write about facts and law that favor your opposition, since your adversary will provide this information to the court. This may appear contradictory, but it is not. Your duty is to tell the court of *controlling* negative precedent, not *all* negative precedent. Authorities are not controlling unless the particular case, statute, or regulation is binding in your jurisdiction. Detail the facts that favor your client. Remember that when you need to include facts which favor the opposition, you can de-emphasize them by stating them briefly, using the passive voice, and selecting weak verbs.

Facts are important in memoranda to the court. Be sure that you include all necessary facts. Be as specific as possible, and avoid conclusions. As with the internal legal memorandum, you should prefer to list incontrovertible facts rather than factual conclusions. No one really knows how "cold" a cold day may be. Instead, list the gale force of the wind and the outside temperature.

After you complete your memo, review it to make sure that you have referred to all of the necessary facts in the fact segment of the document. Remove any facts that you originally included which you do not discuss in the analysis, unless these facts are necessary as background information or unless they help your reader understand your client's position. Be sure to organize the fact segment of your memo, as a disorganized statement of fact is confusing to your judge. No judge will feel compelled to do extra work in order to understand your request. Quite the contrary, it is easy for a judge to deny a request. It is your job to convince the judge, not the judge's job to argue your case. Therefore, be sure to organize your facts. You may wish to begin with a short summary explaining the nature of the case. This will give the judge a skeleton or plan for the entire case. One way to begin is to list the problem briefly, describe the people involved, and then tell the judge what you want him or her to do. You may wish to begin your memo in this manner. Alternatively, you may wish to organize your facts chronologically. Remember to check the Rules of Court in your jurisdiction; sometimes you must follow a particular format.

The analysis section of the memo presents the law to the judge. As with the internal legal memorandum, you will analyze the legal authorities. You should generally begin by presenting the central rule of law. Quote statutes or constitutional provisions if these are not well known. If, however, the constitutional provision is very well known, you may elect to omit the quotation and, instead, refer to the provision. Give case law that illustrates or defines the legal standard. If there are cases which interpret specific statutes or constitutional provisions, you should refer to these cases in your discussion. Be sure to refer to the specifics of the case; do not just list a legal proposition and follow it with a citation. You must discuss the relevance of the cited authority to the legal proposition. Follow this discussion with references to the similarities to or differences from the facts of your client's position. Repeat this for each legal point or rule of law that you discuss. You should also break each statute, rule, constitutional provision, or legal point into its elements and discuss each element separately. Finally, remember to check the rules of court for your jurisdiction to ensure that you comply with page limits or other restrictions and have the proper form and format for your memo.

6.7
THE COMPLEX LEGAL MEMORANDUM

From time to time, you may need to write a more complex document than any of those thus far discussed. If you must address several different issues in a single memorandum, you will need to add several additional sections to the memo. In addition to the heading, statement of the assignment, question presented, conclusion, facts, discussion, and possible recommendations, you will probably have a table of contents, a table of authorities, a summary, and appendices. You may find that you need topic headings within the discussion to provide some visual organization for the memo.

The table of contents lists the major topics in the memo and the pages on which they are found. The table of authorities follows the table of contents and lists every authority used in the memo and the page on which it is found. List the cases alphabetically by name. Follow the cases with a listing of statutes. Finally, list the secondary authorities. If a citation appears on more than one page, include a reference to each page on which it appears.

Following the table of authorities you may wish to include a separate summary when the legal memo is lengthy.

The appendix is used to provide additional supporting information, such as charts, statistical data, pages of transcripts, or the full text of some of the legal authorities. You would usually include in the appendix only legal authority that is difficult to access.

6.8
CAUTIONS

When writing, use the active voice. Save the passive for those special times when you want to lessen the impact of a fact or authority. Also, use positive rather than negative words. Negatives are confusing. Although we learned in algebra that a double negative is the same as a positive, this concept often is difficult to follow. It is easier to read or write that someone must do something. Many find it difficult to learn that they "may not avoid" doing the same thing.

Avoid using the phrase "in fact." Facts are things that can be seen, smelled, tasted, touched, and heard. We perceive facts through our senses. When we write "in fact," we usually do not really mean that we are discussing a fact at all. Facts should be specific. If what you are writing about is not a specific fact, you should avoid using the term "fact."

Do not say the same thing twice. This often means that you should remove an adjective that adds nothing to a description when the word the adjective modifies itself implies the adjective. For example, you should not write that you have a "short synopsis," since a synopsis is a shortened version of a document. Similarly, you should not write about a binding contract or unnecessary cruelty, unless you are also planning to discuss a nonbinding contract or necessary cruelty in the same writing.

Watch your words. Do not use extra words. Unlike Charles Dickens, you are not paid by the word. Shorter is better. When you finish writing, circle every word that you do not need. If you can read a sentence without a particular word, and the sentence says what you want, you do not need that word. Remove it. Look at the words you have circled. You will find that these words are often conjunctions, interjections, "lawyerisms," and adjectives. "Lawyerisms" do not make you sound like a lawyer; rather, they make you sound like an archaic lawyer. Latin is wonderful. Learn it, and you will increase your English vocabulary. Do not use Latin phrases in your writing, however. Phrases or words like *inter alia, ab initio,* and *arguendo* make your writing difficult to understand. Remember that communication is your goal.

Any word that interferes with your ability to communicate should be excised. Remove other "lawyerisms" that are redundant and reminiscent of the days when every document had to be understood by Norman judges and Anglo-Saxon peasants at the same time. You do not need to say "cease and desist," "by and between," "good and valuable," or "full and complete," or similar expressions. Look for terms or phrases joined with the conjunction "and." If the word immediately before the "and" and the word immediately after the "and" mean the same thing, you can probably remove one of the two. Avoid cliches. (A cliche is a trite statement.)

Do not use sexist language unless you are describing a sexist situation. Substitute titles or nouns, or write in the plural. Restructure your sentence, use an article (a, an, the), or the pronoun "it" or "one."

6.9
MODEL STUDENT PAPERS

The following are examples of legal memoranda written by beginning students at the American Institute in Phoenix, AZ. All problems are fictitious, although based on fact. The papers are reproduced as written by the student. Note that legal standards may have changed.

TO: Myra Harris, Attorney at Law
FROM: Rod Elkins, Paralegal
RE: Louise Armourer, #001-11-94
DATE: November 30, 1994

FACTS

Louise Armourer, a convicted murderer currently serving her sentence in Arizona State Prison, read about a recently released study of positron emission tomography (PET) that connected violent criminal behavior in adults with impaired function in the prefrontal cortex of the brain, an area affecting a person's ability to control his or her impulses. Ms. Armourer seeks Rule 32 relief claiming that if a state-funded PET scan of her brain indicates that she has this impaired function, then she should be released because her crime was the result of a mental disorder which she views as a disability, and that to imprison her for a disability violates not only her civil rights, but also her rights under the Americans with Disabilities Act (ADA). Alternatively, Ms. Armourer seeks Rule 32 relief claiming that the study is newly discovered evidence that she was unaware of when she was tried.

ISSUES

Is an impaired brain a disability? Can Ms. Armourer obtain funding for a PET scan? Is the prefrontal cortex theory admissible as newly discovered evidence?

CONCLUSION

The Court probably will not consider an impaired brain a disability in interpreting the ADA's definition of "disability."

Ms. Armourer should be able to obtain funding for a PET scan from the state; if not, she may be able to obtain the funding from the federal government. The prefrontal cortex theory is newly discovered evidence, but whether it will be deemed admissible depends on the admissibility test applied by the Court.

Although Ms. Armourer might not be released, she could possibly have her sentence reduced.

ANALYSIS

42 U.S.C. § 12102(2) (A) defines a "disability" with respect to an individual as "a physical or mental impairment that substantially limits one or more of the major life activities of such individual . . . ." Not being able to control one's impulses surely affects one's "life activities," but as this term is not clearly defined in the statute, the Court may view impulse control as *not* affecting "life activities."

The ADA pertains mainly to discrimination against "disabled" persons in the areas of employment, public transportation, and public accommodations. Being a convict who is not really involved in any of these areas, it would seem that Ms. Armourer cannot use this defense.

Nothing in the Civil Rights of Institutionalized Persons Act seemed to be helpful to Ms. Armourer. See Pub.L. 96-247, May 23, 1980, 94 Stat. 349 (42

U.S.C. § § 1997, 1997a, 1997b, 1997c, 1997d, 1997e, 1997f, 1997g, 1997h, 1997i, 1997j). Amended by Pub.L. 97-256, Title II, S 201, Sept. 8, 1982, 96 Stat. 816 (42 U.S.C. § § 1997b, 1997f).

A.R.S. § 31-222 (B) states: "The [state] department [of corrections] may conduct and supervise research into the causes of detention and treatment of crime . . ." A.R.S. S 31-222 (C) states:

> The [state] department [of corrections] may establish such joint research and information facilities of governmental and private agencies as it shall determine, and in furtherance of such activities may accept funds or other assistance from public or private sources.

Ms. Armourer's request for funding qualifies under these statutes because the PET scan may help to determine her "cause of detention."

If the state refuses Ms. Armourer's request, she may be able to obtain federal funding under 18 U.S.C. § 4352(7) which states:

> [that the National Institute of Corrections has the authority] to conduct, encourage, and coordinate research relating to corrections, including the causes, prevention, diagnosis, and treatment of criminal offenders . . .

And 18 U.S.C. §4353 states "[that the Institute is authorized to appropriate funds]." Ms. Armourer's request qualifies under these statutes because of the above-mentioned reason.

Rule 32.1(e) of the Arizona Rules of Criminal Procedure states that a convicted person may obtain post-conviction relief if:

> Newly discovered material facts probably exist and such facts probably would have changed the verdict or sentence. Newly discovered material facts exist if:
> (1) The newly discovered material facts were discovered after the trial.
> (2) The defendant exercised due diligence in securing the newly discovered material facts.
> (3) The newly discovered material facts are not merely cumulative . . .

The pre frontal cortex theory qualifies because: (1) The theory was not in existence at the time of Ms. Armourer's trial. (2) Ms. Armourer secured the study within a week of its release (*very* diligent). (3) The findings of the study are *not* merely cumulative in that they do not prove something already established.

For 70 years, the test for admissibility of evidence was the "general acceptance" test set forth in *Frye v. United States,* 293 F. 1013, 1014 (D.C. Cir. 1923). In that case, the Court stated:

> Just when a scientific principle or discovery crosses the line between the experimental and demonstrable stages is difficult to define. Somewhere in this twilight zone the evidential force of the principle must be recognized, and while courts will go a long way in admitting expert testimony deduced from a well-recognized scientific principle or discovery, the thing from which the deduction is made must be sufficiently established to have gained general acceptance in the particular field in which it belongs.

This case involved a man who appealed a second-degree murder conviction on the ground that the trial court erred in not admitting evidence of a "systolic blood pressure deception test." The court refused to admit the evidence because the test had not been generally accepted in the scientific community. The Circuit Court affirmed Frye's conviction. This case is very similar to Ms. Armourer's in that it involved a convicted murderer trying to get fairly new medical "evidence" admitted into trial; therefore, if this test is used by the court, the prefrontal cortex theory will probably not be admitted because it is too recent to have been "generally accepted" in the scientific community.

However, in *Daubert v. Merrell Dow Pharmaceuticals, Inc.*, 509 U.S. 579, 113 S.Ct. 2786, 125 L.Ed. 2d 469 (1993), the U.S. Supreme Court held that the "Frye test" was superseded by Rule 702 of the Federal Rules of Evidence, and that admissibility depends on a two-step inquiry: (1) Does expert testimony constitute scientific knowledge? (2) Will the expert testimony assist the trier of fact in understanding the evidence or in determining a fact in issue? The first step requires determination of whether the testimony has been subjected to the scientific method (i.e., whether the testimony is supported by scientific conclusions or studies). The prefrontal cortex theory is supported by the study Ms. Armourer read, and also by a small English study. See N. Volkow and L. Tancredi, "Neural Substrates of Violent Behavior: A Preliminary study with Positron Emission Tomography," 151 British Journal of Psychiatry 668-673d (1987). (These authors or the author of the study Ms. Armourer read would be good choices as "experts" if they could explain the theory in layman's terms—which should not be too difficult because the theory is not that complicated or technical.) This would fulfill the second requirement proposed in *Daubert, id,* and if this test is used, the evidence will probably be admitted.

In *State v. Bible,* 175 Ariz. 549, 580, 858 P.2d 1152, 1183 (1993), the Arizona Supreme Court held that "[W]e are not bound by the United States Supreme Court's non-constitutional construction of the Federal Rules of Evidence when we construe the Arizona Rules of Evidence." The holding in this case (which involved the admissibility of DNA evidence) implies that the Court may use the old "Frye test." This could impact Ms. Armourer's case because the prefrontal cortex theory and DNA both involve genetic concepts, and if DNA is accepted as evidence (after 6 years' use in a criminal context), then the prefrontal cortex theory may also be accepted (but probably not for a few years).

In *State v. Stuard,* 176 Ariz. 589, 863 P.2d 881 (Ariz. 1993), the Arizona Supreme Court reviewed a case in which a man suffered from severe organic brain damage resulting from a boxing career. The defendant's sentence was reduced from death to life in prison because his capacity to conform his conduct to the requirements of the law was substantially impaired. If Ms. Armourer is found to have an impaired prefrontal cortex (an organic brain disorder), she may be able to get her sentence reduced.

A New York court was the first to admit PET scans to determine a defendant's sanity in *People v. Weinstein,* 156 Misc. 2d 34, 591 N.Y.S. 2nd 715 (Sup. Ct. N.Y. County 1992). In this case, the court refused to consider genetic predisposition theories similar to the prefrontal cortex theory; however, the defendant did get his sentence reduced from second-degree murder to manslaughter.

In *State v. Ellevan,* 1994 WL 450086 (Ariz. App. Div. 1), the Arizona Court of Appeals granted Rule 32 relief to a man diagnosed as having AIDS. This is a more serious illness than that claimed by Ms. Armourer, but both would affect a person's "life activities."

In *State v. Jensen*, 153 Ariz. 171, 174, 735 P.2d 781, 784 (1987), a convicted murderer was granted Rule 32 relief on the basis of testimony on the theory of Post Traumatic Stress Disorder (PTSD), which is similar to Ms. Armourer's condition in that it is a mental disorder.

See also *Henry v. Industrial Commission of Arizona*, 157 Ariz. 67, 754 P.2d 1342 (1988), where the Arizona Supreme Court vacated an opinion by the Arizona Court of Appeals which held that a former police officer did not file a claim for Worker's Compensation on time. The claim was based on the diagnosis of PTSD *24 years* after the fact! This case supports the fact that Ms. Armourer "exercised due diligence" because she is filing her claim *23 years* sooner!

In another case involving PTSD, *State v. Bilke*, 162 Ariz. 51, 781 P.2d 28 (1989), the Arizona Supreme Court held that the defendant's diagnosis constituted a "colorable claim" of newly discovered evidence. Again, this is similar to Ms. Armourer's claim in that both conditions are mental disorders.

Similarly, in *U.S. v. Chischilly,* 30 F.3d 114 (9th Cir. 1994), the U.S. Court of Appeals upheld a District Court's admission of DNA evidence. As stated above, Ms. Armourer's condition and DNA both involved genetic concepts.

In *Baker v. State Bar of California,* 49 C.3d 804, 781 P.2d 1344 (1980), the California Supreme Court admitted testimony on an attorney's genetic predisposition to alcoholism, and the testimony was used to mitigate the attorney's punishment for misappropriation of clients' funds. The attorney was relieved of all responsibility and placed on probation. This is similar to Ms. Armourer's claim of genetic predisposition to violent criminal behavior.

MEMORANDUM

To: Myra Harris
From: Betty Leavitt
Re: Ms. Olivia Bewelle, No. 93-8, claim of negligent surgeon's care re-
             sulting in misdiagnosis of breast cancer.
Date: August 23, 1993.

STATEMENT OF ASSIGNMENT

The purpose of this memorandum is to explore what problems Ms. Bewelle will
encounter if she initiates a lawsuit against Dr. Osgoode for failing to diagnose her
breast cancer and for causing her emotional distress.

QUESTIONS PRESENTED

Was Dr. Osgoode negligent in his treatment of Ms. Bewelle? What is the medical
standard of care? Are liability damages appropriate for Ms. Bewelle?

DISCUSSION

Dr. Osgoode is an Arizona licensed surgeon practicing in Phoenix, Arizona. Our
client, Ms. Bewelle, saw him in December, 1991 at the request of her gynecologist because her mammogram indicated a questionable lump in her left breast.
After conducting his own physical examination, reading the radiologist's report,
examining the mammogram and sonogram, Dr. Osgoode concluded that this
lump was a cyst, which was a benign condition. He suggested annual follow-ups
with her gynecologist and to avoid food items containing caffeine, since caffeine
sometimes causes these cysts to develop. Two years later the gynecologist referred Ms. Bewelle, now age 30, back to Dr. Osgoode after her mammogram
showed a questionable lump. After this examination and review of the mammogram report, he surgically removed the lump. The pathology report indicated the
tumor was cancerous and a left radical mastectomy was performed. Since this
cancerous lump was proximal to the original cyst, our client wishes to sue Dr. Osgoode for failing to diagnose her cancer two years ago, and for emotional distress.
      When a physician or surgeon is guilty of malpractice, he or she demon-
strates negligence in performing the necessary skill, care and diligence as required by his or her profession. In addition, the treatment is contrary to accepted
medical standards with injurious results to the patient 70 C.J.S. *Physicians, Surgeons, and Other Health-Care Providers,* § 62,p. 455 (1987). In our case, Dr. Osgoode's duty of care to Ms. Bewelle incorporates the special knowledge and expertise he has in the fields of surgery and oncology. This knowledge and
expertise is compared to other members of his profession within Phoenix, or a
similar community *Kriesman v. Thomas,* 12 Ariz. App. 215,220, 469 P.2d
107,112 (1970).
      Negligence may exist in diagnosis as well as in treatment of a patient. The
standard of care is the same in either case 70 C.J.S. *Physicians, Surgeons, etc.,*

§ 62,p.456(1987). Whether a surgeon is negligent in making a diagnosis must be determined by the existing conditions and facts known at the time; not in knowledge gained through subsequent developments 70 C.J.S. *Physicians, Surgeons, etc.,* § 72,p.471–73 (1987).

Under Arizona law, in a medical malpractice action, the physician causes injury or death by negligence, misconduct, errors, or omissions while delivering health care A.R.S. 12-561.2. Our client must show that Dr. Osgoode failed to follow the accepted standard of care in two ways: first, he failed to exercise the appropriate care and skill expected of a surgeon treating a patient with a lump in her breast; second, this failure was the immediate cause of Ms. Bewelle's resulting cancer A.R.S. 12-563.

Proving this deviation from a medical standard of care rests with our client. To demonstrate inappropriate medical care by Dr. Osgoode, our firm must present expert medical testimony in order to measure Dr. Osgoode's conduct. A jury cannot consider whether Dr. Osgoode acted negligently without first determining what other surgeons would do in a similar situation *Peacock v. Samaritan Health Service,* 159 Ariz. 123,126, 765 P.2d 525 (App.1989).

Patient injury in medical malpractice actions refers to the development of a problem into a more serious condition posing a greater danger to the patient and requiring more extensive treatment. *DeBoeur v. Brown,* 138 Ariz. 168,170, 673 P.2d 912 (1983).

A.R.S. 12-581 defines bodily injury as bodily harm, sickness, disease, emotional or mental distress sustained by an individual. Ms. Bewelle qualifies as a claimant, acquiring bodily injury through disease and emotional distress. If Dr. Osgoode is held liable, the court will make findings for possible past damages and future damages, while deciding the duration of these payments A.R.S. 12-584. Under A.R.S. 12-542, all injury and medical malpractice actions need to be prosecuted within two years after the cause of action occurs.

Boyce v. Brown, 51 Ariz. 416, § 77 P.2d 455, 457 (1938) lays the foundation for general rules governing medical malpractice actions. Although these principles are applicable to our side, unfortunately, they are also useful to the doctor. (1) Dr. Osgoode, licensed to practice medicine, is presumed to possess the degree of skill and learning possessed by another surgeon in good standing in the Phoenix community. If Dr. Osgoode does not possess the necessary skill, or does not apply it, he is guilty of malpractice. (2) Before Dr. Osgoode can be held liable for malpractice he must have neglected to do something which the medical standard in Phoenix requires; i.e., a biopsy of the first lump and timely follow-ups. (3) Negligence by Dr. Osgoode must be proven and never presumed. A jury cannot speculate as to what the required standard is. (4) The testimony of other surgeons declaring they would follow a different course of treatment than Dr. Osgoode is not sufficient to establish malpractice unless the treatment digressed from an approved standard of therapy in the Phoenix community.

We must ascertain that Dr. Osgoode was negligent in failing to perform a biopsy on Ms. Bewelle's original lump. The following eight elements have to be present 11 *P.O.F.2d, Negligence of Biopsy,* 319,p.342(1976). First, we must establish that a physician and patient relationship existed between Dr. Osgoode and Ms. Bewelle. The clinical record containing Dr. Osgoode's physical examination, evaluations of diagnostic test(s), diagnosis, and therapies does this.

Second, we must show a reoccurrence of the symptoms. Two years later on the advice from her gynecologist, Ms. Bewelle returned to Dr. Osgoode because of a lump.

Third, we need to prove a discovery of misdiagnosis when this time the lump was cancerous. Negligence has been supported where a physician failed to do a biopsy in order to determine whether or not a growth was malignant 61 *AmJur2d, Physicians, Surgeons, etc,* § 263,p.405(1981).

Fourth, treatment of malignancy occurred when Dr. Osgoode performed a lumpectomy and subsequent left radical mastectomy.

Fifth, the element of damages is present. Anxiety or worry about a future disease or condition constitutes a proper element of damages if the disease resulted from the injury that Dr. Osgoode is alleged to have caused 61 *AmJur 2d, Physicians and Surgeons,* § 368,p.542(1981). Since breast cancer is often cured with prompt surgical intervention, damages for an improper diagnosis tend to be considerable. If a patient survives in these cases, the treatment of the malignancy may involve amputation of the arm and shoulder as well as the breast. In *MacMahon v. Nelson,* 39 Colo.App. 355, § 568 P.2d 90,91 (App.1977) there was adequate evidence that a surgeon's incorrect diagnosis caused his patient emotional distress when she learned that removal of a cancerous tumor had been delayed eight months. The possibility exists that Ms. Bewelle's original tumor was malignant and untreated for two years resulting in invasive surgical procedures: a lumpectomy, a left radical mastectomy, and chemotherapy treatments.

In *Nussbaum v. Gibstein,* 138 App. Div.2d 193, 531 N.Y.S.2d 276, 283–84, (A.D. 2Dept.1988),app. gr.72 N.Y.2d 810, 534 N.Y.S.2d 938, 531 N.E.2d 658,rev'd on other grds,73 N.Y.2d 912, 539 N.Y.S. 2d 289, 536 N.E.2d 618 (N.Y.1989) damages for the plaintiff included pain and suffering and loss of enjoyment of life. The concept of pain and suffering deals with definitive body injury. In our case, body injury refers to Ms. Bewelle's breast surgeries and future medical treatments. The second concept involves Ms. Bewelle's inability to perform activities which were part of her life prior to the injury-causing event; her surgeries caused her fatigue, loss of weight, unemployment, and a nonexistent social life.

The Arizona Constitution, Art.II, § 31, and Art.XVIII, § 6, affirms there is no limit to the amount of damages recovered for death or injury of a person, and the amount is not subject to statutory limitation. According to the Az. Supreme Court in *Eastin v. Broomfield,* 116 Ariz. 576, 570 P.2d 744, 753 (1977), defendants may introduce evidence of benefits payable to a plaintiff due to injury, i.e., workers' compensation, health insurance, but the court may ignore these collateral benefits when determining damages.

The next two elements are closely related to each other: the standard of care required of physicians and the physician's failure to conform to them. In *Kennedy v. U.S.,* 750 F.Supp 206, 210 (W.D.La.1990), a physician breached his duty of care in the diagnosis and treatment of a breast lump by referring the patient for a mammogram instead of performing a biopsy or needle aspiration. The standard of care relevant to the diagnosis and treatment of breast lumps is discussed. This standard is uniform for internists, oncologists, and surgeons. Additionally, this case declares there are two ways to distinguish a lump in the breast from cancer: by a clinical examination or by a biopsy. Although at the time of the first visit Dr. Osgoode conducted a clinical examination, it is considered inadequate if the lump remained. When a lump remains in the breast over time, a physical examination cannot distinguish the lump from cancer, and a biopsy is mandatory. Medical testimony further concludes that it is never appropriate to use a mammogram as a way to avoid performing a biopsy on a lump in the breast. The fact that a mammogram is negative does not necessarily mean that carcinoma is not present in the breast. *Shapiro v. Burkons,* 62 Ohio App.2d 73, 404 N.E.2d 778,780(App.1978) brings up the question of mammograms performed on women in their early thirties. Dr. Sternen, an expert witness, testified that a mammogram on a woman in that age group tends to be inaccurate since breast tissue is dense and may hide any tumors. Ms. Bewelle was 28 at her initial examination.

Dr. Osgoode made his diagnosis about the "cyst" based on his physical examination and the mammogram results. He did not ask Ms. Bewelle to return after her next menstrual cycle for comparison, or within three months for reevaluation. Nor did he ask her to return to her referring doctor sooner than one year. In *Nussbaum* at 279, a medical specialist testified that Dr. Gibstein diverged from good practice and acceptable medical standards in New York when he failed to follow-up a breast lump in his 32 year old patient by timely reexamination.

Finally, the eighth element is Dr. Osgoode's negligence as the proximate cause of Ms. Bewelle's injuries. In *Nussbaum,* the jury concluded from the evidence presented that Ms. Nussbaum's lesion of 1982 developed into the malignant tumor excised in 1983. The jury considered Dr. Gibstein negligent in failing to order tests and to follow up his initial examination in checking the condition of the lump. These findings parallel our case: a jury might reach the same conclusions about Dr. Osgoode. The "cyst" developed into cancer two years later; Dr. Osgoode was negligent in failing to order a biopsy, to follow up his initial examination, or to ask the gynecologist to follow Ms. Bewelle within three months.

When contemplating the feasibility of initiating a lawsuit against Dr. Osgoode we must take into account the case law which supports his side.

A qualified physician is not liable for an error of judgment if he: (1) applies reasonable skill and care normally exercised by other physicians or surgeons, (2) uses his best judgment (3) keeps within recognized and approved methods of common practice; (4) forms his decision after a careful examination or investigation 70 C.J.S., *Physicians, Surgeons, etc.,* § 73,p.474 (1987); *Weatherman v. White,* 10 N.C.App. 480,179 S.E.2d 134 (App.1971). More crucial for Dr. Osgoode's defense is the following: when there is more than one recognized or approved method of treatment relevant to a case, a physician is not liable for an honest mistake of judgment in selecting a method 70 *C.J.S., Ibid.*

It appears that Dr. Osgoode assumed Ms. Bewelle's original lump to be fibrocystic in nature. This conclusion was based on the facts that Ms. Bewelle had no family history of breast cancer, her age, the doctor's physical examination and the radiologist's report. Expert medical testimony by two surgeons in *Weatherman* indicated that the physician exercised reasonable care and his best judgment in his patient's treatment. Fibrocystic breast disease, or noncancerous breast lumps, is a very common disease in women. The doctor has the choice of removing these lumps or allowing them to remain contingent upon the patient's history, including the size, texture and shape of the lumps. The experts said removing all lumps found in a woman's breast because they are there is not the general standard of care.

Continuing along these lines, Dr. Osgoode could refer to defense counsel's closing argument in *Thor v. Boska,* 38 Cal. App.3d 558, 113 Cal. Rptr.

296,300(App.1974) for his own defense. A physician could biopsy every patient who presented with any kind of a breast irregularity, but that would constitute very poor practice. Women would have excess biopsies and subject themselves to unnecessary surgical risks. Dr. Osgoode did not suspect a malignant lump during Ms. Bewelle's initial consult. In his judgment, the lump did not exhibit characteristics indicative of cancer and he felt no biopsy was necessary. If Dr. Osgoode believed the lump to be benign, he was correct in his clinical evaluation that no surgical intervention of any kind was needed at that time. Therefore, there was no negligence or malpractice on his part.

Regarding his lack of follow-up, Dr. Osgoode could say that being a surgeon he is called only for a specific occasion or service, and is under no duty to continue his visits or treatments since Ms. Bewelle has a primary physician 70 C.J.S., *Physicians, Surgeons, etc.*, § 75,p.476–77(1987).

In *Caputo v. Taylor*, 403 So.2d 551 (Fla. App.1981) the court held there was no evidence that the physician's actions contributed to the patient's condition. The experts testified there was no way to tell within reasonable medical probability whether Ms. Caputo's malignancy found in 1977 was present one year prior. Dr. Osgoode could subpoena surgeons specializing in cancer surgery to testify that a lack of evidence exists to support that the malignancy existed prior to December, 1992. This lack of evidence is due to limited medical knowledge as to the origin, rate of growth, and spread of cancer. Dr. Osgoode may also refute alternative diagnostic procedures by our experts saying that such procedures are not necessarily appropriate for a patient of Ms. Bewelle's age, with her history and initial presenting lump *Beckom v. U.S.*, 584 F.Supp 1471 (N.D.N.Y.1984)

CONCLUSION

We need to establish two facts for a medical malpractice case against Dr. Osgoode. One, the doctor failed to follow the standard of care by failing to follow up and biopsy a suspect breast lump resulting in misdiagnosis. Two, this misdiagnosis led to Ms. Bewelle's breast cancer.

In regards to the first issue, we must establish a standard of care in the diagnosis and treatment of breast cancer or we fail to present a prima facie case of liability. We can show the examination and treatment given by Dr. Osgoode fell below the valid standard for cases like Ms. Bewelle, when compared to qualified surgeons practicing in Phoenix, Arizona and similar communities in 1991. We could say a reasonable method and acceptable medical course of action would have been to watch the area and reexamine it within a month or so. More significantly, Dr. Osgoode did not perform the test(s) necessary for a proper diagnosis of Ms. Bewelle's condition even though he advised her that her condition was benign. As breast cancer problems increase more physicians are ordering biopsies for unexplained breast lumps remaining over a period of time. We can show by expert testimony that the delay in performing a biopsy violated reasonable standards of care, as did lack of follow-up examinations.

Proving that this lack of care and misdiagnosis led to Ms. Bewelle's cancer is more difficult and actually may not be possible if their expert witnesses are more credible to the jury. Case law supports the theory that no one can tell when or where a cancer forms or how long it has been there. I remain doubtful that we can win on this issue.

Liability damages are possible only if the jury finds for Ms. Bewelle. However, Ms. Bewelle's "injury" occurred when the lump began to grow in 1992, not when the misdiagnosis happened in 1991. Her damages would only include present and future damages.

I would suggest telling Ms. Bewelle that she may not be able to win a lawsuit against Dr. Osgoode.

RECOMMENDATIONS

1. File a claim with BOMEX for an investigation into Ms. Bewelle's initial treatment by Dr. Osgoode. The Board decides if the information merits a decree of censure against Dr. Osgoode or a dismissal because the information is without merit.

2. Consider out of court settlement with a claim to Dr. Osgoode's insurance company for damages.

3. Explain to Ms. Bewelle that Dr. Osgoode may file a medical malpractice countersuit on the grounds that the medical malpractice claim was without foundation. Some of these countersuits have been successful at the trial level.

4. Acquire our expert witness team if needed based on the following: (a) surgical oncologist(s) from Phoenix who is respected within the profession; publishes papers and participates in breast cancer studies; holds prominent positions in local, state or national medical associations. (b) surgical oncologist from the City of Hope, California. Not only is the City of Hope an acknowledged leader in cancer care, but it is within our Ninth Circuit. (c) surgical oncologists from Dana Farber Institute, Boston, Massachusetts and Sloan-Kettering Institute, New York City, New York. These cities are known for their high medical standards.

TO: Myra Harris
FROM: Cindie Schwartzberg Edlow
RE: Firm Memorandum File: Censorship and Community Standards
          General Firm File: FF94-059-8
DATE: May 9, 1994

STATEMENT OF ASSIGNMENT

This memorandum of law discusses the concept of library censorship in the context of community standards, and the allowances, implications and restraints of governmental authority as it applies to the matter of obscenity. Also discussed is the situation at the Mesa Public Library with regard to Madonna's book, *Sex*, and other photographic works exhibited as well in the context of obscenity and censorship.

CONCLUSION

The United States Supreme Court has granted to each individual state of the Union the authority to determine materials obscene in nature by utilizing the community standards of that particular state. It allows for the censorship of materials judged to be obscene under applicable state regulations. Any materials defined as obscene under state statute and addressed within the community standards of that state can be legally censored.

QUESTION PRESENTED

What are the laws on obscenity and application of censorship toward obscenity that the people of the United States must subscribe to?

DISCUSSION

It is law that under the freedoms of the First Amendment of the United States all courts must remain sensitive to any infringement on genuinely serious literary, artistic, political or scientific expressions of speech or press. It is also law that the U.S. Supreme Court has decided that obscene material is not protected by the First Amendment. *Kois v. Wisconsin,* 408 U.S. 229, 92 S.Ct. 2245, 33 L.Ed.2d 312 (1972). It is at this juncture that it became the responsibility of the U.S. Supreme Court to establish the standards by which to define and measure obscene material that could be regulated by any state without infringing on the First Amendment rights of the individual.

In the precedent setting case *Miller v. California,* 413 U.S. 15, 93 S.Ct. 2607, 37 L.Ed.2d 419 (1973), the U.S. Supreme Court set the rules for governing obscenity issues that are still adhered to today. It acknowledged the inherent censorship issues of regulating any form of expression and wisely chose to refrain from establishing a "national" community standard of obscenity, leaving it to each state to regulate its own version of obscenity statutes which the citizens of that state must follow. "State statutes designed to regulate obscene materials must be carefully limited . . . (w)e now confine the permissible scope of such regulation to works which depict or describe sexual conduct. That conduct must be specifically defined by the applicable state law, as written or authoritatively construed." *Id.*, at 22-23. The Court drafted a 3-tier structure of basic guidelines on the constitution of obscenity. It stated:

> The basic guidelines for the trier of fact must be:
> (a) whether "the average person, applying contemporary community standards" would find that the work, taken as a whole, appeals to the prurient interest . . .
> (b) whether the work depicts or describes, in a patently offensive way, sexual conduct specifically defined by the applicable state law; and
> (c) whether the work, taken as a whole, lacks serious literary, artistic, political, or scientific value.

Id. at 25.

This 3-tier structure is the backbone by which all case law on the subject of obscenity since the *Miller* opinion has been decided.

The Miller opinion gives each state the authority to define obscenity according to the community of the state's inhabitants. Restrictions or censorships can be enforced by that state's obscenity statutes on materials that the community deems offensive. It is up to the community to determine what it considers "patently offensive" and "prurient". ". . . (t)he primary concern with requiring a jury to apply the standard of "the average person, applying contemporary community standards" is to be certain that, so far as material is not aimed at a deviant group, it will be judged by its impact on an average person, rather than a particularly susceptible or sensitive person—or indeed a totally insensitive one. *Id.* at 33. "It is neither realistic nor constitutionally sound to read the First Amendment as requiring that the people of Maine or Mississippi accept public depiction of conduct found tolerable in Las Vegas, or New York City. . . . People in different States vary in their tastes and attitudes, and this diversity is not to be strangled by the absolutism of imposed uniformity." *Id.* at 33.

With this opinion as authority, library censorship is completely legal and permissible. A library is a city governmental facility (unlike a bookstore or coffeehouse with books) and it follows the statutes laid down by the legislature of the state. Given that there are obscenity statutes on the books for the state of Arizona, what remains at issue is the precise definitions on the meanings of words or phrases in the arena of obscenity. In *State v. Bartanen,* 121 Ariz. 454, 591 P.2d 546 (1979), the court held to the general definition of prurient interest in A.R.S. 13-531.01(2) but went on to clarify for the jury (the setters of community standards) that "A prurient interest in sex is not the same as a candid, wholesome, or healthy interest in sex. . . . An appeal to the prurient interest is an appeal to sexual desire, not an appeal to sexual interest. An interest in sex is normal, but if the material appeals to an abnormal interest in sex, it can appeal to the prurient interest." Further, *Bartanen* goes on to specify the meaning of "sexual activity", and the "appeal" approach to obscenity as distinguished by the "tendency" approach to obscene material. The Supreme Court of Arizona specified graphic phrases with the least amount of discrepancy so that jurors would better see what did or did not come within the boundaries of obscenity in order to pass judgment on particular acts or materials. This is directly connected to the legality of censorship, particularly in a library setting. If a court is going to verbally describe a sexual scene in increasingly particular detail and then state that if that exact scene is descriptively written about or a picture is taken of it, then those materials are illegally obscene and subject to censorship under the community standards of the state. The community has the legal right to be purged indefinitely of those materials.

In *State v. Book-Cellar, Inc.*, 139 Ariz. 525, 679 P.2d 548 (App. 1984), the appellate court went further in holding "The state can impose regulations on the use of obscenity in local commerce and in all place of public accommodation, so long as those regulations do not run afoul of specific constitutional prohibitions." This means that the state of Arizona has the last word on whether or not it will allow what it considers to be obscene material in a place of public accommodation. Some would believe that a library, of all public places that house books, should be the bearer of all written words and published volumes, regardless of the expression of the words and the content of the volumes. That is at the heart of what a library is. To censor the contents of a library, even according to the standards of the community that surrounds it, may be legal, but it is not just. The court is holding that it can mandate what materials cannot be made available in places of public accommodation when those materials are adjudged to be obscene in nature.

In *State v. Lichon*, 163 Ariz. 186, 786 P.2d 1037 (App. 1989), the court reiterated the contemporary state standards of obscenity. It also made a point of telling the jurors that perhaps some of them might not feel "average" as people go, and that to ascertain whether or not a material is obscene, they should judge not according to their own opinion but to the version of an "average" person: ". . . (w)e believe that a juror may consider, as a factor, the views of the average person in the juror's community in arriving at an assessment of the statewide standard." *Id.* at 190. An escalating refinement on definitions of terms and approaches to regulations seems to be manifesting with each new case opinion written on the issues of obscenity and censorship.

A telephone call to the Mesa Public Library proved to be very interesting. As of this writing, the library still does not stock the book *Sex,* a photographic book on Madonna with a variety of pictures involving sexual conduct. The history of the library's reasoning is as follows: They did order the book to be shelved in their collection and before it came in, the City Council was questioned by some members of the community as to whether they were getting it and why. The mayor of the city of Mesa canceled the order on behalf of the constituents who pressured him. Three citizens volunteered to donate the book at no charge to the library. Public meetings were held at City Council chambers, public citizens said they did not want it stocked, and the library board, appointed by the mayor, requested that the library not carry the book. The Mesa Public Library contends that the reason they are not carrying the book is due to the way in which the book is bound (i.e., pages can be ripped, easy to tear out, spiral binding, etc.), not that the contents are offensive to the average person. Do they have other books with spiral bindings?

A volume of Robert Mapplethorpe's books would contain a section of photographs that are extremely sexually graphic and would be considered "patently offensive" and "obscene" under Arizona statute. A public library would not legally be forced to carry the book. If the Mesa Public Library were to order it and the community standards of the people of Mesa and the state of Arizona were to speak up and decry the placement of it on the shelves, the library would most likely back down from stocking the book. This is legal. However, the quality of the paper and the binding and the publication of a Mapplethorpe book is of extraordinarily superior workmanship and the Mesa Public Library would be walking on thin ice if they used that line of reasoning in this instance.

RECOMMENDATIONS

This is an area of law that will consistently be in flux, undergo modifications and the rewritings of supreme law. There will be challenges whenever a fundamental amendment to the people of the United States, to whatever degree, is tampered with. Any form of restriction, be it large or small, tears at the foundation of pure freedoms. This is obvious. But it also allows for persuasive argument on behalf of the pure freedoms of speech and the press in the case of this memorandum. This in turn can ultimately influence the supreme laws of the land. What is unfortunate is that if we prepare a sound case and base it on the immeasurable value of free speech and free press, perhaps we can begin the decrease of some of these archaic restrictions that the state has power to censor over individual right and privilege. As Justice Douglas so eloquently and powerfully stated in his dissenting opinion in *Miller v. California,* "What shocks me may be sustenance for my neighbor. What causes one person to boil up in rage over one pamphlet or movie may reflect only his neurosis, not shared by others. We deal here with a regime of censorship which, if adopted, should be done by constitutional amendment after full debate by the people. . . . If there are to be restraints on what is obscene, then a constitutional amendment should be the way of achieving it. There are societies where religion and mathematics are the only free segments. It would be a dark day for America if that were our destiny. But the people can make it such if they choose to write obscenity into the Constitution and define it. . . . Perhaps the people will decide that the path toward a mature, integrated society requires that all ideas competing for acceptance must have no censor. Perhaps they will decide otherwise. Whatever the choice, the courts will have some guidelines. Now we have none except our own predilections." *Id.* at 45-47.

Pictorial exhibits follow for purposes of persuasion in personal favor of Mr. Douglas' dissenting opinion. What is in the eye of the beholder will always be in that beholder's eye. How a person sees what he sees is an interpretation and not an issue. At issue is the state telling the beholder he can not see what he should have an inalienable right to.

Interoffice Memorandum

To: Myra Harris
From: Alicia Bray
Re: Parents of Susie Student; Client # 007
           Validity of claims of child abuse and infliction of emotional distress
           based on classroom discipline.
Date: May 16, 1994
Statement of Assignment: Research law on reasonableness of discipline in
                            public schools and on infliction of emotional distress.

Questions Presented

Issue 1: Was Mr. Rowver's method of discipline reasonable?
Issue 2: Did Susie suffer emotional distress as a result of Mr. Rowver's disci-
         pline?

Conclusion

Issue 1: No, it is most likely unreasonable to discipline ten year old pupils, in the
         manner he used for minor infractions. Mr. Rowver could be terminated
         on grounds of unprofessional conduct. Mr. Rowver and/or the school
         board could be held responsible for the infliction of emotional distress, if
         a jury so decided.
Issue 2: Probably yes, but this is a question for the jury, pending evidence from a
         psychological examination to determine the nature and origin of Susie's
         emotional distress. Whether the potential reward of damages would be
         worth bringing suit is an important consideration.

Discussion/Analysis

Facts: Mr. Rowver is a fifth grade teacher at a local Arizona elementary school.
He was formerly a marine sergeant, and disciplines his ten year old students with
the same methods he used on new recruits in basic training. He screams "Speak,
Stupid, Speak!" directly into the child's face and then requires the child to provide
a verbal explanation of his or her conduct in front of the class, while Mr. Rowver
jeers and ridicules. The children are subject to this discipline for even minor infractions, such as asking a question out of turn or for momentary lapses of attention. The school board has neither sanctioned this method of discipline with written policy, nor has it taken any actions against Mr. Rowver for his conduct.
    Susie is a ten year old in Mr. Rowver's class; though she has never been
subjected to his discipline, she has witnessed it on two occasions. Since being in
Mr. Rowver's class, Susie has become withdrawn and complains of stomach
aches every morning before school. She is presently receiving psychological
counseling to alleviate her fears and the physical symptoms. Her parents have
contacted our firm to see if they have a cause of action against the school board
and Mr. Rowver. Mr. and Mrs. Student are considering bringing suit against
these two parties for child abuse, intentional infliction and negligent infliction of

emotional distress. They seek damages to pay for Susie's counseling sessions, as well as termination of Mr. Rowver's teaching contract.

Law—Issue 1: The Arizona Revised Statutes establish that one of the duties of teachers is to "hold pupils to strict account for disorderly conduct" 15 A.R.S. § 15-521. 15. A.R.S. § 15-843 gives the governing board authority to "prescribe rules for the discipline, . . . of pupils." The courts hold that the purpose of punishment and discipline is to maintain and encourage an environment conductive to learning, and that the punishment must bear some reasonable relationship to the educational environment, *Martinez v. School Dist. No. 60,* 852 P.2d 1275 (Colo. App. 1992), *Wilson v. Abilene Independent School Dist.,* 190 S.W.2d 406 (Tex. App. 1945). In *Weyl v. Commissioner of Internal Revenue,* 48 F.2d 811 (2d Cir. 1931), the court supplied a broad definition of education that included "the acquisition of knowledge; mental and moral training; cultivation of the mind, feelings and manners." The courts hold that there are limits to punishment, and it must be reasonable within the context it is administered in, *People v. Ball,* 581 II.2d 36, 317 N.E.2d 54 (1974). Punishment should "not exceed the bounds of moderation", and that which does is detrimental to the child's future, *Tinkham v. Kole,* 110 N.W.2d 258 (Iowa 1961). In *Holman v. Wheeler,* 677 P.2d 645 (Okl. 1983), the court relied on the standards of reasonableness for punishment found in the Restatement of Torts 2d § 150. These include, but are not limited to: 1) age, sex, physical and mental condition of the child; 2) nature of the offense and motive; 3) was punishment reasonably necessary and appropriate; 4) was punishment disproportionate to the offense, unnecessarily degrading, or likely to cause serious or permanent harm. A reasonable person could conclude that Mr. Rowver's methods of discipline are unreasonable; especially in light of the age of his students, and the minor infractions they were punished for. The totality of the learning environment, which includes emotional development, in addition to the acquisition of academic knowledge, should also be taken into consideration. Reasonableness is always a question for the jury to determine, *LaFrentz v. Gallagher,* 105 Ariz. 255, 462 P.2d 804 (1969), *Tinkham v. Kole,* 110 N.W.2d 258 (Iowa 1961). In *Roberts v. Santa Cruz Valley Unified School Dist. No. 35,* 161 Ariz. 398, 778 P.2d 1294 (App. 1989), the Arizona court recently affirmed the dismissal of an elementary school teacher on grounds of unprofessional conduct (A.R.S. §§ 15-203, 15-341), citing that his punitive activities "created a situation harmful to the physical, mental and educational well-being of the students." Id at 400. This case is similar to our client's, but not parallel since the *Santa Cruz Valley* case involved an element of physical abuse; both cases do share degrading, public punishment disproportionate to the offenses of young children, as well as promoting an emotionally abusive environment.

Law—Issue 2: Recovery of damages due to infliction of emotional distress is a complex area of tort law; the courts have traditionally been very strict in allowing recovery in hopes of limiting fictitious claims, *Hunsley v. Giard,* 553 P.2d 1096 (Wash. 1976). Emotional distress has been defined as including: fright, worry or apprehension of future consequences, shame, embarrassment and humiliation, 25 C.J.S. § 70, *Roberts v. Saylor,* 230 Kan. 289, 637 P.2d 1175, 1180 (1981). The validity of an emotional distress claim is strengthened if accompanied by physical symptoms that can be documented by expert testimony, 18 Am.Jur.POF3d 103. The Supreme Court of Washington, *Hunsley v. Giard,* 553 P.2d 1096 (Wash. 1976), outlined the standards for recovery of damages from the negligent infliction of emotional distress: 1) did the defendant owe a duty to the plaintiff; 2) did the defendant breach the duty owed to the plaintiff by the infliction, and was the resulting emotional distress foreseeable; 3) was defendant's breach of duty the cause of the plaintiff's emotional distress; 4) is the mental suffering accompanied by physical symptoms; 5) is the plaintiff's reaction that of a reasonable person under the circumstances, or did the defendant have prior knowledge that the plaintiff may be susceptible to emotional distress? Many of these strict standards were applied to cases involving adults; the court may see standards differently for a ten year old child. It is a question for the jury whether, as her teacher, Mr. Rowver owed a duty to Susie; whether he breached his duty, and if the results should have been foreseeable. Even though Susie was not personally subjected to Mr. Rowver's punishment, she was directly affected by the classroom environment he created; so the "Bystander" doctrine (requiring either threat of physical injury, or witnessing the injury of an immediate family member) may be inapplicable, *Long v. PKS, Inc.,* 12 Cal. App. 4th 1293, 16 CA.2d 103, 105 (1993).

   The elements of intentional infliction of emotional distress include: 1) outrageous conduct by the defendant, defined as actions that would be intolerable to civilized society; 2) defendant's intentional or reckless disregard of the probability of causing emotional distress; 3) plaintiff suffers severe emotional distress; 4) defendant's outrageous conduct was the cause of the emotional distress, *Roberts v. Saylor,* 230 Kan. 289, 637 P.2d 1175 (1981), *Steckelberg v. Randolph,* 448 N.W.2d 458 (Iowa 1989). It is unlikely that the court would find Mr. Rowver culpable of intentional infliction, since his discipline was never focused on Susie directly. Likewise the facts probably do not support an allegation of child abuse, since this has been defined as "substantial risk of physical injury which would likely cause . . . protracted impairment of physical or emotional health", *In re C.* (Anonymous) Children, 583 N.Y. Supp.2d 499 (*1992*).

Recommendations

1. Get a forensic psychologist to examine Susie to determine if she is suffering emotional distress, and if Mr. Rowver is the proximate cause. Also to determine if her shyness is within the "normal" range for a child of her age, confronted with a similar situation in the classroom.

   2. Bring an action against the school board for the termination of Mr. Rowver's teaching contract on grounds of unprofessional conduct.

   3. Depending on the results of the psychological examination, consider bringing suit against Mr. Rowver and the school board (under the doctrine of respondent superior, if Mr. Rowver was indeed acting within the scope of his employment) for the negligent infliction of emotional distress. If it can be determined that he should have reasonably known that Susie would have suffered emotional distress as a result of his actions, then he may be held personally liable outside the scope of his employment, *Hunsley v. Giard,* 553 P.2d 1096 (Wash. 1976). The benefits of the possible award of damages should be weighed against the cost of bringing suit.

Invoice

Library research—10 hrs. @ $60.00 per hr.	$600.00
Westlaw research—15 min. @ $4.00 per min.	60.00
Analysis & Write-up—7 hrs. @ $60.00 per hr.	$420.00
Total due******	$1080.00

INTERNAL MEMO

TO: Myra Harris
FROM: Connie Niebling
RE: WePlant Em, Inc., (#1001), Responsibility of property owner under
             EPA requirements for environmental damage caused by prior own-
             ers
DATE: April 29, 1994

QUESTIONS PRESENTED

1. What are the federal and state environmental requirements for the protection
   of land, water & air on property used for agricultural purposes?
2. Is WePlant Em, Inc. in compliance with those requirements and regulations
   and how would noncompliance affect WePlant Em's sale of the property?

CONCLUSION

Federal and state statutes require users of agricultural pesticides and fertilizers
to apply for an aquifer protection permit and to advise the Department of Environmental Quality of the use of pesticides. The State would then be responsible for
monitoring the property for land, water, and air contamination. The use of pesticides does not necessarily indicate land contamination. If the pesticides used are
on government approved lists and are used according to directions, then the
using parties are not held responsible for contamination even if contamination
occurs.

     If Fruit or Plenty, Inc. and Trees R Us, Inc. failed to make proper applica-
tions, it would be prudent of WePlant Em., Inc. to make a report to the Department of Environmental Quality, giving the department appropriate information,
and have the land checked prior to making a sale to another party.

     All statute and case law discovered holds WePlant Em, Inc. liable for any
contamination. The two nursery firms which were actively involved in the pollution are also liable, but their financial history makes WePlant Em, Inc., as owner
of the property, an easier target for clean-up and recovery costs. A sale of the
property to a third party, even with an "as is" clause, would not relieve WePlant
Em, Inc. of their liability.

DISCUSSION

FACTS

The WePlant Em, Inc. pension and profit sharing plan purchased a parcel of ten
acres of land on Broadway at 57th Avenue in 1983. The pension and profit sharing plan purchased the land as an investment and did not actively use the property for any agricultural purpose.

     Two years later, the property was sold to Fruit or Plenty, Inc. who used the
property to grow fruit trees for commercial sale. Fruit or Plenty, Inc. subsequently
sold the acreage to another nursery firm, Trees R Us. Trees R Us also used the

land as an orchard and continued growing and harvesting fruit trees for commercial sale. Pesticides were used in both of the nursery businesses for six years from 1985 to 1991.

In 1991, Trees R Us filed bankruptcy and their corporation was dissolved. The Trees R Us corporate officers have since departed the United States.

Because both Trees R Us and Fruit or Plenty, Inc. defaulted on their payments, WePlant Em, Inc. reacquired title to the property and would now like to sell it to another party. The prospective purchaser wants assurance that the property is in compliance with all federal and state environmental requirements. WePlant Em, Inc. has requested the assistance of this law firm in determining their environmental obligations for this piece of property.

LAW

The environmental quality of the United States is protected by several pieces of legislation and is administered by the Environmental Protection Agency. The major acts which would apply to this situation are: 1) *The Clean Air Act,* 2) *The Comprehensive Environmental Response, Compensation, and Liability Act of 1980,* (CERCLA), 3) *The Federal Water Pollution Control Act,* 4) *The National Environmental Policy Act of 1969,* 5) *The Safe Drinking Water Act,* and 6) *The Federal Insecticide, Fungicide, and Rodenticide Act.*

The Environmental Protection Agency works closely with state and county governments and implementation and enforcement of the various acts take place at these local levels.

Title 49 of the *Arizona Revised Statutes Annotated* provides for State implementation of the Environmental Protection Agency mandates. Specifically *Ariz. Rev. Stat. Ann.* § 49-202 creates the Department of Environmental Quality. This department sets water quality standards, enforces those standards, and is responsible for pesticide contamination prevention.

It is known that Fruit or Plenty, Inc. and Trees R Us, Inc. both employed the use of pesticides in their nursery businesses. According to *Ariz. Rev. Stat. Ann.* § 49-305, "A person who uses a pesticide which has been placed on the groundwater protection list is required to report to the director the use of the pesticide . . ." Additionally, if either of the two nursery firms used nitrogen fertilizers, they are also required to apply for an aquifer protection permit, (*Ariz. Rev. Stat. Ann.* § 49-247).

It is not known if Fruit or Plenty, Inc. or Trees R Us, Inc. filed the necessary reports, or obtained the necessary permits. It also is not known if their actions in the use of pesticides and/or fertilizers would be within the limits established by the Department of Environmental Quality. The use of these products is not prohibited for agricultural purposes, but the amounts are regulated and frequent tests are required to monitor residual amounts in the soil and water.

Quality standards for water are set by the Department and may be in narrative form as opposed to numerical limitations. (See *Ariz. Rev. Stat. Ann.* § 49-221). The use of the water source is taken into consideration when standards are set and less stringent standards are applied to aquifers used only for agricultural use as opposed to those which are sources of drinking water.

The Arizona Department of Environmental Quality also has jurisdiction over the regulation of air quality. Chapter 3 of Title 49 of the *Ariz. Rev. Stat. Ann.,* spells out the State's responsibilities for air quality control. The Department is primarily interested in controlling ozone, carbon monoxide and particulates in the air and the regulations reflect those concerns. Permits and compliance orders are required for entities involved in operating incinerators, heavy equipment, or heavy machinery. (See *Ariz. Rev. Stat. Ann.*, § 49-426). The commercial orchards that previously owned the Broadway acreage did not have to obtain a permit under the air pollution control standards. In any event, any air quality problem is more likely to result from the increased motor vehicle traffic because of the connection of Broadway Road from 51st Ave. to 64th Ave. If air quality is found to be a problem, the vehicle traffic should be investigated as the potential cause.

The Comprehensive Environmental Response, Compensation, and Liability Act of 1980 (CERCLA) speaks directly to response, clean-up and remedial actions. The Arizona Department of Environmental Quality implements this act via Article 5 of Title 49 of the *Arizona Revised Statutes Annotated.*

This brings us to the second question involving the obligations of WePlant Em, Inc. if the Broadway acreage is contaminated. According to *Ariz. Rev. Stat. Ann.* § 49-283, an owner, even though not actively involved in the pollution, can be held responsible for the clean-up if he knowingly allowed others to engage in a business that caused pollution at the site. Additionally, a responsible party is identified as an owner who "reasonably should have known" that a hazardous substance was in use at the site, even if he did not have direct knowledge.

There is one paragraph in *Ariz. Rev. Stat. Ann.* § 49-281 which is favorable to WePlant Em., Inc. Paragraph (D) states that an otherwise responsible party may not be held responsible if the damages to the property result from the application of a pesticide product which was approved by the Federal Insecticide, Fungicide and Rodenticide Act and which was applied according to label directions.

Additionally, if the property is found to be contaminated, and WePlant Em, Inc. is held responsible for the clean-up (according to § 49-285 of the *Ariz. Rev. Stat. Ann.*), WePlant Em, Inc. may enjoin any other responsible parties to contribute to the payment of those costs. Although Trees R Us, Inc. is bankrupt and the owners unavailable for action, apparently Fruit or Plenty, Inc. is still in business and may be enjoined in any action because of their direct involvement in the pollution of the property.

As an owner of the property, statute law holds WePlant Em, Inc. responsible for any pollution clean-up costs even though they are absent owners of the property and were not directly involved in the pollution of the area. Available case law supports the clear wording of similar statutes.

In *Guidice v. BFG Electroplating and Manufacturing Co., Inc.* (BFG), 732 Fed. Supp. 556 (W.D. Penn, 1989), the National Bank of the Commonwealth (Bank) obtained the BFG property when BFG went bankrupt. The property was later found to be contaminated and CERCLA looked to the Bank for reimbursement of clean-up costs. The Bank filed a motion for summary judgment based on the premise that they had no direct liability for the property. The Court's decision indicates that the Bank did not have to be both an owner and an operator to be liable under CERCLA. The court held that releasing the Bank from liability and providing a federally funded clean-up of the site would greatly improve the value of the site and the Bank would benefit from the improved land value. Providing an exemption for the Bank would contradict CERCLA policy as defined in 42 U.S.C. § 9607(a)(2) which holds them a responsible party.

In *Gopher Oil Company v. Union Oil Company, Inc.*, 955 F.2d. 519, (8th Circuit, 1992), Union Oil Company attempted to sell contaminated property "as is" to Gopher Oil Company. Gopher spent $423,272.81 on clean-up of the property and looked to Union Oil Company for reimbursement. Union Oil Company was held responsible for the contamination and was not able to transfer their responsibility for the clean-up to Gopher by selling the property on an "as is" basis.

RECOMMENDATIONS

It is apparent that the potential purchaser of the Broadway property will not purchase the land without some assurance that the land is within environmental standards. Statute and case law indicates that WePlant Em, Inc. will be held responsible for contamination, if any is found, either now, or in the future. WePlant Em, Inc. may want to have an independent testing firm do an evaluation of the property so that they can prepare for any eventual encounters with the State authorities and to determine if the property is marketable without a clean-up.

They may also wish to check the public records of the Department of Environmental Quality to see if either Trees R Us, Inc. or Fruit or Plenty, Inc. made any of the appropriate applications or permit filings for use of pesticides and/or fertilizers.

After receiving a report on the property, if it is found to be contaminated, WePlant Em, Inc. may also wish to put Fruit or Plenty, Inc. on notice of a potential claim for contribution to the clean-up costs.

REVIEW QUESTIONS AND EXERCISES

Review Questions

1. What is the purpose of a legal memorandum?
2. What is the difference between an internal legal memorandum and an external legal memorandum?
3. What is your first job in preparing a legal memorandum?
4. Where can you learn the needed facts?
5. Why should you consider negative facts as well as those facts which support your client's claim?
6. What should you do if you notice that there are gaps in your facts?
7. Why should you note the source of your facts when collecting the necessary facts?
8. What type of legal authority should you prefer?

9. Why should your research include law that supports your adversary?

10. Should you discuss the law that supports your adversary in your legal memorandum?

11. Why should you not rely on headnote research?

12. How should you update your research?

13. Will you necessarily use all of the research you collect? Why?

14. How should you use case law that differs slightly from the facts of the situation you are researching?

15. Why should you write notes on your photocopy of each case?

16. Should you photocopy the cases and statutes you will read? Why?

17. What are the best sources of legal authority?

18. What must you check before using a statute or constitutional provision?

19. Can you ignore contravening authority?

20. How can you de-emphasize law that hinders a point that you would like to advance?

21. How can you organize the law pertaining to each issue that you will address in your writing?

22. List three different approaches to organizing your research.

23. What basic information will you find in most internal (in-house) legal memoranda?

24. What is a memo file?

25. What cautions should you keep in mind when referring to a memo from your law firm's memo file?

26. Why is the "date" section of a memo important.

27. Why should you use a date that is earlier than the original date of a legal memo when updating research from the memo in the firm's memo file?

28. What is the purpose of the statement of assignment?

29. What is the "issue" section of a legal memorandum?

30. Why should you consider placing the conclusion toward the beginning of the legal memorandum?

31. What is the "discussion" section of a legal memorandum?

32. What is the purpose of an internal legal memorandum?

33. What citation form should you use when citing legal authority?

34. What style of writing should you use for an internal legal memorandum? Why?

35. Should you include personal opinions in your legal discussion? Why?

36. What is public policy?

37. Should you include public policy arguments in your legal memorandum? When? Why?

38. Should you include a quotation from every source that you reference?

39. Since judges create law, should you quote lengthy examples of the judge's writing to bolster your argument? Why?

40. What information should you include in the "recommendations" section of a legal memorandum?

41. What information should you avoid in the "recommendations" section?

42. What is an external legal memorandum?

43. What writing style should you use in an external legal memo?

44. Should you quote every statute or constitutional provision to which you refer? Why?

45. Should you do more than cite the authority that supports your position? Why?

46. Why must you discuss the relevance of cited authority?

47. Where can you locate necessary page limits when writing an external legal memorandum?

48. Must you tell the court of authority that contradicts your position? When? Why?

49. What is a complex legal memorandum?

50. What is a table of authorities?

51. What is an appendix?

52. List five mistakes one might make when writing a legal memorandum.

Exercises

1. Using the following authorities, construct a table of authorities for a complex legal memorandum:

    a. *E.F.S. Marketing, Inc. v. Russ Berrie & Co., Inc.,* 21 U.S. P.Q. 1993 (S.D.N.Y. 1991)

    b. *North American Bear Company v. Carson Pirie Scott & Co.,* 1991 WL 259031 (N.D. Ill. 1991)

    c. *Alchemy II, Inc. v. Yes! Entertainment Corporation,* 844 F. Supp. 560 (C.D. California 1994)

    d. *American Charm Corp. v. Omega Casting Corp.,* 211 U.S.P.Q. 635, 1982 Corp. L. Dec. P. 25,353 (S.D.N.Y. 1979)

     e. *Wildlife Express Corporation v. Carol Wright Sales, Inc.*, 18 F.3d 502 (7th Cir. 1994)

     f. *Americana Trading, Inc. v. Russ Berrie & Co.*, 966 F.2d 1284 (9th Cir. 1992)

     g. 15 U.S.C. 1125(a)

     h. *SK&F Co. v. Premo Pharmaceutical Laboratories*, 625 F.2d 1055 (3rd Cir. 1980)

     i. *U.S. v. United Mine Workers*, 330 U.S. 258 (1947)

     j. 28 U.S.C. 1331

     k. 17 U.S.C. 411(a)

     l. Federal Rules of Civil Procedure, Rule 11

2. Draft an internal legal memorandum on the following subjects:

     a. Your law firm represents an eight-year-old boy. The child attends a private school in your local city. This particular school adheres to the idea of corporal punishment. Last month, the child was accused of drawing an improper picture of his third-grade teacher. The teacher found the crumpled picture in the trash can. The words "DO IT TO IT" were written at the bottom of the drawing. The teacher, Mary Doit, compared the handwriting on the paper with that of the third-grade pupils in her room. (Ms. Doit is the third-grade teacher at the school.) Ms. Doit determined that the child, Jon Wapped, was the miscreant involved. She ordered Jon to the front of the room and commanded him to "drop his pants." Although Jon protested, he was told that he was to drop his pants and bend over the desk to receive his punishment. Jon complied and was spanked with a large wooden paddle. The children in the class laughed at him as he received this spanking. Jon, by and through his guardian *ad litem,* would like to pursue a claim against the school and Ms. Doit. The elements of the claim will be assault, battery, false imprisonment, and the intentional infliction of emotional distress. (See Chapter 8 for the actual complaint.) Prepare an internal legal memorandum outlining the law in your jurisdiction on these claims. You may wish to begin your research with the U.S. Supreme Court case, *Ingraham v. Wright*, 430 U.S. 651, 97 S. Ct. 1401, 51 L. Ed.2d 711 (1977) holding that corporal punishment in a school setting is not cruel and unusual. See also Annotation, Teacher's Civil Liability for Administering Corporal Punishment to Pupil, 43 A.L.R.2d 469.

     b. Draft an external legal memorandum to support a motion for summary judgment in the Wapped v. Doit case described in part a. The motion will maintain that the defendant is entitled to judgment as a matter of law as a result of consent and reasonable discipline.

7

The Appellate Brief

7.1
INTRODUCTION

The appellate brief is a lengthy document that an attorney submits to an appellate court in support of a client's claim. These writings have the appearance of small books and are never done casually. In this chapter, we will focus on the structure and form of an appellate brief and assume that the procedural steps, such as docketing the appeal and designating the record on appeal, have already been done.[1] Although paralegals usually do not write briefs, they often assist in the preparation of a brief. Attorneys may delegate specific research tasks to a paralegal, or the paralegal may work at assembling the facts that will be used to support the appeal.

You begin the appellate process by indicating to the appellate court that you would like the court to consider your appeal and review the decision or determination of the lower court. In some instances, you may have the right

---

[1]Remember to consult your jurisdiction's appellate rules before beginning any appellate work. Failure to comply with the rules can cause the court to refuse your work. You must file the proper request for an appeal and indicate to the court what lower court records you would like the appellate court to consider. Failure to designate a record (those documents which the lower court used, created, or considered) may preclude the appellate court from considering the record.

to an automatic appeal. In other situations, the appeal may be discretionary, and the court may be free to refuse a particular case. Most appeals to the U.S. Supreme Court are discretionary and proceed by a writ of certiorari. The United States Supreme Court denies most of these requests. The party requesting the appeal is often called the *appellant* or the *petitioner*. The party responding to the appeal is the *appellee* or *respondent*.

Each appeal centers on the record and issues that were first raised at the lower court. If an issue is not first raised at the lower court, it cannot be raised at the appellate level for the first time. A trial court must have had the opportunity to rule on the issue before an appellate court will consider ruling on it. Appellate courts are concerned with trial court errors and will consider only legal issues. By contrast, trial courts rule on factual grounds, and their determinations usually cannot be appealed. Appellate courts deal only with the significance of legal rulings and with how these legal principles can or should be applied to the facts of a particular situation.[2]

Every appellate brief follows a predetermined format. You must first consult your jurisdiction's appellate rules to ensure that you do not inadvertently omit a required section of the brief. Each jurisdiction has its own rules for appellate procedures. These rules dictate the length of the brief, the form the brief must take, the style of typing that must be used, the format of the cover, and the time limits for filing the brief. There are also other rules that must be followed. Remember that you must read and abide by your jurisdiction's appellate rules. Many briefs follow a relatively standard form of organization. You will, of course, use this format only as a model and change the format wherever necessary, remembering that when you make changes, you must still make sure that the brief conforms to court rules.

7.2
TABLES

Each brief will have a table of contents with page references to the different sections of the brief. The table of contents is followed by a table of cases and authorities, which refers to all of the legal authorities that are cited in the brief. This table lists the cases alphabetically and gives page references to where in the brief the cases are cited. The table also lists statutes, constitutional provisions, and secondary authorities and gives page references to

---

[2]Criminal appeals, particularly those dealing with death penalty cases, may use different standards regarding the issues the court will consider.

them. The table of contents and table of cases and authorities are the same as their counterparts in the complex legal memorandum.[3]

7.3
STATEMENT OF JURISDICTION

The second portion of the brief is usually a statement of jurisdiction. This section tells the court why it has jurisdiction over a particular dispute. As with other sections of the brief, you should be prepared to cite relevant statutes when writing the statement of jurisdiction.[4]

7.4
STATEMENT OF THE CASE

The statement of the case indicates the nature of the case and summarizes the procedures that occurred at the lower court. This section refers to the trial court's disposition. It also refers to the dates of the judgment and the dates for the filing of the notice of appeal. The section should indicate that the notice of appeal was filed in a timely fashion.

7.5
STATEMENT OF FACTS

The facts necessary for the appeal are included in the "Statement of Facts" section. Before writing this section, you must cull the record for the necessary facts. Read the lower court transcripts, and organize the facts so that you know the procedural steps and which facts are necessary. Note where in the record you find each item, as you will need to give exact references when you write the statement of facts. Give heed to both favorable and prejudicial references. You have two purposes in reading and noting the record: to present the record accurately and to find every useful fact in the record. You will also look for references in the record that would support your adversary's position, as you will need to assess your opponent's case. Once you have re-

---

[3]Local rules may change the order of the items in your brief.

[4]Since appellate courts are courts of limited jurisdiction, you must, in each case, say why the court can hear the case.

viewed the trial court record and assembled the needed facts, you can begin drafting the statement of facts. Be prepared to redraft this section after you finish the argument component, as you must be sure that you include all the facts which will support your claim. If you refer to a fact in your argument, you must first reference the fact in the "Statement of Facts" section. Double-check and be sure that all facts are included in this section. You may also wish to delete some facts from the section if you did not refer to them and if they will not provide additional assistance to the appellate court. Remember that you must comply with page limitations and therefore do not want extraneous material. Courts prefer to read fewer pages. Say what you need to say, and stop once you have finished. As with the external legal memorandum, be sure that the facts are factual. Avoid conclusory facts, which hint at rather than specifically state what occurred. Remember that facts are identified though our senses of hearing, seeing, smelling, tasting, and touching. Be specific.

When drafting your statement of facts, remember that you wish to be accurate and complete. You also wish to advocate your client's position at all times. Avoid irrelevant facts, and use strong language to portray your client's claim. Do not include names, numbers, or dates unless the name, number, or date is important. Explain the importance of the facts you select. The appellate court is unfamiliar with the case and will learn about it from your brief and the brief your adversary files. Emphasize the favorable facts. This is not the time to give an expository statement of the case. You are not neutral, and the court does not expect you to be. If you write in a dry, explanatory manner, the court will still assume that you are acting as an advocate and will believe that your position is not very strong. Remember that you are arguing your client's case at all times. Do not, however, go to the extreme of misstating any facts. You must be truthful at all times. If there is no evidence to support a particular fact, say so. Use affirmative language to advance your best points. Paint a word picture for your judge so that he or she can "see" what occurred. Remember that detailed facts provide this picture.

You must include adverse facts. You cannot simply ignore those facts which hinder your claim. Omitting unfavorable facts can discredit your entire brief. Courts not only appreciate, but demand, candor. You or your opponent can completely discredit a brief by pointing out to the court that the brief has omitted important facts. Here, however, "creative language"—particularly the passive voice and weaker verbs—will minimize the impact of these negative facts. Nonetheless, do not *present* your opponent's case. Do not begin your facts by reciting what your opponent would say or has said. If you do, you will only emphasize your adversary's claim. Instead, write about the facts of the case, and emphasize the facts that favor your client.

Remember to check your grammar and spelling when you write. Do this both electronically and manually. Remember, however, that an incorrect word or word form may not always be found using electronic grammar or spell checkers. Using a wrong word can dilute the impact of an otherwise good statement of facts.

A well-drafted statement of facts helps the court understand the case. Occasionally, the statement of facts may even be incorporated into the judges' opinion. Whatever the situation, the statement of facts must be easy to understand: You want the judges to understand the facts the first time they read them. Accordingly, organize your facts into a logical sequence—perhaps chronologically. A second approach would be to organize the facts around the issues that you will raise later in the brief. In either instance, you may need special sections dealing with areas requiring expertise, such as engineering or medical details. Describe the events or transactions. Consider using descriptive headings where the facts are complex. These headings will provide an internal structure to the section and help readers understand the events. Here, remember that the court is unfamiliar with the case. You, on the other hand, are probably quite familiar with it, since you may actually have lived a portion of it. Your job will be to simplify the events and make them understandable to others. One way to begin is to write your statement of facts from memory. Those facts which you remember about the case will be the most important ones. Next, read your statement of facts, and add any other facts that give details about the event. Add any needed record references.[5] Remember to double-check so that you include all facts relevant to the issues you will address.

Annotate your facts. Include references to the correct page and line from the trial and/or deposition transcripts and from other exhibits. This allows readers to check your facts, as well as quickly locate additional pertinent facts if necessary. If you use abbreviations to identify particular transcripts, include a footnote or endnote reference identifying each abbreviation. Check your local rules for the correct format for your jurisdiction. You should have a factual reference for each fact you assert. If documents are identified by record references be sure to use these referencing numbers or terms to identify the document to the appellate court. If you have no specific record references, you can create your own abbreviations. Tell the court the meaning of each abbreviation.

---

[5]*Record reference* refers to the document, and often includes the specific page and line of the document.

7.6
RESPONDING TO A BRIEF

If you are responding to a brief instead of writing the original or opening brief, you may wish to write your own statement of facts or you may wish to accept the appellant's version of the facts. In many instances, you will wish to write your own facts so that you can emphasize those facts which favor your side. Many appeals are fought on the facts. If you do not present your own version, you will hamper your ability to fight the appeal successfully. Your statement of facts will follow the same format as the appellant's. Be specific, and here, too, avoid arguing your adversary's case. State *your* facts rather than controverting your opponent's facts.

7.7
QUESTIONS PRESENTED

Your first step in any appeal is to determine the issues you will present to the court. The issues are the heart of the appeal and the reason why the court is hearing the case. You may, however, need to select only a few of the possible issues that you could bring forth. Focus on those issues which have the greatest chance of interesting the appellate court and of resulting in a successful outcome. Weak issues detract from an otherwise strong brief. Do not succumb to the temptation to include marginal issues.

If you have several minor issues that you would like to bring to the court's attention, you can consider including them as factors bearing on a stronger central issue or combining them into a major request. You should also be aware of "hot potatoes." These are issues which create difficult legal questions that courts may not wish to address because of their sensitivity. If your case contains a "hot potato," you should investigate to see whether there is another issue the court might find acceptable, but not as sensitive.[6] Remember your goal(s) at all times.

---

[6]Courts generally like to decide cases on a limited basis. They often go to great lengths to avoid changing or defining broad areas of the law. A court will often look for a way to issue an opinion that avoids a major legal change. Sometimes, however, a court will look for a case as a vehicle for changing the law.

7.8
CRIMINAL APPEALS

You may experience difficulties when preparing appeals for criminal cases. From time to time, you may be faced with a criminal appeal, but be unable to discover an appealable issue. Nonetheless, you may be required to file an appeal. Remember that you can always file an Anders brief, citing *Anders v. California*, 386 U.S. 738, 87 S. Ct. 1396, 18 L. Ed.2d 493 (1967). This case allows the attorney to claim that he or she has not found an appealable issue and to invite the court to search the record for a viable claim. Criminal defendants tend to want to raise every possible issue. Although courts allow more leeway in the number of issues, you should still select your issues with as much care as possible.

When you draft your "Issues Presented" section, remember to refer to relevant facts that favor your client's position. Do not include unnecessary details. However, your question must be phrased with reference to the circumstances of the case. Be concise and avoid repetition. You must also avoid any tendency to stretch the issue(s) beyond recognition in an attempt to argue your case. Remember that the judges will read your adversary's brief as well. When one side of the case bears no relation to the other, warning flags wave in the judges' brains. The judges may believe that the attorney(s) simply do not know or understand the case or that the case is weak. Your issues must be complete enough for the judges to understand the case.

7.9
THE ARGUMENT

The argument discusses the applicable law and how it applies to the facts of the case. You present precedent to support your claim, as well as policy arguments that argue for fairness and justice. Decide the order of the arguments that you will present. You may have subsidiary arguments that accompany the primary issues. These must be placed near the main argument. You may wish to put your strongest argument either first or last. Some writers prefer a strong beginning. Others like to finish on a strong note and place their strongest arguments at the end. Still others prefer a chronological discussion. Once you determine the appropriate order for your argument, you may draft the argument. Remember that the order for the argument must match the order for the "Issues Presented." If these two sections do not match, change the order of one of them. Remember that one section of the argument will lead to another. Your arguments should be drafted in a logical fashion.

Use argument headings to separate major divisions. These headings should preface the section to which they refer and should persuasively discuss the issues and facts pertinent to the division. Argument headings are another opportunity for persuasive writing. View them as a quick way to apprise the court about your client's position. Your argument heading must be complete and stand on its own.

The argument proper follows each argument heading. Here you present your legal argument and authority to the court. Remember that the court does not know the facts of your case. Most judges are familiar with many legal principles and precedents, particularly those decisions which they themselves have authored. Avoid discussing basic general principles. Instead, emphasize those principles which the judges may not know. For example, you would probably waste valuable space in informing judges about the tenets of the U.S. Constitution. You would be better off emphasizing the controlling precedents that affect your case and how this law applies to your specific facts.

Precedent is crucial in the argument section. However, you must select the precedent you actually use. If you have fully researched your issue, you may have located more precedents than you can actually use. Be selective. Do not simply cite case after case without discussing the relevance of the cases you list. A continuous string of citations (string citing) is not persuasive.

By choice, you want to cite binding law. If you are aware of any relevant law decided by the court that will be hearing the case, be sure and include references to this law. You must also include controlling law even when the law does not favor your position. The ABA Ethical Rules, Rule 3.3(a) (3) [identical to Disciplinary Rule DR 7-106(B) (1)] require that attorneys disclose any legal authority from the controlling jurisdiction that is directly adverse to the client's position if the law was not disclosed by the adversary. If you have no binding law, look for persuasive primary authority. If you have a lot of law from a variety of jurisdictions, you may wish to include a selection of cases so that you can argue that the legal point is widely accepted. To avoid the problem of string citing, you may wish to include some of these cases in an appendix. If you locate conflicting law and there is a split of authority, you should select the best case from each side and then tell the court why your position should be favored. Do not simply ignore contrary law, as your adversary is sure to point out the omission and comment that you failed to mention these precedents to the court.

Perform your research thoroughly. Complete research not only provides the best support for your claims, but also may help develop new arguments that you may elect to pursue. Furthermore, judges may elect to use sections of a well-researched and well-written brief as parts of the case opinion. Research the law before beginning the appeal. Then, as the last step before submitting your brief, recheck all of the law you have used. You want to be up to date. Remember to check all of your citations. This should include a computerized cite check using Instacite or Autocite in addition to Shepard's. Remember that if you are using Instacite as your cite-checking modality, you will not locate any cases that overruled your authority if the case was overruled prior to 1972.

Do not use too many quotations. Remember that quotations can distract your reader from your legal argument. You do not want to unduly focus your judges' attention on the problems faced by someone in another case. You want the judicial panel to consider your client's problems. Judges use precedent to substantiate legal ideas. Judges need to determine how the precedent applies to your client's facts. Writing a brief is not and should not be a *Bartlett's Familiar Quotations of Case Law*. Judges often care more for the substance of a case than the language. Indeed, you should quote language from another case only when it "sings" to you. When a judge has written a passage so beautifully that the language forms a vibrant word picture, you may elect to quote from that case. Otherwise you will be better advised to paraphrase the opinion and discuss how the cited case relates to your factual situation.

You must apply your precedent to the facts of your case. Continually reference your own facts. Remember that judges decide cases more on facts then on law. The law (or precedent) establishes the rules of the game. The facts indicate how the game should and will be played. Without the facts there is no "game," no case, and no appeal. Parallel the facts of the illustrative cases with the facts of your own case. Show how the holdings of your precedent compel the judges to rule in your favor. If you are dealing with unfavorable legal precedent, tell the judges how and why this precedent should be distinguished from the current situation or overruled. You may want to address your precedent in three steps: an initial paragraph detailing the legal principle, a second paragraph applying the legal principle to your facts, and a concluding paragraph indicating the result you desire. Alternatively, you may wish to begin this process with the result you wish and then discuss the facts and the law. In some instances, you will need to integrate a number of cases because you have no legal authority directly on your point. Remember that when you are writing about the facts, you must remain with those documents and facts which are part of the record on appeal. You can never add facts or evidence that does not appear in the record. You can cite nonlegal authorities in support of your position, as well as secondary authority, but you must take care to apply these sources to your facts. Double-check to be sure that you have referred to each fact you use in your argument in the "Statement of Facts" section of the brief.

Remember the rules of grammar. Clear writing is effective writing. Avoid lengthy briefs. You want to write as concisely as possible. Judges do not reward you for lengthy scholarship. They just want to know which legal principles you feel best advance your case and how these principles apply to your factual situation. Omit conclusory language. Judges are not interested in your opinion. They want to know what happened and then draw their own conclusions. Tell the judge what happened, and then argue why the decision was correct or incorrect. Edit your brief when you finish. Make sure that your argument parallels your "issues" statements. Your goal is to have someone who knows little or nothing about the law or your case fully understand your argument. If this is not so, you have failed. Proofread, Shepardize, and cite check. Even small errors may discredit your entire brief.

Finally, do not use many footnotes. Avoid them altogether, if at all possible, since they are usually either ignored or distracting. If ignored, the footnotes serve no purpose. If the footnotes distract the reader from your argument, you will need to work to regain the reader's attention. Neither choice is desirable. Remember to use simple words. Your goal is not to impress the judge with your brilliance, but to have the judge finish the brief and conclude that you are correct. A well-written document captures your attention at the beginning and flows until you reach the end. The reader's attention should not wander, but instead, should be naturally directed along with no real effort on the reader's part.

7.10
RESPONSE BRIEFS

When responding to a brief, you employ many of the same techniques as when you write a brief. In responding to a brief, however, you want to remember that your goal is not just to refute the opening brief; rather, you want to advance your own client's position. Write affirmatively. Advance your position; do not simply negate the appellant's contentions. If the opposition has misquoted or misstated facts or the law, say so clearly and strongly. Then leave the problem. Do not dwell on it.

If you have raised a cross-appeal, you will effectively be writing an opening brief for those issues. Apply the standard we have already discussed for the opening brief.

7.11
REPLY BRIEFS

You may elect to reply to a response brief. The reply brief gives the appellant the opportunity to respond to the appellee's contentions. Although the format of the reply brief is similar to that of the opening brief or the response brief, the content is limited. You use the same technique of persuasive language. You fully research your position. However, you must limit your comments and research to those issues which were raised in the response brief. You cannot raise new issues in a reply. Even if the law you cite is correct and well stated, you cannot argue new issues. Courts simply will not consider issues raised for the first time in a reply brief. You may rebut any point raised in the response brief, but this is all. Answer only those contentions which are important. Spending limited space on minor issues may emphasize those issues in the court's eyes.

If the response brief leaves questions that the appellant would like to clarify for the court, then write a reply. However, remember that reply briefs are optional. Do not reserve points of contention for oral argument that you have not briefed for the court. All of your points should first be written. Oral argument will reinforce your strong points. However, you want the court to have written documentation before the argument is given orally, so that the court can consider all of your claims. Also, you want the court to have such documentation after the argument is presented orally, because then your brief will be a reminder of what you maintained in court.

Finally, in writing any brief, remember that you want to leave the court with the impression that you have the stronger case. Rarely will you demolish every argument your adversary advances. Many cases are close. Therefore, do not clutter your brief with attempts to denigrate each of your opponent's claims. Concentrate instead on reinforcing your strong points and indicating your opposition's weaknesses, so that, on balance, the law and equity favor your side.

7.12
SUMMARY AND CONCLUSION

You should include a summary at the end of your brief. The summary is a short (1-2 pages) review of the substance of your claims. This is your final chance for advocacy. Remember that you will want to write as persuasively as possible and emphasize your strongest points. Strive for closure. You should resolve contradictions. Avoid raising any new issues. Never put concepts, arguments, or law in your summary that you did not include in the main part of your brief. Finally, write a conclusion that includes the behavior you would like to see the court take. If you wish the court to remand the case, say so. If you wish a particular ruling to be reversed, ask the court for the reversal.

7.13
THE APPENDIX

If your local rules allow, you may wish to include an appendix to your brief. Here is where you can attach more complete portions of a transcript, jury instructions given or refused, and copies of relevant case law, statutes, constitutional provisions, or hard-to-find materials that might aid the judges in their understanding of your brief. Remember that although these materials may be available as part of the record on appeal or in the library, the judge will not necessarily have ready access to them at the time he or she is reading your brief. If you believe that there are documents that would help the court understand your arguments, include copies of these materials as appendices. Judges will not usually seek out additional materials. Provide any documents you think a judge may need, so that the judge has ready access to them.

7.14
SAMPLE APPELLATE FORMS

SUPERIOR COURT OF ARIZONA

MARICOPA COUNTY

JOHNNY DIDWELL,	
Plaintiff,	No. _____
v.	NOTICE OF APPEAL
JANE UPSET,	
Defendant.	

Notice is given that the plaintiff (defendant) appeals to the Court of Appeals (other appellate court) from the judgment (denial of motion for a new trial, other order) entered on April 1, 1995, in favor of defendant (plaintiff).

Dated:

_____
Attorney Name and Address
State Bar No.
Attorney for _____

Copy of the foregoing
mailed (delivered) this
_____ day of _____, 1995,
to (Opposing Counsel)

By _____

SUPERIOR COURT OF ARIZONA

MARICOPA COUNTY

JOHNNY DIDWELL,

                    Plaintiff,

v.   No. _____

                                            Designation of Record
JANE UPSET,   on Appeal

                    Defendant.

Pursuant to Rule _____ of the _____ (Rules of Appellate Procedure) (plaintiff, defendant, name of party) designates the following as the record on appeal.

Plaintiff (defendant) intends to present the following issues on appeal.

1.

2.

Dated:

                                            _____
                                            Attorney Name and Address
                                            State Bar No.
                                            Attorney for _____

Copy of the foregoing
mailed (delivered) this
_____ day of _____, 1995,
to (Opposing Counsel)

By _____

IN THE COURT OF APPEALS

STATE OF ARIZONA

DIVISION I

JOHNNY DIDWELL,

      Appellant,

v.

JANE UPSET,

      Appellee.

No. _____

Motion for Extension of
Time to File Brief

    Appellant (appellee) requests an extension of time within which to file its

opening (answering, response, reply) brief from (date) until (date) for the reasons

that:

1.

2.

    Dated:

                 _____

                 Attorney Name and Address
                 State Bar No.
                 Attorney for _____

Copy of the foregoing
mailed (delivered) this
_____ day of _____, 1995,
to (Opposing Counsel)

By _____

IN THE COURT OF APPEALS

STATE OF ARIZONA

DIVISION I

JOHNNY DIDWELL,

               Appellant,

v.

JANE UPSET,

               Appellee.

No. _____

Motion to Exceed Page Limitations

Pursuant to Rule _____ of the Rules of _____ Appellate Procedure, appellant (appellee) requests permission to file an extended brief that exceeds the allowed page limitations for the following reasons:

1.
2.

If the Court denies this request, appellant (appellee) requests this Court to extend the time for filing the brief for _____ days to allow the edition of the brief to conform to the page limitations set forth in rule _____ of the Rules of Appellate Procedure.

Dated:

                                        _____

                                        Attorney Name and Address
                                        State Bar No.
                                        Attorney for _____

Copy of the foregoing
mailed (delivered) this
_____ day of _____, 1995,
to (Opposing Counsel)

By _____

Attach an affidavit if required by your rules.

TABLE OF CONTENTS

Page

Statement of the Case

Statement of Jurisdiction

Statement of Facts

Questions Presented

Argument

Request for Attorney Fees (if applicable)

Summary

Conclusion

Appendix

Affidavit of Service

TABLE OF CITATIONS

Page

Cases (arranged alphabetically)

Statutes and Rules

Regulations

Secondary Authority

IN THE COURT OF APPEALS

STATE OF ARIZONA

DIVISION I

JOHNNY DIDWELL,
 	
          Appellant,
 	
v.
 	
JANE UPSET,
 	
          Appellee.
	No. _____
	
	Request for Oral Argument

        Pursuant to Rule _____ of the _____ Rules of Appellate Procedure, appellant (appellee) requests oral argument in this matter.

        Dated:

                                      _____
                                      Name and address
                                      State Bar Number
                                      Attorney for _____

Copy of the foregoing
mailed (hand delivered)
this _____ day of _____,
1995, to:
(Opposing Counsel)

By _____

IN THE COURT OF APPEALS

STATE OF ARIZONA

DIVISION I

JOHNNY DIDWELL,

                    Appellant,

v.

JANE UPSET,

                  Appellee.

No. _____

List of Supplemental Authorities

      Appellant (appellee) respectfully submits the following supplemental citations not contained in its opening (response, answering, reply) brief in support of its position on page _____ of that brief. This submission is made pursuant to Rule _____ of the _____ Rules of Appellate Procedure.

      (List the citations. Do not include any argument.)

      Dated:

                                          _____

                                          Name and address
                                          State Bar No.
                                          Attorney for _____

Copy of the foregoing
mailed (hand delivered)
this _____ day of _____,
1995, to:
(Opposing Counsel)

By _____

IN THE COURT OF APPEALS

STATE OF ARIZONA

DIVISION I

JOHNNY DIDWELL,

                Appellant,   No. _____

v.

                                      Motion to Strike Opening
                                      (Responsive, Reply) Brief

JANE UPSET,

                Appellee.

Appellant (appellee) requests that the answering (opening, response, reply) brief of appellee (appellant) be stricken and that the matter be submitted for consideration by this court for the following reasons:

1.

2.

Appellant (appellee) further requests that the appellant/appellee be ordered to file a replacement brief that conforms with the mandates and requirements of the _____ Rules of Appellate Procedure.

        Dated:

                                          _____

                                        Name and address
                                        State Bar No.
                                          Attorney for _____

Copy of the foregoing
mailed (hand delivered)
this _____ day of _____,
1995, to:
(Opposing Counsel)
By _____

REVIEW QUESTIONS AND EXERCISES

Review Questions

1. What is an appellate brief?
2. How do you begin the appellate process?
3. Why must you consult the appellate rules for the jurisdiction in which you will file the appellate brief?
4. What is designating a record on appeal?
5. What is the effect of failing to designate a record on appeal?
6. List one court where appeals are usually discretionary.
7. What name is given to the party requesting an appeal?
8. Why must an issue first be raised at the trial court?
9. What areas of law does an appellate court handle?
10. What is a table of contents, and what information does it contain?
11. What is a table of cases and authorities, and what information does it contain?
12. Compare a table of cases and authorities in an appellate brief with a table of cases and authorities in a complex legal memorandum.
13. What is a statement of jurisdiction?
14. Why must you include a statement of jurisdiction in an appellate brief?
15. What is the statement of the case?
16. What information should you include in the statement of the case?
17. Why should you note where in the record you found the facts that you include in your statement of facts?
18. Why do you read and note the record?
19. Why should you look for references to the record that support your adversary's position?
20. When should you redraft the statement of facts?
21. What writing style should you use when drafting your statement of facts?
22. Why must you include unfavorable facts?
23. How can you minimize the impact of adverse facts?
24. How should you organize your facts?
25. How can you structure your facts so that they are easier to read and understand?

26. Why would you want to write your own statement of facts when responding to a brief?

27. Should you include every possible issue in a brief? Why?

28. Do courts prefer major legal changes?

29. When and why might you cite *Anders v. California*, 386 U.S. 738 (1967)?

30. Why must you phrase your issue(s) or question(s) with reference to the facts of your case?

31. What is the argument section of an appellate brief?

32. How can you support your claim?

33. Where should you put your strongest argument?

34. Why should you use argument headings?

35. What function(s) can these headings serve?

36. Should you begin each section with a thorough discussion of the basic principles of law? Why?

37. Should you cite all the precedents you find?

38. When should you select the precedent you use in your brief, and what criteria should you use to determine which precedent to select?

39. What is string citing?

40. Must you include controlling law that favors your adversary? Why?

41. When should you use quotations in a brief?

42. Is it preferable to paraphrase a judge's language or to quote the actual language from the case? Why?

43. Why are the facts so important to the judge's final determination?

44. Under what conditions can you add facts or evidence that do not appear in the record?

45. How important are footnotes to the briefing process?

46. What is the purpose of a response brief?

47. What is the purpose of a reply brief?

48. What is a summary?

49. What writing style should you use in writing the summary?

50. Why should you avoid introducing new arguments in the summary?

51. What information should you include in the conclusion?

52. What information would you include in the appendix?

Exercises

1. Locate the appellate rules of your state.
2. Locate the appellate rules of the Circuit court in your area.
3. Structure an outline for an appellate brief.

8 *Drafting Pleadings and Other Legal Documents*

8.1
INTRODUCTION

As a paralegal, you may have occasion to draft a variety of legal documents, from pleadings to contracts. With these documents, you will often consult a form to help you with your drafting. Your first step in this process is to find the correct form to use as a model. Many law firms keep files of forms. Consult these files first. You may also wish to look in any of a number of form books, which you can find in your law library. Consult your library card catalog for a listing of applicable books. Once you have selected your form books and located the correct model form (using the index to the set of books you chose), you can begin the initial stages of your drafting. Determine whether the set of books is specific to your jurisdiction. If the set or the form is not specifically written for the court or jurisdiction in which you work, you will need to check the jurisdiction's rules and law to ensure that the form you have in mind is acceptable for use. Some courts require specific types of forms or language. You must include this "magic" language if your writing is to be acceptable. You will also need to research any legal standards and be sure that those expressed in the form are in accord with the standards used in your jurisdiction. Remember that many legal form books have selections of forms from the entire United States, and the form may, and probably will, need to be adapted to suit the legal standards for your jurisdiction. Forms are just guidelines.

Once you determine that the law is correctly stated, you must adapt the form to conform to your client's facts. Most forms are written with blank spaces in which you can fill in relevant material. Other forms are examples of how a particular kind of document can or should be drafted. You will need to adapt these forms to your facts.

Forms can help you by giving you a skeleton around which you can support your writing. Forms give you a place to start, not a place to finish. You will almost always need to do a substantial amount of editing to make the form suit your particular purpose. Once you finish adapting the form, double-check the changes that you made.

If you cannot find a form, or if you elect not to use one, you can draft each document independently. If you are drafting pleadings, be sure to consult your procedural rules so that you comply with jurisdictional requirements. You will also want to research the area of the law that you are working with before you draft any specifics, so that you do not inadvertently violate any legal requirements. Write clearly, and be sure that you know what you want to state. If you are drafting a contract, double-check to make sure you include all of the provisions the parties want. You must be equally sure that you do not include anything that the parties want to exclude. Also, make sure that you include necessary general provisions such as a default clause, a choice-of-law clause, and the dates the contract is to become effective and is to end. Draft carefully and read your document when you finish. You are responsible for the finished product.

Make sure that you follow all of the rules of clear writing that have been explained in this book. When you finish drafting the document, you should set it aside for a day or two if you have the time. Then pick it up again, and read it carefully to see whether it still seems to say what you want it to say. Make any necessary changes and do a final review. You may want to have a colleague read the document for you as well. It never hurts to get another opinion.

8.2
SAMPLE PLEADING: A COMPLAINT

IN THE SUPERIOR COURT OF THE STATE OF ARIZONA

IN AND FOR THE COUNTY OF MARICOPA

JOHN WAPPED, a minor by and through his guardian ad litem, Plaintiff, v. MARY DOIT and ROBERT DOIT, husband and wife, and ALLFAITHS RELIGIOUS ACADEMY, a Corporation, Defendants.	No. CV95-1234 COMPLAINT (Tort Non Motor, Misc. Civil)

Plaintiff alleges,

ALLEGATIONS COMMON TO ALL COUNTS

I. The Plaintiff is a resident of Maricopa County, Arizona.
II. Upon information and belief, the individual Defendants are residents of Maricopa County, Arizona.
III. The Corporate Defendant is an Arizona Corporation.
IV. The actions complained of took place within Maricopa County, Arizona.
V. The Plaintiff is a minor and is appearing through his duly appointed guardian *ad litem.*
VI. The individual defendants are teachers at the school operated by the corporate defendant.
VII. Defendant MARY DOIT was the teacher assigned to the third grade at the ALLFAITHS RELIGIOUS ACADEMY.
VIII. Plaintiff was a third-grade student in the school.
IX. On January 4, 1995, while in the third-grade class at ALLFAITHS RELIGIOUS ACADEMY, Mary Doit found a drawing in the trash can with a caricature of a female teacher and the words "Do it to it" at the bottom.
X. The drawing was not complimentary.
XI. Mary Doit compared the handwriting on the note with the handwriting of her students.
XII. Mary Doit determined that the Plaintiff had authored the note.
XIII. Plaintiff was called to the front of the room.
XIV. Upon reaching the front of the room, Plaintiff was told to pull down his pants and lean over the desk.
XV. The Plaintiff protested.

XVI. Plaintiff was told that he would either comply or be expelled from school.

XVII. Plaintiff was further told that he could not leave until the paddling was administered.

XVIII. Corporal punishment is commonly used at the school.

XIX. The Plaintiff pulled down his pants and leaned over the desk, whereupon Defendant Mary Doit administered a paddling consisting of five whacks with a wooden paddle.

XX. The paddling left the Plaintiff severely bruised.

XXI. The Plaintiff was next told to sit down despite his crying that he could not sit down without great pain.

XXII. During the paddling, the Plaintiff heard some of the girls in the class snickering.

XXIII. Since the paddling, the Plaintiff has had problems with his classmates and, in particular, with the girls who are in his class.

COUNT I—BATTERY

XXIV. Plaintiff was spanked.

XXV. Plaintiff did not consent to the spanking.

XXVI. Plaintiff found the spanking to be painful.

XXVII. Plaintiff was bruised as a result of the spanking.

WHEREFORE Plaintiff prays for relief as follows:

1. For judgment against the Defendants in such amount as the court shall determine is reasonable and just.
2. For the costs of this action.
3. For interest on the judgment at the maximum rate allowable by law.
4. For such other and further relief as the court deems just and reasonable.

COUNT II—ASSAULT

XXVIII. Plaintiff was afraid that he would be spanked.

XXIX. Plaintiff did not consent to the spanking.

XXX. Plaintiff was spanked within minutes of being called to the front of the room.

XXXI. Plaintiff knew or had reason to believe that the spanking would be painful.

WHEREFORE Plaintiff prays for relief as follows:

1. For judgment against the Defendants in such amount as the court shall determine is reasonable and just.
2. For the costs of this action.
3. For interest on the judgment at the maximum rate allowable by law.
4. For such other and further relief as the court deems just and reasonable.

COUNT III—FALSE IMPRISONMENT

XXXII. Plaintiff was a third-grade student at the time of the alleged incident.

XXXIII. Plaintiff did not believe that he could leave the room at the time of the alleged incident.

XXXIV. Plaintiff remained in the room because of duress.

XXXV. The teacher told Plaintiff that he could not leave the room.

WHEREFORE Plaintiff prays for relief as follows:

1. For judgment against the Defendants in such amount as the court shall determine is reasonable and just.
2. For the costs of this action.
3. For interest on the judgment at the maximum rate allowable by law.
4. For such other and further relief as the court deems just and reasonable.

COUNT IV—INTENTIONAL INFLICTION OF EMOTIONAL DISTRESS

XXXVI. Plaintiff was publicly spanked.

XXXVII. Plaintiff was greatly embarrassed by the spanking.

XXXVIII. Defendant knew or should have known that a public spanking would humiliate Plaintiff.

XXXIX. Plaintiff has suffered and continues to suffer from the jibes of his classmates.

WHEREFORE Plaintiff prays for relief as follows:

1. For judgment against the Defendants in such amount as the court shall determine is reasonable and just.
2. For the costs of this action.
3. For interest on the judgment at the maximum rate allowable by law.
4. For such other and further relief as the court deems just and reasonable.

DATED this _____ day of _____, 1995.

Jon Cheetem, Esq.
Cheetem and Much
Attorneys for Plaintiff
1234 Main Street
Temple City, Arizona 88888
(520) 654-3210

REVIEW QUESTIONS AND EXERCISES

Review Questions

1. What is a law firm form file?
2. What is a form book?

3. Why would you consult a form book before drafting a document?
4. Where can you find a form book?
5. Can you always use the form in a form book as it is written?
6. Why must you research legal standards before using a form?
7. Must you always use a form book?

Exercises

1. Draft a complaint for a negligence action where an attorney failed to file an answer in a timely manner. The opposing side took a default judgment against the client.

2. Draft a contract for your client who is entering a new business as a private investigator. Your client would like to arrange with his two partners to develop a business as a private investigator. The client is licensed by your local state. The potential partners do not have the training necessary to obtain private investigator licenses, but will work under your client's supervision. Your client will retain 52 percent of the business, and each partner will have 24 percent of the business. Income will be divided on an equal basis after all of the business debts are paid and a reserve account of $25,000.00 is established. Your client must approve all cases that the firm undertakes, since the firm will be operating under his or her license.

Appendix A: Vocabulary Builders

English is composed of words and word roots from many languages. Greek and Latin roots are common in English, and learning a few of the following terms can aid your vocabulary.

a, ana   *negative prefix*

ab   *go away from*

ad, ag   *to, forward*

adelphos   *brother*

agogos   *leader or leading*

algos   *pain*

alter   *other*

alumnus, alumna   *graduate (plural: alumni, alumnae)*

ambi   *both*

andros   *male*

anglus   *English*

anthropos   *mankind*

anti   *against*

asketes   *monk*

astron   *star*

autos   *self*

baros   *weight*

bi   *two*

biblion   *book*

bios   *life*

botane   *plant*

centrum   *center*

chiro   *hand*

chronos   *time*

con   *with*

corrigo   *correct or set straight*

datum, data   *information*

deca   *ten*

demos   *people*

derma   *skin*

dexter   *right hand*

dicha   *in two*

dis   *against*

droit   *right hand*

e, ex   *out*

ego   *self, I*

en, em   *in*

endo   *inner, within*
epi   *on*
-er   *one who*
escence   *growing or becoming*
extro   *outside*
gamos   *marriage*
gauche   *left hand*
ge, geo   *earth*
genesis   *birth or origin*
geras   *old age*
geron   *old man*
graphein   *to write*
gyne   *woman*
hypos   *under*
iatria   *medical healing*
-ic   *adj. suffix*
ician   *expert*
in   *prefix meaning not, or else* inside
internus   *inside*
intro   *inside*
-ion   *noun suffix*
-ist   *one who*
-itis   *inflammation*
-ity   *quality or condition*
-ium   *place where*
-ize   *verb suffix*
jure   *law*
kakos   *bad, harsh*
kalos   *beauty*
kardia   *heart*
kentron   *center*
laud   *praise*
lingua   *tongue*
logos   *study of, science*
mancy   *prediction*
mania   *madness*
mat   *kill*
metron   *measure*
misein   *hate*
monos   *one*
nautes   *sailor*
ne   *negative prefix*
-ness   *noun suffix*
neuron   *nerve*
nomos   *arrangement, order*
notus   *known*

octo   *eight*
oculus   *eye*
odontos   *tooth*
omnis   *all*
ophthalmos   *eye*
opsis, optikos   *view, vision, sight*
orthos   *straight*
-osis   *abnormal or diseased condition*
osteon   *bone*
-ous   *suffix*
paidos   *child*
pathos   *feeling, suffering, diseased*
pede   *foot*
peri   *around, surrounding*
philien   *love of*
photos   *light*
platys   *flat, broad*
podos, pous   *foot*
polys   *many*
pre   *before*
pseudo   *false*
psyche   *spirit, soul, mind*
pulcher   *beauty*
pyge   *buttocks*
sciens   *knowing*
scio   *know*
se   *apart*
sectus   *cut*
senex   *old*
sinister   *left hand*
socius   *companion*
soma   *body*
sophos   *wise*
sphygmos   *pulse*
summus   *highest*
syn, sym   *with, together*
tele   *distance*
therme   *heat*
tome   *a cutting*
tri   *three*
un   *negative prefix*
verto   *turn*
vetus   *old*
-y   *practice or custom of*
zoion   *animal*

Appendix B: Cases and Materials for the Exercises

The following materials are included to help you with the exercises in this book.

Auto-Cite (R) Citation Service, (c) 1995 Lawyers Cooperative Publishing

CITATION YOU ENTERED:

In re Rosenkrans*1, 84 N.J. Eq. 232, 94 A. 42 (1915)

ANNOTATIONS CITING THE CASE(S) INDICATED ABOVE WITH ASTER-ISK(S):

1 Negligence, inattention, or professional incompetence of attorney in handling client's affairs as ground for disciplinary action, 96 A.L.R.2d 823, secs. 5, 9, 27 (superseded by Negligence, inattention, or professional incompetence of attorney in handling client's affairs in estate or probate matters as ground for disciplinary action—modern cases, 66 A.L.R.4th 342, and by Attorney's delay in handling decedent's estate as ground for disciplinary action, 21 A.L.R.4th 75, and sec. 27 superseded by Negligence, inattention, or professional incompetence of attorney in handling.

In re ROSENKRANS.

No. 39/653.

Court of Chancery of New Jersey.

April 30, 1915.

In the matter of Addison P. Rosenkrans, a solicitor of the Court of Chancery of New Jersey. On order to show cause why respondent should not be disbarred or otherwise disciplined and punished. Respondent suspended.

(Syllabus by the Court.)

1. ATTORNEY AND CLIENT k44—MISCONDUCT OF ATTORNEY—DELAY IN PROSECUTING SUIT—FRAUD.

Mere delay in prosecuting a client's cause, unless, perhaps, it is so long continued as to be evidence of fraudulent conduct, does not afford the basis for disciplining a solicitor beyond reprimand and an admonition to proceed; but, when a solicitor receives a fee, especially when it is all he asks, upon a promise to speedily prosecute, and then does nothing whatever to that end—does not even start—but, on the contrary, when asked by his client for information as to the status of the cause, he falsely informs her that it is pending and is being prosecuted with all convenient speed, in whatever words the idea is conveyed, he is guilty of fraud upon his client, and for this he should be disciplined.

[Note.—For other cases, see Attorney and Client, Cent. Dig. ss 55, 56, 62, Dec. Dig. k44.]

2. ATTORNEY AND CLIENT k42—MALPRACTICE—PROCUREMENT OF FALSE AFFIDAVIT.

A solicitor who counsels and procures a client to make an affidavit 'that she is the petitioner named in the foregoing petition,' and also 'that the matters and things therein set forth are true, to the best of her knowledge and belief,' when, in fact, there is no petition in existence, with intent to annex the affidavit to a petition thereafter to be drawn and filed (which would have aggravated the matter, involving uttering a false affidavit and imposing the same upon the court), is guilty of professional misconduct amounting to malpractice.

[Ed. Note.—For other cases, see Attorney and Client, Cent. Dig. s 54; Dec. Dig. k42.]

3. ATTORNEY AND CLIENT k38—PROCEEDINGS TO DISCIPLINE—MALPRACTICE.

Professional malpractice is of three kinds—ignorant, negligent, and willful. While disciplinary proceedings may not be taken against a solicitor for ignorant malpractice, for negligent malpractice he can be censured by the court, and in gross cases disciplined; and for willful malpractice he can be disciplined even to the extent of disbarment.

[Ed. Note.—For other cases, see Attorney and Client, Cent. Dig. ss 51, 61; Dec. Dig. k38.]

4. ATTORNEY AND CLIENT k58—GROUND FOR SUSPENSION—MALPRACTICE.

The offense of the respondent is of a dual character: (a) Obtaining money from a client upon the promise of prompt professional service, without rendering any service, accompanied by false representations that her cause was being prosecuted with all convenient speed, extending over a period of seven months; and (b) counseling and procuring her to make an affidavit false in fact in the sense that the alleged fact did not exist, but not false in that it was contrary to existing fact, with intent to make use of the affidavit. Both offenses were deliberately—that is to say, willfully—committed.

These offenses, singly or together, amount to malpractice in a solicitor, and for both of them suspension from practice for a period of two years is a proper penalty under all the facts and circumstances of the case at bar.

[Ed. Note.—For other cases, see Attorney and Client, Cent. Dig. ss 76–78]

5. ATTORNEY AND CLIENT k44—'MALPRACTICE'

The violation of a promissory obligation, followed up with the false assertion, oft repeated, that the promise was being performed, is malpractice, in a solicitor who has received a fee from a client for professional service.

[Ed. Note.—For other cases, see Attorney and Client, Cent. Dig. ss 55, 56, 62; Dec. Dig. k44.

For other definitions, see Words and Phrases, First and Second Series, Malpractice.] *233 Nelson B. Gaskill, of Trenton, for the prosecution.

Clifford L. Newman, of Paterson, for respondent.

WALKER, Ch.

Upon complaint of Mrs. Stella Van Dien accusing Addison P. Rosenkrans, a solicitor, with unprofessional conduct in not prosecuting, while he represented to her that he had commended and was prosecuting in the Court of Chancery, a proceeding to obtain for her maintenance for her child after a decree of divorce already made in her favor against her husband, which had been obtained by another solicitor, an order to show cause was made which recited substantially as follows: That he (Rosenkrans) was charged with malpractice as a solicitor of the Court of Chancery, in that he, being such solicitor, was consulted by Mrs. Van Dien for the purpose of obtaining his advice with respect to her proposed action for support of her child, who related to him the circumstances in which she found herself after the decree of divorce, and being without other means for her support than the income from her own labor, which was insufficient to maintain herself and her child, because of which it was necessary for her to take some steps to compel her former husband, Arthur G. Van Dien, to contribute to the support of the child, and to pay Mrs. Van Dien such sums in the nature of alimony as the court might award, whereupon he (Rosenkrans) agreed to undertake the cause for Mrs. Van Dien, and received a retaining fee in the sum of $5, and, thereafter failing in an attempt to obtain or enforce a voluntary agreement for alimony and support, he`(Rosenkrans) requested Mrs. Van Dien to call at his office; that she did so on or about the 10th day of February, 1914, and was informed by him of the impossibility of obtaining an agreement for support and alimony, that it would be necessary to institute proceedings for that purpose, and that if she (Mrs. Van Dien) would give to him (Rosenkrans) the sum of $25, he would start the proceedings that afternoon, and push the matter with all possible speed, and that the cause would come up in Paterson in about two weeks' time, that he would conduct the proceedings as cheaply as possible, do all he could in her behalf, and urged upon her that he would do all that was right in the premises; and Mrs. Van Dien, not then being in possession of the sum of $25 was required by Rosenkrans as preliminary to the institution of proceedings, was obliged to borrow and become indebted for that amount, and did so, and on the 17th day of February, 1914, paid Rosenkrans the sum, and obtained therefor a receipt signed by him acknowledging the payment thereof for his services in procuring an order for alimony and support for her child, under the final decree in the action for divorce of Stella Van Dien against Arthur G. Van Dien, already concluded; that Rosenkrans, having received the $25, thereafter neglected and failed to institute any proceedings in behalf of Mrs. Van Dien against her former husband for alimony and support, filed no papers or proceedings in the Court of Chancery, and wholly neglected and failed to prosecute the cause which she had placed in his hands, and for which she had paid him the fee requested, and thereafter neglected and refused to inform her accurately and truthfully concerning the status of the matter, and on several occasions made appointments with her, but postponed and failed to keep the same, or to advise her of the exact state of the proceedings; that in March, 1914, Rosenkrans wrote Mrs. Van Dien that he would be ready very shortly, but that matters of more immediate and pressing importance had delayed her cause; that subsequently Charles W. Vreeland, making inquiry of Rosenkrans, at the solicitation of Mrs. Van Dien, received a post card written and signed by Rosenkrans, dated the 10th day of April, 1914, stating that the taking of proofs in the Van Dien matter would be postponed until Saturday, the 18th, and on the 17th Rosenkrans again wrote Vreeland stating that as soon as he had the testimony in another matter he would fix a day to take proofs in the Van Dien case; that he (Rosenkrans) subsequently stated to Forrest Mackey, who visited him on behalf of Mrs. Van Dien, that the hearing in her cause would be held on Saturday, July 18, 1914, but no hearing was, in fact, held at any time, nor was any petition or other proceeding filed by Rosenkrans in the cause of Mrs. Van Dien, and that Rosenkrans was not, either at the time of the writing of the post cards to Vreeland, or the statements to Mackey, in a position to take proofs or otherwise forward the cause as indicated by the post cards, or the statements to Mackey, and that Rosenkrans, although repeatedly urged by Mrs. Van Dien to proceed with her case, or return to her the money which she paid to him as her solicitor in that behalf, neither instituted nor forwarded her cause, and had not returned to her the money so paid.

Nelson B. Gaskill, Esq., was assigned to prosecute the order to show cause, and the matter came on for hearing before me in his presence, and in the presence of the respondent himself, and of Clifford L. Newman, Esq., his counsel. Mrs. Van Dien, Forrest Mackey, John M. Weaver, Charles W. Vreeland, and the respondent, Rosenkrans, were examined as witnesses. There was no dispute—at least no material dispute—concerning the essential facts recited in the order to show cause and above set forth.

Mr. Rosenkrans, the solicitor, testifying in his own behalf, said that he was admitted to the bar of this state in June, 1907, and had practiced since that date; that Mrs. Van Dien's object in calling upon him was to learn whether or not there was an agreement in writing signed by her former husband in which he bound himself to pay her $3 a week toward the support of their child (no provision for maintenance having been made in the decree which she had obtained), and to learn whether, notwithstanding there was a divorce, she might institute proceedings of some sort by which she could oblige her husband to continue to make payments towards her child's support, her husband having paid $3 a week with more or less irregularity, and being then in arrears; that he told her it was not too late to proceed in a supplemental way in her divorce case; that, if she would send him $25, he would undertake the matter for her, she paying him $5 then for his advice and to cover his inquiries as to whether a written agreement was in existence.

Mrs. Van Dien paid a second visit to Rosenkrans, and took him her decree nisi and final decree. Rosenkrans said that at this interview the affidavit was drawn and signed by Mrs. Van Dien. This was new matter—came as a surprise; the affidavit was called for by me and produced by Rosenkrans. It was sworn to as well as subscribed. It was offered in evidence, and will be adverted to later. The interview between Mrs. Van Dien and Rosenkrans at which the affidavit was made occurred on February 10, 1914. Asked why, after February 10th, a petition was not filed or some proceeding taken, Rosenkrans said that he had intended to get it all ready for the late afternoon of that day, after the close of the register's office, where he was making a search; that he intended getting an order or reference to some master in Paterson to take testimony on Mrs. Van Dien's application on the supplemental petition; that he expected to move before me for an order of reference ex parte and as of course, instead of giving notice to the defendant. Such an order he could not have obtained.

It is strange that Rosenkrans should have thought that a defendant against whom a final decree had passed without an award of alimony or maintenance in it could afterwards be visited with an order or decree for alimony without an opportunity to be heard.

On February 17th $25, which Mrs. Van Dien was obliged to borrow to the knowledge of Rosenkrans, and which he says was a final payment of what he asked, was paid to him, and yet up to the date of the order to show cause, September 16, 1914, which was seven months afterwards, he had instituted no proceeding on his client's behalf.

On April 3, 1914, Rosenkrans visited Mrs. Van Dien's home at Upper Macopin, N.J., being in that neighborhood to obtain witnesses in another cause, and, allusion being made to her matter, he said that he had not yet got ready to take care of it, and that he had been very busy from the time he got the money until a certain homicide case in which he was counsel was disposed of, and had been very busy since, and said that he would take care of her case, and might be able and ready to start by Saturday, April 17th, and had it in mind to go down to Trenton with a verified petition and get an order of reference to some master in chancery in Paterson who would hear the matter. He appears not to have known that he could have applied to any vice chancellor for an appropriate order to show cause upon the delinquent husband.

Vreeland and Mackey were interested in behalf of Mrs. Van Dien, and it was with them, and not with her directly, that Rosenkrans corresponded and talked about her matter. On May 29, 1914, Rosenkrans wrote Mackey as follows:

'In suggesting the 30th instant, in the Van Dien matter, I hit upon Decoration Day, which neither Mr. Vreeland nor I then thought of as a holiday. We can take care of the matter almost any day next week; but on account of the sittings of the circuit court and the uncertainty as to the list of causes, I think that we had better fix upon next Saturday, when every one concerned will be free. If that date is satisfactory to your people, it will be satisfactory to me.'

And on April 10th he wrote Vreeland as follows:

'We will postpone taking of proofs in the Van Dien matter till Saturday, the 18th. Will explain occasion for postponement when I see you.'

And on April 17th he again wrote Vreeland as follows:

'As soon as I have testimony in the Sisco case, I will fix a day to take proof in the Van Dien case. One trip will cover both cases, and require no other.'

Thus two or three dates were fixed for the taking of testimony and on the day before word would be sent by Rosenkrans that the matter would go off, and that another day would be set.

At last, in despair, Mrs. Van Dien, on July 21, 1914, wrote Rosenkrans as follows:

'As we see you are not going to attend to my buness As you promised Mr. Mackey you would sure, have the hearing last Saturday, July 18 We have gave you long enought time, It has bin since Jan. 6 Now I want my money I will give you till Saturday July 25, 1914, to return my money or I will send some one that will collect it for me.'

Rosenkrans did not answer this letter, but shortly thereafter saw Vreeland and told him that he had received it, and said that, as Mrs. Van Dien was dissatisfied, he would ask him (Vreeland) to go to his (Rosenkrans') office and get a check from him to return her the money, and that he (Vreeland) asked him (Rosenkrans) to wait; that he would see her, and did not want to receive it for her. On the day following the service of the order to show cause upon Rosenkrans, Vreeland called at his office, and was told by him that he (Vreeland) had advised him (Rosenkrans) badly, and he gave him a check for $25 to take to Mrs. Van Dien, which he (Vreeland) tendered to her, and she declined to receive it. Mrs. Van Dien says she told Vreeland that she would not take the money until she saw her lawyer, a Mr. McDavitt of New York whom she had consulted; he (McDavitt) having told her not to accept it. On the hearing Rosenkrans offered to repay the $25 to Mrs. Van Dien, and I advised her to accept it, which, I understand, she afterwards did.

No petition for maintenance was ever drawn by Rosenkrans, and no proceeding of any kind was instituted by him on Mrs. Van Dien's behalf for the support of her child. The matter is at an end between them, and their relation of solicitor and client has terminated. As already stated, Rosenkrans testified that at the interview with Mrs. Van Dien on February 10, 1914, he had her make an affidavit, which was called for and offered in evidence. It reads as follows:

'State of New Jersey, County of Passaic—ss.:

'Stella M. Van Dien, being duly sworn to law, on her oath says that she is the petitioner name in the foregoing petition, and that the matters and things therein set forth are true, to the best of her knowledge and belief.

Stella M. Van Dien.

'Sworn to and subscribed before me this tenth day of February, A. D. 1914.

'John H. Collier,

'Master in Chancery of New Jersey.'

Here we have a case of a solicitor of this court counseling and procuring a client to make an affidavit 'that she is the petitioner named in the foregoing petition,' when, in fact, there was no petition in existence, and also 'that the matters and things therein set forth are true, to the best of her knowledge and belief.' It is hard to characterize this conduct of Rosenkrans, or, rather, it is hard to refrain from reprobating it as it deserves to be. It is more than strange that Rosenkrans should procure Mrs. Van Dien to subscribe and swear to an affidavit which was untrue in point of fact. He says he intended to draw a petition and annex the affidavit to it. This would have aggravated the matter. If he had done so, and had filed the petition he would have uttered and imposed upon the court a false affidavit. His conduct in this regard amounts to malpractice. Without raising any question as to whether either Rosenkrans or Mrs. Van Dien were guilty of an infraction of the criminal law with reference to this affidavit, it is enough for the purpose of this inquiry to say that Rosenkrans counseled and procured his client to subscribe and swear to an affidavit false in fact—a thing intolerable.

The Supreme Court in Re McDermit, 63 N. J. Law, 476, 43 Atl. 685, reprobates the breach of that highest trust and confidence which obtains between counsel and client, under which a duty to observe the strictest integrity in his dealings with a client is enjoined, and disbarred a lawyer who had been unfaithful to the instructions of his clients, obtaining from them money for which he failed and neglected to render any adequate service, and retained for his own use money which he had received from them for another purpose.

[4] Measured by the standard here set up, Rosenkrans, it will be seen at a glance, has in a great degree abused the trust and confidence of his client, Mrs. Van Dien, and has not observed the strictest integrity in his dealings with her or justly regarded her interests. Nor has he rendered any adequate service to his client for the money which she paid him in the expectation of receiving such service. In fact, he rendered her no service at all.

The Supreme Court, in Re Simpson, 82 Atl. 507, disbarred an attorney and counselor who received and retained for himself the sum of $15 to commence divorce proceedings (he having actually prepared the petition and had his client swear to it), and subsequently obtained for his services and expenses in the proceedings various sums, during a period of eight months, aggregating $50, making $65 in all. The case was not pending (never having been commenced), but counsel, nevertheless, wrote his client in September, having been retained in March, six months before, that the case would be proceeded with; the court having reopened. Late in October he wrote that he would be in Trenton then soon, and would advise when the case would be heard. As stated, although the petition was actually prepared and sworn to, it was never filed. The respondent to the rule was disbarred.

The Supreme Court, in Re Bedle, 87 Atl. 100, disbarred an attorney who collected $150 for his client, and converted it to his own use, and also obtained $160 for fees and costs to bring a divorce suit and prosecute it to a decree, but for more than six years did nothing but file a petition, although afforded every opportunity and often pressed to proceed. The delay in the Bedle Case was six years, but the delay in the Simpson Case was only eight months. The delay in the matter at bar was seven months. And the amounts varied, being $160 in the Bedle Case, $65 in the Simpson Case, and only $25 in the case under consideration. But there is no rule as to the amount of money that counsel obtains to prosecute a suit, nor as to the length of time that must elapse without such prosecution before proceedings can be taken to discipline the solicitor for his faithlessness in that regard. Each case depends upon its own facts and circumstances.

[1] Mere delay in prosecuting a client's cause, unless, perhaps, it is so long continued as to be evidence of fraudulent conduct, does not afford the basis for disciplining a solicitor. Mere delay, without more, if brought to the attention of the court, would, of course, result in a reprimand and an admonition to the solicitor to proceed; but, when a solicitor receives a fee, especially when it is all he asks, upon a promise to speedily prosecute a client's cause, and then does nothing whatever to that end—does not even start—but, on the contrary, when asked by his client for information as to the status of the cause, he falsely informs her that it is pending, and is being prosecuted with all convenient speed, in whatever words the idea is conveyed, he is guilty of a fraud upon his client.

The Supreme Court, in Re Cahill, 67 N. J. Law, 527, 50 Atl. 119, laid down three rules which justify the disbarment of an attorney, the last one of which is 'such intentional fraud upon the court or a client as shows evidence of moral turpitude,' remarking that 'for less offenses such temporary suspension as the court may deem proper punishment will be imposed.'

The offense of respondent to this rule is of a dual character: (1) Obtaining money from a client upon the promise of prompt professional service without rendering any service; and (2) counseling and procuring her to make an affidavit false in fact in the sense that the alleged facts did not exist, but not false in that it was contrary to existing facts, with intent to make use of the affidavit. See the remarks as to the sacredness and solemnity of an oath in my opinion in the matter of Breidt and Lubetkin, filed simultaneously with this. In the Cahill Case it was not held that disbarment must follow either one of the three offenses which would justify it; only that such punishment might be inflicted.

[3, 5] Nor does Rosenkrans' offense fall within that in the Simpson Case, where the respondent from time to time obtained money from his client under the false pretense that he was prosecuting for her a suit which he had never commenced. In the matter at bar the respondent certainly made false representations to his client as to what he was doing, but did not obtain money upon the strength of those particular promises. He had obtained his fee for work to be done, and then failed to do the work he promised to do. To violate a promissory obligation and follow that up with the false assertion, oft repeated, that the promise was being performed, is, in a solicitor, malpractice. In Webster's New Int. Dic. 'malpractice' is defined to be: any professional misconduct or any unreasonable lack of skill or fidelity in the performance of professional or fiduciary duties; wrongdoing. A question of professional malpractice or negligence is determined by what might be reasonably required under the circumstances of the case.'

With reference to physicians, 'malpractice,' in Bouv. Law Dic. (Rawles Rev.) vol. 2, p. 669, is defined as being either willful, negligent, or ignorant. These degrees are equally attributable to the conduct of attorneys and solicitors. While disciplinary proceedings may not be taken against a solicitor for ignorant malpractice, for negligent malpractice he certainly can be censured by the court, and in gross cases disciplined; and for willful malpractice he can be disciplined even to the extent of disbarment.

This case, like that of Breidt and Lubetkin, was considered at a conference of all the judges of the Court of Chancery, and in their unanimous opinion, suspension from practicing as a solicitor for the term of two years is the proper punishment to be meted out to Rosenkrans for his willful malpractice in the Van Dien matter, and such will be the order. If the order should be violated, the respondent will be permanently debarred from practicing in the Court of Chancery.

N.J.Ch. 1915

IN RE ROSENKRANS

END OF DOCUMENT

FISHER v. LOWE
333 N.W.2d 67 (Mich.App. 1983)

122 Mich.App. 418

William L. FISHER V., Plaintiff-Appellant,

Karen LOWE, Larry Moffet and State

Farm Mutual Automobile Insurance

Company, Defendants-Appellees.

Docket No. 60732.

Court of Appeals of Michigan.

Submitted Nov. 3, 1982.

Decided Jan. 10, 1983.

Released for Publications May 6, 1983.

A wayward Chevy struck a tree
Whose owner sued defendants three.
He sued car's owner, driver too,
And insurer for what was due
For his oak tree that now may bear
A lasting need for tender care.
The Oakland County Circuit Court,
John N. O'Brien, J., set forth
The judgment that defendants sought
And quickly an appeal was brought.
Court of Appeals, J.H. Gillis, J.,
Gave thought and then had this to say:
1) There is no liability
   Since No-Fault grants immunity;
2) No jurisdiction can be found
   Where process service is unsound;
   And thus the judgment, as it's termed,
   Is due to be, and is,

     Affirmed.

1. Automobiles ☞251.13

Defendant's Chevy struck a tree—
There was no liability;
The No-Fault Act comes into play
As owner and the driver say;
Barred by the Act's immunity,

No suit in tort will aid the tree;
Although the oak's in disarray,
No court can make defendants pay.
M.C.L.A. § 500.3135.

2. Process ⊶4
No jurisdiction could be found
Where process service was unsound;
In personam jurisdiction
Was not even legal fiction
Where plaintiff failed to well comply
With rules of court that did apply.
GCR 1963, 105.4.

William L. Fisher, Troy, in pro. per.

Romain, Donofrio & Kuck, P.C. by Ernst W. Kuck, Southfield, for defendants-appellees.

Before BRONSON, P.J., and V.J. BRENNAN and J.H. GILLIS, JJ.

J.H. GILLIS, Judge.

[1,2] We thought that we would never see
A suit to compensate a tree.

A suit whose claim in tort is prest
Upon a mangled tree's behest;

A tree whose battered trunk was prest
Against a Chevy's crumpled crest;

A tree that faces each new day
With bark and limb in disarray;

A tree that may forever bear
A lasting need for tender care.

Flora lovers though we three,
We must uphold the court's decree.

Affirmed.[1]

---

[1]Plaintiff commenced this action in tort against defendants Lowe and Moffet for damage to his "beautiful oak tree" caused when defendant Lowe struck it while operating defendant Moffet's automobile. The trial court granted summary judgment in favor of defendants pursuant to GCR 1963, 117.2(1). In addition, the trial court denied plaintiff's request to enter a default judgment against the insurer of the automobile, defendant State Farm Mutual Automobile Insurance Company. Plaintiff appeals as of right.

The trial court did not err in granting summary judgment in favor of defendants Lowe and Moffet. Defendants were immune from tort liability for damage to the tree pursuant to § 3135 of the no-fault insurance act. M.C.L. § 500.3135; M.S.A. § 24.13135.

The trial court did not err in refusing to enter a default judgment against State Farm. Since it is undisputed that plaintiff did not serve process upon State Farm in accordance with the court rules, the court did not obtain personal jurisdiction over the insurer. GCR 1963, 105.4.

Fla. App. 311 So.2d 381
Johnny Diamond HELTON, Appellant,

v.

STATE of Florida, Appellee.

No. W–217.

District Court of Appeal of Florida,
First District.

April 24, 1975.

Defendant was convicted in the Circuit Court, Alachua County, Wayne Carlisle, J., of escape, and he appealed. The District Court of Appeal, Boyer, Acting C. J., held that intent to avoid lawful confinement was an element of the crime of escape; and that where defendant remained outside of lawful custody for approximately one month, two weeks after specifically promising to return, defendant had requisite intent to escape, notwithstanding contention that his original departure from custody was rendered unintentional by reason of intoxication.

Affirmed.

1. Escape ⊶1

Elements of crime of escape are physical act of leaving or not being in custody and intent to avoid lawful confinement. West's F.S.A. § 944.40.

2. Escape ⊶10

Intent to escape may be proven by circumstantial evidence. West's F.S.A. § 944.40.

3. Escape ⊶1

In escape prosecution, State is not required to show that intent to escape existed prior to or even contemporaneously with the physical act of escape. West's F.S.A. § 944.40.

4. Escape ⊶1

Where defendant remained outside of lawful custody for approximately one month, two weeks after specifically promising to return, defendant demonstrated requisite intent to escape, notwithstanding contention that original departure from custody was unintentional by reason of intoxication. West's F.S.A. § 944.40.

Alan R. Parlapiano, Asst. Public Defender, for appellant.

Robert L. Shevin, Atty. Gen., and A. S. Johnston, Asst. Atty. Gen., for appellee.

BOYER, Acting Chief Judge.

We here consider an issue of first impression in this State: What degree of intent, if any, is the State required to prove in order to convict an accused of the crime of escape?

Appellant, defendant below, charged with escape as defined by F.S. 944.40, was convicted, and sentenced to serve three years in the State Penitentiary. It seems that on the night of December 24, 1973, appellant was lawfully incarcerated in Cell Block "E" of the Alachua County Adult Detention Center. The next morning, appellant and seven other inmates left Cell Block "E" without permission and did not immediately return. Approximately two weeks later, appellant made several calls to the Alachua County Sheriff's office from Louisville, Kentucky, and agreed that he would come back to Gainesville and turn himself in, in exchange for the Sheriff's office promise not to notify the authorities in Louisville for two days. Rather than turning himself in within two days, appellant surrendered himself to the authorities two weeks after his conversations with the Sheriff's office, or approximately one month after leaving the Detention Center.

At trial, the trial judge refused to allow the defense to introduce evidence of intoxication, on the ground that intent is not an element of the crime charged. The proffered evidence showed that the jailer at the Detention Center gave vodka to the inmates on the night of the escape. The effect of the inebriating beverage on the appellant and his fellow inmates was colorfully portrayed by defense counsel in closing argument to the jury as follows:

"Twas the night before Christmas, when all through the jail

Not an inmate was stirring, they couldn't make bail.

The stockings were hung by the cell door with care

In hopes that St. Nicholas would soon be there:

The inmates were huddled alone in their beds

While visions of freedom danced in their heads

And guards in their uniforms and John in his rack

Had just settled down for a long winter's nap,

When up on the roof there arose such a clatter,

John sprang up from his bed to see what was the matter.

Away to the window he flew like a flash,

Tore open the cell door and threw up the sash.

When what to his wondering eyes should appear

But a miniature sleigh and eight tiny reindeer,

With a little old driver, so lively and quick

He knew in a moment it must be St. Nick.

More rapid than eagles his courses they came,

And he whistled and shouted, and called them by name:

Now, Macquire, now Bass, now Fillingame, Newman,

On, Ingram, on Suggs, on Crosby, and Helton.

To the top of the porch, to the top of the wall

Now dash away, dash away, dash away all."

We have been cited to no definitive Florida case as to whether intent is a necessary element to the crime of escape, and independent research has failed to reveal any. We must, therefore, turn to other jurisdictions for purposes of analysis. It should first be noted that the jurisdictions are split on this issue. Some have ruled that intent is not an inherent element of the crime of escape: State v. Kiggins, 86 S.D. 612, 200 N.W.2d 243 (1972). People v. Spalding, 17 Mich.App. 73, 169 N.W.2d 163 (1969); State v. Leckenby, 260 Iowa 973, 151 N.W.2d 567 (1967); Wiggins v. State, 194 Ind. 118, 141 N.E. 56 (1923); Alex v. State, 484 P.2d 677 (Alaska 1971); State v. Marks, 92 Idaho 368, 442 P.2d 778 (1968). Other courts have held contra: Riley v. State, 16 Conn. 47 (1843); Gallegos v. People, 159 Colo. 379, 411 P.2d 956 (1966); State v. Morton, 293 A.2d 775 (Me.1972); State v. Hendrick, 164 N.W.2d 57 (N.D.1969); Cassady v. State, 247 Ark. 690, 447 S.W.2d 144 (1969); United States v. Nix, 501 F.2d 516 (7th Cir. 1974). A slight numerical majority exists in favor of the proposition that intent is not an element of the crime.

[1] In considering this issue, we are not concerned with the weight of sheer numerical superiority: We look instead to justice and fairness, and on that foundation conclude that the crime of escape necessarily entails as an essential element thereof the intent to escape as well as the act of leaving, or being absent from, lawful custody. (See United States v. Nix, supra)

Assume the case of a prisoner, X, who, as a member of a road gang, falls asleep under a shady oak tree during a rest break and is left behind by a negligent guard. Upon waking up, X realizes what has happened and dutifully sets forth upon the highway in an effort to return to his place of imprisonment. In the meantime, however, the authorities have discovered X's absence and have begun searching for him. Under these circumstances if intent is not a necessary element of the crime, X could be convicted of escape. As another example, assume that while X is being returned to his place of confinement the vehicle in which he is being transported is involved in an accident and the driver is severely injured. Is X to be convicted of escape if he leaves the scene in search of help? We think not.

Our conclusion is buttressed by the line of cases which have recognized the "narrow but time-honored defense of necessity available to a prisoner whose escape has been motivated by sufficiently perilous circumstances . . ." 16 Cr.L.Rptr. 2375. In California, where intent has been held not to be an element of escape, a Court of Appeal has held that two women prisoners would be allowed to claim necessity as a defense to the crime of escape where the proffered evidence showed that the two women had been threatened by a group of lesbian inmates who told them they were to perform lesbian acts. (People v. Lovercamp, 43 Cal.App.3d 823, 118 Cal.Rptr. 110, opinion filed December 11, 1974) A Michigan Court of Appeal has also held that necessity may, under severely limited circumstances, constitute a valid defense to escape. [People v. Harmon, 53 Mich.App. 482, 220 N.W.2d 212 (1974)] These cases implicitly recognize that a prisoner should not be punished for escape where he or she does not leave confinement with the intent of eluding lawful authority.

[2,3] We therefore hold that there are two elements to the crime of escape: The physical act of leaving, or not being in, custody coupled with the intent to avoid lawful confinement. We hurriedly note that in providing intent, the State may rely on circumstantial evidence. (Simpson v. State, 1921, 81 Fla. 292, 87 So. 920; Edwards v. State, Fla.App.3rd 1968, 213 So.2d 274) Intent may be inferred from the circumstances. (Thompson v. State, Fla.App. 1st, 310 So.2d 448, opinion filed April 9, 1975) Nor is the State required to show that the intent to escape existed prior to, or even contemporaneously with, the physical act of escape. Even though a defendant may not possess the necessary mental element at the time he leaves confinement or custody, he may subsequently do so and thereby render himself criminally liable. [Chandler v. United States, 378 F.2d 906 (9th Cir. 1967); Parent v. State, 31 Wis. 2d 106, 141 N.W.2d 878 (1966)] As the Court noted in the Chandler case, "If defendants left the camp inadvertently while wandering in an intoxicated condition, they may not have had the intent to escape at the moment they left the confines of the prison camp. However, if they thereafter decided to seize the opportunity to take off for more hospitable climes, they would be guilty of escape or attempted escape, notwithstanding tardy formulation of the idea."

[4] We do not here find it necessary to decide whether intoxication may be relied upon to prove lack of intent; nor do we decide whether, if intoxication may be relied upon, such intoxication must have been involuntary as distinguished from voluntary. It is clear that in either event appellant's conviction must stand. Whether he did or did not intend to escape at the time he followed the jingle bells of Christmas, the facts remain that he remained outside of lawful custody for approximately one month, two weeks after specifically promising to return. Intent therefore ceased to be a viable issue. (Chandler v. United States, supra)

We have considered the other points raised by appellant on appeal and find them to be without merit.

Affirmed.

McCORD and MILLS, JJ., concur.

531 N.E. 2d 549

403 Mass. 501

COMMONWEALTH

v.

MARITIME UNDERWATER SURVEYS, INC.

Supreme Judicial Court of Massachusetts,
Barnstable.

Argued Sept. 15, 1988.

Decided Dec. 12, 1988.

Salvager of abandoned shipwreck within coastal waters of Massachusetts sought and obtained preliminary injunction, restraining Massachusetts from granting or extending any additional permits within one mile of salvager's permit area. Thereafter parties filed cross motions for summary judgment regarding title to vessel and applicability of statute requiring permit. The Superior Court, James J. Nixon, J., granted salvager's motion and Commonwealth appealed. The Supreme Judicial Court, Lynch, J., transferred case from Appeals Court and held that salvager was not required to comply with Massachusett's statutory scheme requiring permit for exploration, recovery, or salvage of underwater archeological resources.

Affirmed.

1. Abandoned and Lost Property ☞10
Law of finds grants title to first party to discover and reduce to possession things found in sea which have never been owned or property which is long lost or abandoned.

2. Abandoned and Lost Property ☞10
Under American Rule, title to recovered property or treasure rests in finder absent legislative exercise of sovereign prerogative.

3. Admiralty ☞1.20(1)
Shipping ☞213
Salvager of abandoned shipwreck within coastal waters of Massachusetts was not required to comply with Massachusett's statutory scheme requiring permit for exploration, recovery or salvage of underwater archeological resources; federal maritime law of finds applied, and title to wreck consequently vested in salvager. M.G.L.A. c. 91, § 63.

Carolyn V. Wood, Asst. Atty. Gen., for Com.
Allan H. Tufankjian, Scituate (James P. McMahon, with him) for defendant.

Before HENNESSEY, C.J., and WILKINS, ABRAMS, NOLAN and LYNCH, JJ.

LYNCH, Justice.

History, legend, and the evolution of our legal and governmental systems converge in this tale of shipwreck and sunken treasure which begins in the early Eighteenth Century. In April, 1717, the notorious pirate ship "Whydah," laden with plundered cargo, crashed and capsized in a raging storm off the Cape Cod coast, disappearing beneath the sea, and evading discovery and salvage for the next two hundred sixty-five years. While all but two sailors perished in the wreck, the Whydah's legend survived, and the remains of the vessel were apparently located in 1982 after extensive research and searching.[1] Giving spectral significance to the observation of Roger Byam, the narrator of "Mutiny on the Bounty," that a ship seems "at times to have the very breath of life," the ill-fated Whydah, nearly three centuries later, has sailed into this court's jurisdiction as the subject of a dispute between contemporary treasure seekers and the would-be modern sovereign of the coastal waters—a conflict mired in competing claims of title to the shipwreck and its cargo, involving issues of Federal maritime and admiralty law, and disputed dominion over submerged lands in the marginal sea.[2]

The parties submitted a statement of agreed facts. In November, 1982, Maritime Underwater Surveys, Inc. (Maritime), discovered an unidentified, wrecked, and abandoned vessel one mile off the coast of Wellfleet under approximately fourteen feet of water and five feet of sand within the coastal waters of Massachusetts. The Commonwealth was neither actively searching for nor aware of the location of the wreck. Shortly after its discovery, Maritime filed an in rem admiralty action in the United States District Court for the District of Massachusetts, seeking title to the abandoned vessel, or the grant of a salvage award. The District Court issued a warrant for arrest in rem, and appointed Maritime substitute custodian of the vessel. The United States Marshal executed the warrant. The Commonwealth contested Maritime's claim of ownership to the vessel through the filing of a restricted appearance, asserting that, since the Commonwealth itself claimed title and no other parties had appeared to contest Maritime's claim, the Federal court therefore lacked jurisdiction under the Eleventh Amendment to the United States Constitution to adjudicate what was essentially a suit against the State. The District Court agreed, dismissed the action on jurisdictional grounds, and was subsequently upheld on appeal. *Maritime Underwater Surveys, Inc. v. Unidentified, Wrecked and Abandoned Sailing Vessel*, 717 F.2d 6 (1st Cir.1983).

The Commonwealth simultaneously instituted an action in Superior Court seeking a confirmation of its title in the vessel and cargo, and a declaration that

---

[1] Maritime Underwater Surveys, Inc., claims the wreck it discovered is the Whydah. The Commonwealth does not dispute that contention.

[2] An historical account of the infamous blackguard, Captain Samuel Bellamy, who captured the Whydah and steered the ship into a course of pillaging and plundering, is ably and dramatically told in the opening section of the Superior Court judge's memorandum of decision, reproduced in the Appendix to this opinion.

Maritime was obliged to comply with the Commonwealth's statutory scheme requiring a permit for exploration, recovery, or salvage of underwater archeological resources. G.L. c. 91, § 63 (1986 ed.). The Superior Court judge entered an order of custody, assented to by the Commonwealth, appointing Maritime temporary custodian of the wreck. Under protest, and reserving its right to contest the applicability of the statute, Maritime applied to the Board of Underwater Archaeological Resources (board) for a permit to salvage the vessel pursuant to c. 91, § 63. Maritime began excavation and salvage operations under a subsequently-issued permit to explore and salvage within a limited area, and since 1983 has successfully recovered numerous artifacts. Maritime also applied for, and was granted, a permit from the Army Corps of Engineers, allowing it to perform certain excavation procedures as long as it abided by "strict historic and archaeological standards." Pursuant to 16 U.S.C. § 470*l* (1982), the permit was issued after consultation with the Federal Advisory Council on Historic Preservation and the State Historic Preservation Officer.

Believing that wreckage or cargo, known as "scatter," from the Whydah might have settled beyond the limited area delineated in its State permit, Maritime requested, but was denied, an extension of the search area. The board's regulations provide for permits to explore and salvage *areas* rather than wrecks, and limit the number of permits which can be granted to a single permittee to a total of one excavation and one reconnaissance permit. See 312 Code Mass.Regs. § 2.08(2) (1986). Third parties had applied for, and received, permits to explore and excavate adjacent areas which Maritime believed to contain scatter from the Whydah.[3] Maritime therefore sought, and in February, 1986, obtained, a preliminary injunction, restraining the Commonwealth from granting or extending any additional permits for sites within one mile of Maritime's permit area. The parties thereafter filed cross-motions for summary judgment regarding title to the vessel and the applicability of G.L. c. 91, § 63. The judge denied the Commonwealth's motion, and, in granting Maritime's motion, declared that title to the vessel is vested in Maritime and that, since G.L. c. 91, § 63, conflicts with Federal maritime law, Maritime is not obliged to comply with the statute's requirements, 1987 A.M.C. 2590. The Commonwealth appealed from this judgment, and we transferred the case here on our own motion. Since the Superior Court judge's decision rests on a statement of agreed facts and governing principles of law, we may draw our own inferences and decide the case according to our judgment as to the questions of law. *Newburyport Soc'y for the Relief of Aged Women v. Noyes*, 287 Mass. 530, 532–533, 192 N.E. 54 (1934). See *Simon v. Weymouth Agricultural & Indus. Soc'y*, 389 Mass. 146, 148–149, 449 N.E.2d 371 (1983).

The conflicting assertions of title to the Whydah rest on two complementary principles of admiralty law. Maritime claims title to the vessel under the law of finds, or, alternatively, an award for recovery of the wreck under the law of salvage. The Commonwealth claims ownership of the Whydah through the legislative assertion of title in G.L. c. 6, § 180 (1986 ed.), to all underwater archaeological resources,[4] contending that the statute evinces the Commonwealth's

---

[3]One of these, Old Blue Fishing Co., Inc., was allowed to intervene.

[4]The parties agree that the Whydah meets the statutory definition of an underwater archaeological resource.

exercise of sovereign prerogative, and that any salvage operations and award must be governed by the statutory scheme and board regulations requiring a permit.

[1,2] The law of salvage is an ancient maritime doctrine which, unlike traditional common law, was meant to encourage the rescue of imperiled or derelict marine property by providing a liberal reward to those who recover property on or in navigable waters. See 3A Norris, Benedict on Admiralty, § 1 (7th ed. 1983 & Supp.1986). "Compensation as salvage is not viewed by the admiralty courts merely as pay . . . but as a reward given for perilous services . . . and as an inducement. . . . Public policy encourages the hardy and adventurous mariner to engage in these laborious and sometimes dangerous enterprises." *The Blackwall,* 10 Wall. 1, 14, 19 L.Ed. 870 (1869). This doctrine assumes that the property is owned and has not been abandoned. The law of finds, on the other hand, grants title to the first party to discover and reduce to possession things found in the sea which have never been owned or property which is long-lost or abandoned. Benedict on Admiralty, *supra* at § 158. The application of admiralty law to a claim regarding derelict property, "[u]nder usual circumstances . . . would lead to an award *either* of outright ownership of the recovered goods (applying the law of finds) *or* of entitlement to an appropriate salvage award" (emphasis added). *Cobb Coin Co., Inc. v. Unidentified, Wrecked & Abandoned Sailing Vessel,* 525 F.Supp. 186, 198 (S.D.Fla.1981). See *Treasure Salvors, Inc. v. Unidentified, Wrecked & Abandoned Sailing Vessel,* 640 F.2d 560, 567 (5th Cir.1981) (*Treasure Salvors III*); *Rickard v. Pringle,* 293 F.Supp. 981, 984 (E.D.N.Y.1968) (since ship's propeller had lain abandoned on ocean floor for sixty years, ownership vested by operation of law in first finder lawfully reducing it to possession). American courts have applied the law of finds, rather than the law of salvage, in cases involving ancient shipwrecks where no owner is likely to come forward. See, e.g., *Treasure Salvors, Inc. v. Unidentified, Wrecked & Abandoned Sailing Vessel,* 569 F.2d 330, 336–337 (5th Cir.1978) (*Treasure Salvors I*); *Wiggins v. 1100 Tons, More or Less, of Italian Marble,* 186 F.Supp. 452, 456 (E.D. Va.1960). Cf. *Hener v. United States,* 525 F.Supp. 350, 355, 358 (S.D.N.Y.1981) (despite preference for law of salvage, court may properly apply law of finds where all parties assume property has been abandoned and no prior owner is likely to appear). The English common law approach to the law of finds is that title to abandoned property found on the seas is the prerogative of the crown. *Treasure Salvors I, supra* at 340–341. The so-called American Rule is that title to recovered property or treasure rests in the finder absent a legislative exercise of the sovereign prerogative. *Id.* at 341–343.

We conclude that, since the Whydah has rested undisturbed and undiscovered beneath the sea for nearly three centuries, it is proper to consider the wreck abandoned and accordingly to apply the law of finds. *Martha's Vineyard Scuba Headquarters, Inc. v. Unidentified, Wrecked and Abandoned Steam Vessel,* 833 F.2d 1059, 1065 (1st Cir.1987) ("given the passage of so many decades after the sinking," District Court did not err in applying law of finds). Title to the wreck therefore vests in Maritime unless the sovereign prerogative has been exercised. The Commonwealth claims that G.L. c. 6, § 180, is its assertion of sovereign prerogative, and that the Whydah was therefore owned by the Commonwealth and *not* abandoned at the time of Maritime's discovery of the wreck. Maritime contends that the United States, and not the Commonwealth, is sovereign of the submerged lands along the coast, and that c. 6, § 180, is therefore ineffective as a legislative assertion of title or sovereign prerogative. A threshold question, therefore, and one correctly decided by the Superior Court judge, concerns whether the Federal government or the Commonwealth is the sovereign.

The Commonwealth's claim of sovereignty rests in part on the State's Marine Boundaries Act, G.L. c. 1, § 3 (1986 ed.), which declares that the territorial limits of the Commonwealth "shall extend seaward to the outer limits of the territorial sea of the United States," and on c. 1, § 2, which declares that "the sovereignty and jurisdiction of the Commonwealth shall extend to all places within its boundaries." The question whether the United States government has paramount rights in the submerged lands beneath navigable waters within the boundaries of the coastal States was considered by the United States Supreme Court in a controversial 1947 case in which the Court held that notwithstanding the State's ability to exercise its police power over the three-mile marginal belt within its boundaries, the Federal government had "paramount rights in and power over this area." *United States v. California,* 332 U.S. 19, 36, 67 S.Ct. 1658, 1667, 91 L.Ed. 1889 (1947). This decision arose out of an attempt by the Federal government to enjoin California from executing leases for the drilling for petroleum and mining of other natural resources in the offshore seabed. The conclusion that States had no interest in the oil or mineral deposits along the coast resulted in passage of the Submerged Lands Act of 1953, 43 U.S.C. §§ 1311 et seq. (1982) (Act), which vested in the States title to the lands and natural resources under the navigable waters extending three miles from their respective coastlines. *United States v. Alaska,* 422 U.S. 184, 187, 95 S.Ct. 2240, 2245, 45 L.Ed. 2d 109 (1975).

The Commonwealth contends that its Marine Boundaries Act, G.L. c. 1, § 3, is consistent with the Federal Submerged Lands Act, and that it accordingly has complete dominion and sovereignty over the land in which the Whydah now lies. Maritime argued, and the Superior Court judge agreed, that the Submerged Lands Act was intended only to transfer title to and concomitant development rights in natural resources, without disturbing the sovereignty of the Federal government over the marginal sea. We agree. "The Act left congressional power over commerce and the dominant navigational servitude of the United States precisely where it found them." *United States v. Rands,* 389 U.S. 121, 127, 88 S.Ct. 265, 269, 19 L.Ed.2d 329 (1967). See *Cobb Coin Co., Inc. v. Unidentified, Wrecked & Abandoned Sailing Vessel,* 525 F.Supp. 186, 215–216 (S.D.Fla. 1981) (the Act "does not empower the State, through legislation which purports to derogate both federal jurisdiction and the application of admiralty principles, to lay claim to abandoned wreck sites"). The Act itself explicitly cautions that nothing therein should "be construed as the release or relinquishment of any rights of the United States arising under the constitutional authority of Congress to regulate or improve navigation," 43 U.S.C. § 1311(d) (1982), and expressly retains for the United States "all its navigational servitude and rights in and powers of regulation and control of said lands and navigable waters for the constitutional purposes of commerce, navigation, national defense, and international affairs." *Id.* at § 1314(a). These rights and powers "shall be paramount to, but shall not be deemed to include, proprietary rights of ownership . . . use and development of the lands and natural resources." *Id.* In 1975, the Supreme Court expressly declined to overrule the *California* decision which had led to passage of the Act, stating that its "constitutional underpinnings" and rule "that paramount rights to the offshore seabed inhere in the Federal Government" as an incident of Federal sovereignty, were "embraced rather than repudiated by Congress" through passage of the Act. *United States v. Maine,* 420 U.S. 515, 524, 95 S.Ct. 1155, 1160, 43 L.Ed.2d 363 (1975).

That the Federal government granted ownership rights only, while retaining paramount sovereignty, and that the Act did not contemplate a transfer of rights in underwater archeological treasures or artifacts, is evidenced in the Abandoned Shipwreck Act of 1987 (enacted in April, 1988), in which title to any abandoned shipwreck embedded in the submerged lands of any State is asserted by the United States, 43 U.S.C. § 2105(a) [Pub.L. No. 100–298, 102 Stat. § 432 (1988)], and "transferred to the State in or on whose submerged lands the shipwreck is located." *Id.* at § 2105(c). The Abandoned Shipwreck Act also expressly provides that neither the law of salvage nor the law of finds shall apply to any shipwreck to which its provisions apply. *Id.* at § 2106(a). While the Abandoned Shipwreck Act by its terms does not affect any legal proceeding brought prior to the law's enactment, § 2106(c), its provisions are consistent with the view that title to or rights in ancient wrecks were *not* conveyed in the Submerged Lands Act and that the constitutional power to take control of and assert title to abandoned wrecks remained in the Federal government after passage of the Act.

[3] Since we have concluded that the Commonwealth is *not* the sovereign, and that its assertion of sovereign prerogative is therefore ineffective, and since we decide that the Federal maritime law of finds applies and title to the wreck consequently vests in Maritime, Maritime is not subject to the Commonwealth's statutory scheme (G.L. c. 91, § 63), in its salvaging of the wreck. We need not decide whether the Commonwealth's statutory scheme requiring licensing of salvage projects impermissibly intrudes upon or violates Federal admiralty law, because the salvage statute, which presupposes the Commonwealth's ownership of the resources to be salvaged, is wholly inapplicable in this case. Rather, under Federal admiralty law regarding abandoned maritime property, the first successful finder or salvor has "possession of the distressed property with which no one can interfere." *Rickard v. Pringle,* 293 F.Supp. 981, 985 (E.D.N.Y.1968). See *Treasure Salvors III, supra* at 567. The judge was therefore correct in declaring that Maritime is not obliged to comply with G.L. c. 91, § 63, and that it has the right to exclude other salvors from recovering the remains of the Whydah or its treasure. Thus, the claim of the Commonwealth founders on the shoals of Federal sovereignty as surely as the Whydah foundered on the shoals off Wellfleet, ironically suffering the same fate as the 1717 proclamation of the Colony's Royal Governor Samuel Shute, which claimed the wreck for the Crown.

Judgment affirmed.

APPENDIX.

"Historical Background

"In April, 1717, the great pirate ship "Whydah", loaded with gold, indigo and other purloined treasure, crashed hard against a sand bar amid a temptest off the coast of Cape Cod. The ship capsized almost at once, and within minutes all of its crewmembers were struggling in the raging sea. One hundred and forty four men perished (only two survived), including the captain of the craft, the infamous Samuel Bellamy, 'as notorious a pirate as ever sailed the Spanish main.' Edward R. Snow, *Great Storms and Famous Shipwrecks of the New England Coast,* 51 (1946). As the great ship went down, its great plundered cargo also was swallowed up by the violent sea.

"The story of Bellamy and his ill-fated capture of the "Whydah" has been often told. In 1716, Bellamy ventured to the West Indies in hopes of salvaging a sunken vessel. Frustrated by the complete failure of this 'legitimate' endeavor, Bellamy and another disappointed salvor, Paulsgrave Williams, decided to become pirates or, in the lexicon of the trade, to 'go on the account.' George F. Dow, *Pirates of the New England Coast,* 116 (1923). They joined with two other ambitious marauders, Benjamin Horngold and Louis Lebous, and, with a crew of 140 men, set off to pillage the seas.

"In the months ahead, Bellamy captured several vessels off the Virgin Islands and St. Croix. One such ship, the "Sultana", was made into a galley, the command of which was given to Paulsgrave Williams. From another ship, the "St. Michael", the pirates forced four men to join their crew. Among them was Thomas Davis, who turned out to be 'the only white man to escape drowning when Bellamy was afterwards wrecked on Cape Cod.' Dow, *Pirates of the New England Coast* at 116.

"Bellamy first spotted the "Whydah" sailing through the Windward Passage between 'Porto Rico' and Cuba in late February, 1717. A London galley fresh from a successful slaving voyage, the "Whydah" was loaded with a rich cargo of indigo, Jesuit's bark, elephant's teeth, gold dust, sugar and other valuables. Bellamy pursued the "Whydah" for three days before finally sailing close enough to fire a shot at the galley. To Bellamy's amazement, the single shot ended the chase, and Captain Lawrence Prince quickly lowered the ship's flag in surrender. As a reward for his lack of resistance, Captain Prince was given the "Sultana", and Bellamy, now piloting the "Whydah," led his crew toward the Capes of Virginia, plundering more ships along the way.

"About this time a great storm struck, blowing with such violence that the "Whydah" nearly capsized. At Bellamy's skillful command, the ship survived the four-day gale, but this near-disaster proved a harbinger of what awaited the crew on the hard sandbars of Cape Cod.

"When this storm finally abated, Bellamy changed course and headed toward Rhode Island. On the way he overtook a sloop commanded by Captain Beer, who was ordered on board the "Whydah" while his sloop was being plundered. Both Bellamy and Williams wanted to give Captain Beer his sloop again, but were outvoted by the rest of the crew and the sloop [was] sunk. After the vote was taken, Bellamy made the following now-famous speech to Captain Beer:

> Damn my blood. I am sorry they won't let you have your Sloop again, for I scorn to do any one a Mischief, when it is not for my advantage; damn the Sloop, we must sink her, and she might be of Use to you. Tho', damn ye, you are a sneaking Puppy, and so are all those who will submit to be governed by laws which Rich Men have made for their own

Security, for the cowardly Whelps have not the Courage otherwise to defend what they get by their knavery; but damn ye altogether: Damn them for a Pack of crafty Rascals, and you, who serve them for a Parcel of henhearted Numskuls. They villify us, the soundrels do, when there is only this difference, they rob the Poor under the Cover of Law, forsooth, and we plunder the Rich under the Protection of our own Courage. . . .

Dow, *Pirates of the New England Coast* at 121, quoting Johnson's *History of the Pirates* (1727).

"Bellamy made one more noteworthy capture before disaster struck. On April 26, 1717, he took the pink "Mary Anne" of Dublin, laden with a cargo of wine from Madeira. Seven pirates were sent upon the captured vessel, while the pink's captain, Andrew Crumpstey, and five of his hands were ordered upon the "Whydah." At this point Bellamy, now commanding a four-ship fleet, resumed his course northward, allowing the "Mary Anne" to lead the way.

"Just what stroke of fate led the fleet into the rough waters of Cape Cod is not entirely clear. It appears that the pirates on the pink imbibed heavily of the wine on board, which may have led to some sloppy navigating. By one account, largely discredited today, Captain Crumpstey was permitted to pioneer the lead ship and intentionally led the fleet into dangerous waters, unbeknownst to the intoxicated pirates on board.

"What is clear is that by the evening of April 26 the pirates had come upon another raging storm. 'The wind blew from the east, it lightened and rained hard and the vessels soon lost sight of each other.' Dow, *Pirates of the New England Coast* at 123. The "Mary Anne" was tossed against heavy breakers, then ran ashore on the south side of Cape Cod in what is now the town of Orleans. At daybreak, those aboard the pink managed to jump directly off the boat onto land. The pirates on board made great haste toward Rhode Island. News of the wreck soon reached Joseph Doane of Eastham, a justice of the peace who, with a deputy sheriff and posse of men, pursued the fleeing pirates, and captured them at the Eastham tavern.

"Meanwhile, the "Whydah" strayed into turbulent waters ten miles north of where the "Mary Anne" ran aground. An anchor was dropped, but the force of the sea was so great that 'the cable was cut and the attempt made to work off shore but she soon drove on the bar. A quarter of an hour after she struck, the mainmast went by the board and in the morning the fine new ship was a tangled mass of wreckage.' Dow, *Pirates of the New England Coast* at 125. Her entire contents, crewmen and cargo alike, spilled like pebbles into the sea. Only two men, Davis, who had been forced aboard in December, and John Julian, a Cape Cod-born Indian, managed to swim to safety.

"By the next morning, the remains of the ship washed ashore, and Davis, Julian and some twenty others salvaged the few valuables that had washed up. The next day Davis and Julian were arrested for piracy and placed with the seven pirates from the "Mary Anne" in the Barnstable jail.

"Meanwhile, Royal Governor Samuel Shute, upon learning of the wrecked vessel, issued a proclamation taking possession of everything of value from the wreck on behalf of the crown, and dispatched his 'most trusted mariner, Captain Cyprian Southack, to the scene of the disaster.' Snow, *Great Storms and Fa-*

mous Shipwrecks at 54. The colorful Captain Southack was just the man for the job, for he had produced a map of the Boston shoreline before 1700, and knew more about the treacherous Massachusetts coastline than any other mariner of his generation.

"Nonetheless, Southack's mission proved a dismal failure. By the time he arrived at the wreck site, local residents had picked the shoreline clean of valuables. And most residents defied Governor Shute's order to turn over all such goods to Captain Southack. ' . . . His Majesty's "loving subjects" refused to disgorge. "They are very wise and will not tell one nothing of what they got on the Rack" wrote the complaining captain.' Dow, *Pirates of the New England Coast* at 128.

"The local residents' displeasure with Captain Southack deepened when mangled bodies began to wash ashore from the wreck. The local coroner ordered that the bodies be buried and demanded that Captain Southack pay the costs of interment. Utterly discouraged both by his failure to find any treasure and by the uncooperativeness of the local inhabitants, Captain Southack loaded what goods he could find aboard the sloop "Swan" heading for Boston. As fate would have it, the "Swan" was plundered by pirates.

"The following October, the nine jailed pirates were brought to trial in Boston. All were condemned to death except Davis and Thomas South, who were freed. Julian later died in jail, but the remaining six were hanged before a 'large and fascinated crowd' at Charlestown Ferry on November 15, 1717. Snow, *Great Storms and Famous Shipwrecks* at 56.

"The vast riches on board the "Whydah", which, Davis testified, 'were laid together in one head,' Dow, *Pirates of the New England Coast* at 125, were never retrieved. Nor were they ever forgotten. John Newcomb, a Wellfleet oysterman, once told Henry David Thoreau that he had seen the 'iron caboose' of the Whydah 'during an extremely low run of tides.' Snow, *Great Storms and Famous Shipwrecks* at 56. Around 1863, according to one historian, the wreck was exposed again, but still eluded salvage. During the middle of the last century, Thoreau and a companion found a few coins on the bar near the wrecksite.

"But the first major breakthrough in uncovering the great treasure of the "Whydah" came in 1982, when the defendant in this case, Maritime Underwater Surveys (Maritime), reported discovery of the vessel about a mile off the beach of Wellfleet, in approximately fourteen feet of water and under approximately five feet of sand. Maritime has since undertaken excavation efforts, uncovering numerous artifacts, including a ship's bell bearing the inscription "THE *WHYDAH* *GALLEY* 1716".

"It should be noted that the luckless Captain Southack, though he failed miserably in his own efforts to secure the treasure, aided significantly in Maritime's successful search efforts by accurately mapping the site of the wreck."

535 F.2d 1219
Mary ROE, on behalf of herself and all other persons similarly situated, Appellant,

v.

Honorable Calvin L. RAMPTON, Individually and in his capacity as Governor of the State of Utah, and Honorable Vernon B. Romney, Individually and in his capacity as Attorney General of the State of Utah, Appellees.

No. 75–1555.

United States Court of Appeals,
Tenth Circuit.

Argued and Submitted March 24, 1976.

Decided June 4, 1976.

Woman who was pregnant by a man other than her husband and who wanted an abortion brought suit to enjoin the operation of state statute requiring physician to notify the husband or parents of a woman on whom an abortion is to be performed. A three-judge District Court, District of Utah, Central Division, Aldon J. Anderson, J., 394 F.Supp. 677, abstained and dismissed the action, and plaintiff appealed. The Court of Appeals held that the order of abstention and dismissal was proper, since, relative to abstention, the state statute had several ambiguities which, when considered by the state courts, might eliminate the federal constitutional question, and since, relative to dismissal, it would be inappropriate for the state court to have only half of the case with the federal court retaining the other half.

Affirmed.

1. Courts ⬥518(1)
Where three-judge district court did not resolve the merits of constitutional claim, appeal to the Court of Appeals, rather than to the Supreme Court, was proper. 28 U.S.C.A. § 1253.

2. Courts ⬥260.4
With respect to request of woman, who was pregnant by a man other than her husband, for injunctive relief against operation of state statute requiring the husband or parents of a woman to be notified by a physician that the woman is going to have an abortion, three-judge district court order of abstention and dismissal was proper, since, relative to abstention, the state statute had several am-

biguities which, when considered by the state courts, might eliminate the federal constitutional question, and since, relative to dismissal, it would be inappropriate for the state court to have only half of the case with the federal court retaining the other half. U.C.A.1953, 76–7–304(2).

David S. Dolowitz, of Parsons, Behle & Latimer, Salt Lake City, Utah, for appellant.

William T. Evans, Asst. Atty. Gen., Salt Lake City, Utah, for appellees.

Before SETH and McWILLIAMS, Circuit Judges, and MORRIS, Chief Judge.*

PER CURIAM.

A three-judge court sitting as the United States District Court for the District of Utah in an action challenging a Utah statute relative to abortions entered an order which in part stated:

" . . . This court . . . now enters its order abstaining and dismissing the above entitled action to allow the state courts to decide the questions, including the determination of a class, presented by this case."

The plaintiff has taken an appeal to this court from the above order, urging that abstention was erroneous, and that the action should not have been dismissed.

The appeal has been taken to this court on the theory that the three-judge court did not decide the merits. Thus under 28 U.S.C. § 1253, since there was no "resolution of the merits of the constitutional claim," there was no direct appeal to the Supreme Court. *MTM, Inc. v. Baxley,* 420 U.S. 799, 95 S.Ct. 1278, 43 L.Ed.2d 636; *Gonzalez v. Automatic Employees Credit Union,* 419 U.S. 90, 95 S.Ct. 289, 42 L.Ed.2d 249.

[1] There were three opinions filed by the judges, two of which agreed upon abstention, and the third dissented. There is some discussion of the merits in each of the opinions, but we must rely upon the order entered which is quoted in part above. From this order, the disposition is clear, and we hold that there was no resolution of the merits of the constitutional claim. Thus appeal to this court was proper.

[2] The appellant urges that the doctrine of abstention was not properly applied. The two majority opinions present somewhat different reasons for abstention, but the fact they did not agree on this makes no difference. We are of the opinion that abstention was not improper nor was the dismissal of the action improper.

The state abortion statute need not be quoted at length. The challenged provision relates to "notice" to be given the parents of a minor woman or to her husband. Section 76–7–304(2), Utah Code Annotated 1953, provides in part:

"To enable the physician to exercise his best medical judgment, he shall:

* * * * * *

---

*Of the United States District Court for the Eastern District of Oklahoma, sitting by designation.

"(2) Notify, if possible, the parents or guardian of the woman upon whom the abortion is to be performed, if she is a minor or the husband of the woman, if she is married."

The record shows that the plaintiff was a minor, separated from her husband, and had started divorce proceedings. She was pregnant by someone other than her husband. The doctor had no objection to giving "notice," but the woman objected. She later had an abortion.

The challenge is based on *Roe v. Wade,* 410 U.S. 113, 93 S.Ct. 705, 35 L.Ed.2d 147, on the theory that the notice provision was a "regulation" by the State on the doctor in his exercise of a medical judgment. The appellant repeatedly asserts that this is a challenge of the state statute "on its face." It is a challenge of the statute brought by a plaintiff who found herself in the fact situation above recited. It is not a theoretical, abstract proposition, but is brought by a particular, real person and the application of the statute is to be made to her. She is the only party plaintiff, and is the only person represented by the attorneys for the plaintiff.

The application of the state statute to the plaintiff in her situation raises several problems of construction which make abstention proper. The first of these is whether under the statute the "husband" means the "father," as it is apparent that the "father" is the person who has an interest in the abortion. The plaintiff objected to the "husband" being notified. Also does the statute mean that both the husband, the father, and the parents be notified? When should the notice be given? It would appear that it may be given *after* the decision to abort has been made. Thus it would then have nothing to do with an abortion but is instead a related matter of disclosure of the act. If it is such, it is not a *Roe v. Wade* situation, and no constitutional issue may be involved. The notice, without a time indication, may thus be a non-abortion problem entirely. The statute has these several ambiguities, and others, which when considered by the state courts may eliminate the federal constitutional questions. Thus abstention was not in error. *See Henrie v. Derryberry,* 358 F.Supp. 719 (N.D. Okl.), and the general authorities on ambiguities therein referred to.

Also we must hold that dismissal was proper. The Supreme Court in *Harris County Comm'rs Court v. Moore,* 420 U.S. 77, 95 S.Ct. 870, 43 L.Ed.2d 32, ordered dismissal in a comparable abstention case, and we hold it is proper here. The state court should not have half of such a case with the federal court retaining the other half. Thus the dismissal was proper.

AFFIRMED.

431 N.E.2d 118
Art CARROLL, Appellant (Plaintiff Below),

v.

William LORDY, Appellee (Defendant

Below),

v.

Edwin J. SIMCOX, Appellee
(Cross-Defendant Below).

No. 4–581A13.

Court of Appeals of Indiana,
Fourth District.

Jan. 20, 1982.

Trademark action was filed in which plaintiff sought temporary restraining order, injunctive relief and damages and defendant filed counterclaim. Defendant filed motion for summary judgment. The Superior Court, Madison County, Alva Cox, Special Judge, granted summary judgment upon complaint and entered default judgment upon counterclaim against plaintiff, and plaintiff appealed. The Court of Appeals, Conover, J., held that: (1) affiants were competent to form opinions about term "elephant ears," a deep fried pastry; (2) "elephant ears" is a descriptive term, incapable of trademark registration, and should be stricken from record of the Secretary of State; (3) trial court erred in ruling that finding of Commissioner of Patents and Trademarks was res judicata on generic nature of the term "elephant ears"; and (4) entry of default judgment on counterclaim filed against the plaintiff was improper because default was never applied for and he never received written notice of the default.

Affirmed in part, reversed in part and remanded.

1. Trade Regulation ⊶621
Where "elephant ears" was used in a descriptive manner to describe a deep fried pastry and has been used in that manner since 1965, plaintiff was not entitled to an order restraining defendant from use of that term in his business.

2. Evidence ⊶472(1), 506
A trial judge may in an appropriate case, permit opinion testimony on any ultimate fact issue.

3. Appeal and Error ⊶946
An abuse of discretion which would permit a reviewing court to overturn ruling of the trial court is an erroneous conclusion and judgment, one clearly against the logic and effect of facts and circumstances before the court or the reasonable, probable and actual deductions to be drawn therefrom.

4. Judgment ⊶185(3)
Affidavits in support of defendant's motion for summary judgment in trademark action did not contain inadmissible conclusions, where affiants were competent to form opinions about the term at issue and opinions contained in affidavits were self evident and proper subjects of lay opinion.

5. Trade Regulation ⊶578
In trademark action, consideration of advertising in newspaper articles was not error, where evidence was not offered to prove truth of the matters asserted therein but was probative of the reaction of the average consumer.

6. Appeal and Error ⊶1050.1(11)
Evidence ⊶318(2)
Cover letter from attorney attached to record of proceedings before Patent and Trademark Office did not constitute inadmissible hearsay in trademark action, where letter was merely collateral and did not carry any probative weight on matter of genericness of term at issue; furthermore, even if admission of letter was error, it would be harmless because it did nothing to prejudice rights of plaintiff.

7. Evidence ⊶318(2)
Trade Regulation ⊶587
Letter containing a description of "elephant ears," a deep fried pastry, as well as a multiple hearsay narrative concerning a phone conversation with a baker about "elephant ears" was inadmissible hearsay in trademark action raising issue of genericness of term "elephant ears"; however, even excluding this letter from affidavit, record contained adequate evidence of the genericness of the term.

8. Trade Regulation ⊶17
Once a term is found to express the name of a product rather than the source of the product then that term is incapable of trademark registration. IC 24–2–1–3 (1976 Ed.)

9. Trade Regulation ⊶15
Evidence was sufficient to support conclusion that "elephant ears" was a descriptive term for a deep fried pastry, incapable of trademark registration, and should be stricken from records of the Secretary of State.

10. Judgment ⊶668(2), 669
When determining identity of parties for res judicata purposes, courts look beyond mere nominal parties and hold estopped only those parties whose inter-

ests were directly involved in prior litigation concerning the same subject matter or claim.

11. Appeal and Error ⊶1073(1)
Judgment ⊶678(1), 707

Trial court in trademark action erred in ruling that finding of the Commissioner of Patents and Trademarks was res judicata on the generic nature of the term "elephant ears," a deep fried pastry, where defendant neither opposed registration nor was he in privity with those who did; however, error did not mandate reversal as court independently found that term "elephant ears" was generic term.

12. Judgment ⊶113, 122

Entry of default judgment on counterclaim filed against plaintiff in trademark action was improper because the default was never applied for and he never received written notice of the default. Trial Procedure Rule 55(B).

13. Judgment ⊶123(1)

Strict adherence to language of trial rule governing default judgments is required. Trial Procedure Rule 55.

14. Trade Regulation ⊶671

Since damages were awarded defendants in trademark action pursuant to defaulted counterclaim filed against plaintiff which was previously set aside, no valid judgment was left to support award of either compensatory or punitive damages.

15. Appeal and Error ⊶238(5)

Before a motion to correct errors becomes appropriate there must be a final judgment or an appealable final order entered.

16. Appeal and Error ⊶78(1), 238(6)

Since court did not express in writing that there was no just reason for delay of appeal process until judgment was final, default and summary judgments of July 25, 1980, were not final judgments within meaning of trial rule, and thus appeal was not inappropriate even though motion to correct was filed beyond 60-day limit. Trial Procedure Rules 56(C), 59.

Thomas L. Hulse, Al S. Woolbert, Woolbert, Cunningham & Hulse, Anderson, for appellant.

Fred G. Yelton, Jr., Anderson, for appellee.

CONOVER, Judge.

STATEMENT OF THE CASE

Appellant Art Carroll filed a complaint in the Madison Superior Court, Division 1, charging William Lordy with violations of Carroll's registered trademark "elephant ears." The complaint asked for a temporary restraining order, injunctive relief and damages. A restraining order was granted on July 3, 1979, and notice was given of a hearing to be held on July 11, 1979. At that hearing Lordy was found to be in violation of the restraining order. The case was continued to permit Lordy to retain counsel. Lordy's motion to dissolve the restraining order was granted on December 7, 1979.

Lordy filed a motion to join the Indiana Secretary of State as a third party defendant. This motion was granted and Lordy cross-complained against the Secretary of State asking that the term "elephant ears" be declared a generic term and its registration cancelled. Lordy answered Carroll's complaint and filed a counterclaim on December 14, 1979. The counterclaim alleged that Carroll intentionally and maliciously sought and obtained a restraining order without notice against him without complying with the requirements of Trial Rule 65. Lordy asked for compensatory and punitive damages.

Lordy filed a motion for summary judgment on June 17, 1980, upon the complaint, cross-complaint and counterclaim. On July 25, 1980, the court granted the motion for summary judgment upon the complaint and cross-complaint and entered a default judgment upon the counterclaim against Carroll for not making a responsive pleading. The summary judgment held there was no material issue of fact, the previous determination of the United States Commissioner of Patents and Trademarks declaring "elephant ears" to be a generic term was res judicata, and that "elephant ears" was a generic term under the laws of Indiana. The court ordered cancellation of the Indiana trademark registration and set a trial date on the issue of damages. Trial was held on November 14, 1980, and judgment entered on December 12, 1980, awarding Lordy actual and punitive damages. Carroll timely filed his motion to correct errors which was overruled and now takes this appeal.

We affirm in part, reverse in part and remand.

ISSUES PRESENTED FOR REVIEW

1. Did the trial court err in granting Lordy's motion for summary judgment?

2. Was there error in entry of the default judgment?

3. Were punitive damages improperly awarded?

4. Was Carroll's motion to correct errors timely filed?

Both appellant Carroll and appellee Lordy are engaged in the business of selling a pastry known as elephant ears. Like many other itinerant vendors, Carroll and Lordy travel the fair circuit vending their goods to patrons of these fairs. It was during the Anderson Free Fair in 1979 that Carroll filed a complaint against Lordy for using his registered Indiana trademark "elephant ears" to identify Lordy's products.

Lordy was served with a temporary restraining order prohibiting him from using the term "elephant ears" to describe his pastry. Lordy changed the name on his signs to "Monster Ears." Although other vendors at the Anderson fair were selling under the name "elephant ears" Lordy was the only one upon whom a restraining order was sought.

The evidence shows that "elephant ears" first became the subject of Indiana trademark registration in August, 1972. The trademark was registered to Larry and Karn Bosley who assigned the trademark to Carroll in October 1973.

After changing his signs Lordy testified that his business declined sharply. After leaving the Anderson Fair Lordy changed his signs back to "elephant ears" even though the restraining order was issued statewide. Lordy also testified he was forced to abandon his planned Indiana fair schedule and take fair dates in other states where elephant ears are less popular.[1] As a result of the changed schedule Lordy claims he lost thousands of dollars in profits and damage to his advertising signs.

In the affidavits submitted pursuant to their motion for summary judgment Mr. and Mrs. Lordy both stated they had been familiar with the term "elephant ears" used to describe a pastry product since 1965. They also stated they had observed at least ten other "elephant ears" concessions at the Anderson fair in addition to Lordy and Carroll.

A third affidavit was submitted by John Libbert, a member of the Board of Directors of the Outdoor Amusement Business Association, Inc. In his affidavit Libbert asserted that he had been familiar with a fried pastry product known as elephant ears since the late 1960's. Libbert and the Lordys all stated they believed the term "elephant ears" to be generic. Attached to Libbert's affidavit were numerous exhibits supporting his sworn statements. These exhibits were comprised of letters, pictures and excerpts from newspapers. These affidavits and exhibits formed the basis for the ruling that "elephant ears" was a generic term. Libbert's exhibits also contained material relating to a previous ruling by the Commissioner of Patents and Trademarks holding that "elephant ears" was incapable of federal registration as a generic term. This is apparently the material that supported the court's ruling that the finding of the Commissioner of Patents and Trademarks was res judicata.

After the entry of summary judgment and default judgment trial was held on the issue of damages. Lordy was awarded $2,750.00 actual damages and $4,250.00 punitive damages.

I. SUMMARY JUDGMENT

Carroll makes several arguments concerning the propriety of entering summary judgment. They will be treated in turn.

A. Material Issue of Fact

When a motion for summary judgment is made it is the duty of the moving party to show that no material issue of fact remains in dispute. Ind.Rules of Procedure, Trial Rule 56. When reviewing a grant of summary judgment we must determine if the movant has shown the absence of a material issue of fact and if the law was correctly applied by the trial court. *Lynch v. Indiana State University*

---

[1]Indiana, it appears, is the leading market for elephant ears.

Board of Trustees, (1978) Ind.App., 378 N.E.2d 900, 902. Any doubts are resolved against the movant. *Barr v. State,* (1980) Ind.App., 400 N.E.2d 1149, 1150. Although Carroll did not oppose the motion for summary judgment this does not entitle Lordy to an automatic summary judgment. The moving party still bears the burden of showing the propriety of summary judgment. T.R. 56(C); *Levy Co., Inc. v. State Board of Tax Commissioners,* (1977) 173 Ind.App. 667, 365 N.E.2d 796, 798; *Tekulve v. Turner,* (1979) Ind.App., 391 N.E.2d 673.

Carroll contends the affidavits of the Lordys and Libbert do not demonstrate a lack of any material issue of fact. A fact is "material for purposes of summary judgment if it facilitates resolution of any of the issues involved." *Carrow v. Streeter,* (1980) Ind.App., 410 N.E.2d 1369. The factual issue resolved by the summary judgment was the genericness of the term "elephant ears." Therefore we must look to the affidavits submitted to determine if they settle the question of the generic use of the term elephant ears.

[1] The affidavits consistently testify that "elephant ears" is used in a descriptive manner to describe a deep fried pastry and has been used in that manner since 1965. The exhibits attached to Libbert's affidavits present an overwhelming and uncontradicted witness to the use of "elephant ears" as a generic term. Nothing in the record opposes the evidence and we are forced to conclude the factual issue was not in dispute after the submission of the affidavits, all that remained for the court to do was to apply the law to the facts.

B. Affidavits

Carroll makes two related arguments concerning the affidavits submitted with the motion for summary judgment. He challenges the affidavits as containing inadmissible conclusions and opposes certain documents attached to Libbert's affidavit as inadmissible hearsay.

[2] Carroll's position is that conclusions or opinions are never admissible in evidence. While this rule was once followed inflexibly by the courts of Indiana, the rule has been modified so substantially that the former rule is now the exception. A trial judge may in an appropriate case, permit opinion testimony on any ultimate fact issue. *State v. Bouras,* (1981) Ind.App., 423 N.E.2d 741, 745. In *Rieth-Riley Construction Co., Inc. v. McCarrell,* (1975) 163 Ind.App. 613, 325 N.E.2d 844, the court, after noting the continual erosion of the rigid exclusionary approach to opinions said,

> "Thus the *per se* exclusion rule has been abrogated, and the trial judge at his discretion, may in an appropriate case, permit such evidence. In exercising his discretion, the trial judge should consider the nature of the issue and the offered opinion in light of all attendant circumstances of the particular case. This court will review such an exercise in judicial discretion only for an abuse thereof."

Id. 325 N.E.2d at 852–53.

[3] An abuse of discretion which would permit a reviewing court to overturn the ruling of the trial court is "an erroneous conclusion and judgment, one clearly against the logic and effect of facts and circumstances before the court or the reasonable, probable and actual deductions to be drawn therefrom." *Godfrey v.*

State, (1978) Ind.App., 380 N.E.2d 621, 623; *Dunbar v. Dunbar*, (1969) 145 Ind.App. 479, 483, 251 N.E.2d 468, 471.

[4] The genericness of a term is an ultimate fact issue. Any given term's proper categorization is a factual issue. *Salton, Inc. v. Cornwall*, (D.N.J.1979) 477 F.Supp. 975. The affiants were competent to form opinions about the term "elephant ears." They have traveled the fair circuit and have had ample opportunity to observe personally the use of "elephant ears." Nothing included in their opinions is "clearly against the logic and effect of facts and circumstances before the court."

Also, the issues are so clearly drawn in most trademark actions that the admission of an opinion carries very little prejudice with it. The following statement from a federal trademark decision describes opinion evidence in trademark cases:

> "The opinion of an interested party respecting the ultimate conclusion involved in a proceeding would normally appear of no moment in the proceeding. Moreover, it is known at the outset. One may assume, for example, that an opposer believes confusion likely and that a defending applicant does not. That a party earlier indicated a contrary opinion respecting the conclusion in a similar proceeding involving similar marks and goods is a fact, and that fact may be received in evidence as merely illuminative of shade and tone in the total picture confronting the decision maker."

Interstate Brands Corp. v. Celestial Seasonings (Cust. & Pat.App.1978) 576 F.2d 926, 929; rehearing denied August 10, 1978. We do not think the judge committed an abuse of discretion by considering the opinions contained within the affidavits. The opinions contained therein were self-evident and proper subjects of lay opinion.

[5] In a trademark action, newspaper articles and advertisements may be considered non-hearsay evidence. The evidence is not offered to prove the truth of the matters asserted therein but is probative of the reaction of the average consumer. "To hold otherwise would be to separate the concept of the average prospective purchaser from the world of reality." *Application of Abcor Development Corp.* (Cust. & Pat.App.1978) 588 F.2d 811, 814. Consideration of the advertising and articles was not error.

[6] Carroll also challenges the use of letters attached to the Libbert affidavit. The first letter from an attorney is merely a cover letter attached to the record of the proceedings before the Patent and Trademark Office. This letter is merely collateral and does not carry any probative weight on the matter of genericness. Even if we were to hold that admission of the letter was error it would be harmless because it did nothing to prejudice the rights of Carroll.

[7] The other letter challenged by Carroll is clearly inadmissible hearsay. The letter contains a description of elephant ears as well as a multiple hearsay narrative concerning a phone conversation with a baker about elephant ears. This is clearly hearsay of the first rank and inadmissible. However, even when we exclude this letter and the cover letter from the affidavit, the record still contains more than an adequate amount of evidence to support the granting of summary judgment.

C. Application of the Law[2]

Carroll maintains that Indiana law permits registration of generic terms. The pertinent statutory section reads:

"24-2-1-3 Registerability

"Sec. 3. A trade-mark by which the goods or services of any applicant for registration may be distinguished from the goods or services of others shall not be registered if it

"(e) consists of a mark which, (1) when applied to the goods or services of the applicant, is merely descriptive or deceptively misdescriptive of them, or (2) when applied to the goods or services of the applicant is primarily geographically descriptive or deceptively misdescriptive of them, or (3) is primarily merely a surname: Provided, however, That nothing in this section (e) shall prevent the registration of a mark used in this state by the applicant which has become distinctive of the applicant's goods or services. The secretary of state may accept as evidence that the mark has become distinctive, as applied to the applicant's goods or services, proof of substantially exclusive and continuous use thereof as a mark by the applicant in this state or elsewhere for the five (5) years next preceding the date of the filing of the application for registration; . . . "

The purpose of a trademark is to identify the source of the product, not the product itself. When a trademark becomes primarily the identifier of a product rather than the source then the trademark has become descriptive of the goods. The following quotation from the Ninth Circuit illustrates the reason for not registering descriptive terms.

"The law is that a word which is in the primary meaning merely descriptive of the goods to which it is applied may not be appropriated as the exclusive trademark of a single seller, since one competitor will not be permitted to impoverish the language of commerce by preventing his fellows from describing their own goods. *Bada Co. v. Montgomery Ward & Co.* (9th Cir. 1970) 426 F.2d 8. Loss of the ability of a trademark to identify the source of goods is called a 'common descriptive name of an article or substance' in federal law. 15 U.S.C. 1064(c). Courts have come to equate 'common descriptive name,' with the shorthand expression 'generic term.' *Anti-Monopoly, Inc. v. General Mills Fun Group* (9th Cir. 1979) 611 F.2d 296, 301; *Abercrombie & Fitch Co. v. Hunting World* (2d Cir. 1976) 537 F.2d 4, 9."

[8] The courts of Indiana have not been forced to interpret the words "merely descriptive" or "generic" since the present trademark statute was enacted. We are convinced the language "merely descriptive" and "generic" speaks of the same concept as the words "generic" and "common descriptive term" do in federal law. That is, once a term is found to express the name of a product rather than the source of the product then that term is incapable of trademark registration.[3] Once registered a trademark registration may be cancelled if the term becomes descriptive. The pertinent Indiana statute states:

[2]Unlike patent and copyright law, the Lanham act does not pre-empt state trademark law. Preemption arguments have been expressly rejected by the Third Circuit Court of Appeals, *LaChemise Lacoste v. The Alligator Company, Inc.* (3d Cir. 1974) 506 F.2d 339, 346 and the Ninth Circuit, *Golden Door, Inc. v. Odisho* (9th Cir. 1980) 646 F.2d 347, 352; repudiating contrary dicta in *Mister Donut of America, Inc. v. Mr. Donut, Inc.* (9th Cir. 1969) 418 F.2d 838, 844.

[3]The following list is exemplary of terms which are generic:
Aspirin—*Bayer Co. v. United Drug Co.* (1921 DCNY), 272 F. 505.
Brassiere—*Charles R. DeBevoise Co. v. H. & W. Co.* (1905) 69 N.J.Eq. 114, 60 A. 407.
Escalator—*Haughton Elevator Co. v. Seeberger* (1950 Comm.Pat) 85 U.S. Patent Quarterly 80.
Shredded Wheat—*Kellogg Co. v. National Biscuit Co.,* (1938) 305 U.S. 111, 59 S.Ct. 109, 83 L.Ed. 73.
Yo-Yo—*Donald F. Duncan, Inc. v. Royal Tops Mfg. Co.* (1965 7th Cir.) 343 F.2d 655.

"24–2–1–10 Cancellation

Sec. 10. The secretary of state shall cancel from the register:

(4) Any registration concerning which a court of competent jurisdiction shall find

(a) that the registered trade-mark has been abandoned,

(b) that the registrant is not the owner of the trade-mark,

(c) that the registration was granted improperly,

(d) that the registration was obtained fraudulently;

(5) When a court of competent jurisdiction shall order cancellation of a registration on any ground."

This statute grants very broad power to the courts to review trademark registration. This is due to the fact that the trademark statute does not confer any enforcement or review rights on the Secretary of State. Remedies are left to the parties to work out through traditional legal avenues. And as we have noted, the courts have liberal power to adjudicate trademark validity.

We turn to the evidence used by the court to support a ruling that "elephant ears" was a generic term. We are convinced that the ruling was proper. All of the affidavits and materials submitted with the motion for summary judgment speak with a unitary witness. "Elephant ears" describes a fried pastry topped with sweetened cinnamon. These pastries are sold in commercial mixtures as well as prepared items. The demand for "elephant ears" is especially keen in Indiana. There are a number of itinerant vendors who travel the fair circuit selling similar pastries as "elephant ears."[4]

[9] The only conclusion that could be drawn from such persuasive evidence is that "elephant ears" is a descriptive term, incapable of trademark regis-

---

[4]The following recipe was submitted as characteristic of the use of the term "elephant ears" by the consuming public.

"Several Indiana schools use this recipe for elephant ears sold at school carnivals and fundraisers.

ELEPHANT EARS

1 ½ cups milk
2 tablespoons sugar
1 teaspoon salt
6 tablespoons shortening
2 packages dry yeast
4 cups flour
  Oil for deep frying
  Sugar mixture (recipe follows)

Heat together, but do not boil, milk, sugar, salt and shortening until shortening is melted. Cool to lukewarm. Add yeast, stir until dissolved. Stir in flour, two cups at a time, beating after each addition until smooth.

Put into a greased bowl; cover with a damp cloth and let rise until double, about 30 minutes.

Heat oil to 350 degrees or hot, but not smoking. Dust hands with flour. Pinch off pieces of dough about the size of a golf ball. Stretch each dough ball into a thin 6 to 8-inch circle. Drop stretched dough, one at a time into hot oil. Fry until it rises to the surface, turn and fry other side until light golden brown.

Remove with a slotted spoon; drain on absorbent paper. Sprinkle generously with sugar mixture. SUGAR MIXTURE: Mix 1/2 cup sugar with 1 teaspoon cinnamon."

tration and should be stricken from the records of the Secretary of State.[5] Having found no error in the finding of the court that "elephant ears" is a generic term, we affirm that portion of the judgment and order the Secretary of State to cancel the registration of "elephant ears."

D. Res Judicata

We are more amenable to Carroll's argument that the judge misapplied the law when he ruled the finding of the Commissioner of Patents and Trademarks was res judicata on the generic nature of the term "elephant ears."

> "The basic elements of the doctrine of res judicata are: 1) the former judgment must have been rendered by a court of competent jurisdiction; 2) the matter now in issue was, or might have been, determined in the former suit; 3) the particular controversy adjudicated in the former action must have been between parties to the present suit or their privies; and 4) the judgment in the former suit must have been rendered on the merits."

Glass v. Continental Assurance Co., (1981) Ind.App., 415 N.E.2d 126, 128.

[10] When determining identity of parties for res judicata purposes, courts look beyond mere nominal parties and hold estopped only those parties whose interests were directly involved in prior litigation concerning the same subject matter or claim. *Union Insurance Co. v. State ex rel. Indiana Department of Insurance,* (1980) Ind.App., 401 N.E.2d 1372. A "party" is one "who is directly interested in the subject matter and had a right to make defense or to control the proceedings and to appeal from the judgment." *Mayhew v. Deister,* (1969) 144 Ind.App. 111, 244 N.E.2d 448.

[11] The action before the examiner in the Patent and Trademark office did not involve Lordy. Carroll's application for Lanham Act[6] registration was opposed by a Mrs. Rohr and Gold Medal Products, Inc. Lordy neither opposed the regis-

---

[5]Carroll's trademark was used in connection with the following cartoon figure. Our decision relates only to the use of the words "elephant ears." We express no opinion as to the possibility of Carroll gaining some commercial protection for the cartoon elephant.

[6]15 U.S.C. 1050 et seq.

tration nor was he in privity with those who did. It is fundamental to the rule of res judicata that the party seeking to benefit from the rule must have been a party to the original action or in privity with those who were. *Speedway Realty Co. v. Grasshoff Realty Corp.,* (1965) Ind.App., 206 N.E.2d 632; rev'd on other grounds 248 Ind. 6, 216 N.E.2d 845. While other courts have abandoned the identity of parties requirement, Indiana still retains it as an element of res judicata. *Indiana State Highway Commission v. Speidel,* (1979) Ind.App., 392 N.E.2d 1172, 1176. It was error for the court to hold that the findings of the Commissioner of Patents and Trademarks was res judicata. However, this error does not mandate a reversal as the judge independently found that the term "elephant ears" was a generic term under Indiana law.

II. DEFAULT JUDGMENT

[12] Carroll argues that entry of a default judgment adverse to him was improper because the default was never applied for and he never received written notice of the default. We agree.

Our trial rule 55 is specific and narrowly drawn respecting default judgments.[7] The party seeking a default judgment must apply for it. Written notice must also be served upon the defaulting party. The record submitted on appeal does not show that Lordy made every application for default or that Carroll received written notice of an application for default judgment. The first mention of a default judgment is in the last paragraph of the summary judgment order where it states:

"IT IS FURTHER ORDERED, ADJUDGED AND DECREED by the court that the issue of damages presented by the counterclaim of William Lordy against Art Carroll be and the same is hereby continued and set for hearing at 1:30 P.M., August 8, 1980, the court noting at this time that the Plaintiff, Art Carroll, having failed to file a responsive pleading to the counterclaim of William Lordy, said Defendant and Counterclaimant, William Lordy, is now entitled to the default of the Plaintiff, Art Carroll."

[13] Lordy reasons that since a trial on the issue of damages was held and attended by Carroll it is self-evident that Lordy applied for a default judgment and served written notice. We cannot accept such reasoning. In effect, the Appellee is asking this court to treat the important matters of notice and application for default as if they were mere surplusage in T.R. 55. Strict adherence to the language

[7]Ind.Rules of Procedure; Trial Rule 55(B):

"**Default judgment.** In all cases the party entitled to a judgment by default shall apply to the court therefor; but no judgment by default shall be entered against a person known to be an infant or incompetent unless represented in the action by a general guardian, committee, conservator, or other such representative who has appeared therein. If the party against whom judgment by default is sought has appeared in the action, he (or, if appearing by a representative, his representative) shall be served with written notice of the application for judgment at least three [3] days prior to the hearing on such application. If, in order to enable the court to enter judgment or to carry it into effect, it is necessary to take an account or to determine the amount of damages or to establish the truth of any averment by evidence or to make an investigation of any other matter, the court may conduct such hearing or order such references as it deems necessary and proper and shall accord a right of trial by jury to the parties when and as required."

of T.R. 55 is required. In *Hiatt v. Yergin,* (1972) 152 Ind.App. 497, 498, 284 N.E.2d 834, 841, the court said, "even if a party has failed to plead or otherwise comply with the rules, no default judgment is proper against such a party until an application for a default is filed. . . ."[8] Omission of the application for or written notice of default is reversible error. The entry of a default judgment against Carroll must be reversed.

III. DAMAGES

[14] Since the damages were awarded pursuant to the defaulted counterclaim which was previously set aside, no valid judgment is left to support the award of damages. Therefore, the award of damages, both compensatory and punitive, must be reversed.

IV. MOTION TO CORRECT ERRORS

Lordy contends that Carroll's appeal is inappropriate because the motion to correct errors was filed beyond the 60 day limit permitted by Trial Rule 59. Lordy's calendar begins running on July 25, 1980, the date the default and summary judgments were entered. The last day on which the motion to correct errors could be filed was September 23, 1980. Since the motion to correct errors was not filed until February 3, 1981, 199 days after the entry of summary judgment, Lordy claims we should not entertain this appeal.

Ind.Rules of Procedure, Trial Rule 56(C) states:

> "A summary judgment may be rendered upon less than all the issues or claims, including without limitation the issue of liability or damages alone although there is a genuine issue as to damages or liability as the case may be. A summary judgment upon less than all the issues involved in a claim or with respect to less than all the claims or parties shall be interlocutory unless the court in writing expressly determines that there is not just reason for delay and in writing expressly directs entry of judgment as to less than all the issues, claims or parties."

[15, 16] Before a motion to correct errors becomes appropriate there must be a final judgment or an appealable final order entered. This is for the benefit of the court. Delaying the appeal process until judgment is final obviates the problem of having to deal with an appeal in a piecemeal fashion. Since the court did not express in writing that there was no just reason for delay, we cannot hold that the judgment of July 25, 1980, was a final judgment within the meaning of T.R. 59(C). *Federal Insurance Co. v. Liberty Mutual Insurance Co.,* (1974) 162 Ind.App. 242, 319 N.E.2d 171, 173. Having found that summary judgment was appropriate and default judgment improperly entered, we affirmed the decision of the court finding "elephant ears" to be a generic or descriptive mark and incapable of registration under Indiana trademark law. As to the default judgment we reverse and remand for further proceedings consistent with this opinion.

MILLER, P. J., and YOUNG, J., concur.

---

[8]One exception to the notice rules of 55 is extant.

When the defaulting party has not appeared in the action or where the appearance of counsel has been withdrawn, a default judgment may be entered without notice of a hearing. *Stewart v. Hicks,* (1979) Ind.App., 395 N.E.2d 308, 309, 312.

Fla. App. 342 S.2d 1053
Ingrid CARDOZO and Joseph Cardozo,
her husband, Plaintiffs,

v.

Norma TRUE a/k/a Norma A. True and
Ellie's Book and Stationery, Inc.,
Defendants.

No. 76–1623.

District Court of Appeal of Florida,
Second District.

Feb. 23, 1977.

Rehearing Denied March 24, 1977.

The Circuit Court, Sarasota County, Gilbert A. Smith, J., certified questions to District Court of Appeal as to whether retail book dealer was liable to purchaser of cookbook for injuries caused by lack of adequate warnings as to poisonous ingredients used in recipe. The District Court of Appeal, Scheb, J., made answer that retail book dealer was not liable under Uniform Commercial Code to purchaser of cookbook for injuries and damages caused by improper instructions or lack of adequate warnings as to poisonous ingredients used in recipe; and that absent allegations that bookseller knew that there was reason to warn public as to contents of book, implied warranty in respect to sale of books by merchant who regularly sells them is limited to warranty of physical properties of such books and does not extend to material communicated by book's author or publisher.

Questions answered.

1. Sales ⬥10
Definition of "goods" under Uniform Commercial Code is sufficiently broad to include books. West's F.S.A. § 672.105.

See publication Words and Phrases for other judicial constructions and definitions.

2. Sales ⬥266
Book merchant impliedly warranted the tangible, physical properties; i. e., printing and binding, of books sold. West's F.S.A. § § 672.105, 672.314(1), (2)(c).

3. Libel and Slander ⊶74

Distributors of newspapers and periodicals cannot be held legally responsible for defamatory material contained therein where dealer did not know and reasonably could not have known that publication contained defamatory material.

4. Sales ⊶418(19)

Retail book dealer was not liable under Uniform Commercial Code to purchaser of cookbook for injuries and damages caused by improper instructions or lack of adequate warnings as to poisonous ingredients used in recipe. West's F.S.A. §§ 672.105, 672.314(1), (2)(c).

5. Sales ⊶266

The Uniform Commercial Code, in codifying the law of sales, did nothing to restrict common-law doctrine of implied warranty under state law. West's F.S.A. § 672.314.

6. Sales ⊶279

Absent allegations that book seller knew that there was reason to warn public as to contents of book, implied warranty in respect to sale of books by merchant who regularly sells them is limited to warranty of physical properties of such book and does not extend to material communicated by book's author or publisher. West's F.S.A. § 672.314.

John Patterson of Livingston & Patterson, and James W. Cullis of Icard, Merrill, Cullis, Timm & Furen, Sarasota, for plaintiffs.

Andrew D. Owens, Jr. of Dart, Dickinson, O'Riorden, Gibbons & Quale, Sarasota, for defendant Ellie's Book and Stationery, Inc.

SCHEB, Judge.

The Circuit Court for Sarasota County certified the following questions to this court pursuant to Fla.App. Rule 4.6(a):

I. IS A RETAIL BOOK DEALER LIABLE UNDER SECTION 672.314, FLORIDA STATUTES, TO A PURCHASER OF A COOKBOOK FOR HER INJURIES AND DAMAGES CAUSED BY IMPROPER INSTRUCTIONS OR LACK OF ADEQUATE WARNINGS AS TO POISONOUS INGREDIENTS USED IN A RECIPE?

II. IS A RETAIL BOOK DEALER LIABLE UNDER THE COMMON LAW OF IMPLIED WARRANTIES TO A PURCHASER OF A COOKBOOK FOR HER INJURIES FOR LACK OF ADEQUATE WARNINGS AS TO POISONOUS INGREDIENTS USED IN A RECIPE?

The plaintiffs' amended complaint set forth the essential facts which the trial court has summarized as follows:

"Norma True authored a book entitled 'Trade Winds Cookery', an anthology of recipes selected and prepared by her using tropical fruits and vegetables. It was published by a Virginia corporation, which sold the book to Ellie's Book and Stationery, Inc. Ellie's was and is a retail book dealer located in Sarasota, Florida.

On September 15, 1971, Ingrid Cardozo purchased a copy of 'Trade Winds Cookery' from Ellie's. Four days later, Mrs. Cardozo was using the book and following a recipe in it for the preparation and cooking of the Dasheen plant, commonly known as 'elephant's ears'. While preparing the roots for cooking, she ate a small slice and immediately experienced a burning of the lips, mouth, throat and tongue, coughing and gasping, and intense stomach cramps. This persisted over several days, despite medical care.

Defendant True did not answer plaintiff's complaint, and is not involved in this certificate. As to defendant Ellie's Mrs. Cardozo and her husband alleged that the book did not have adequate instructions; that it failed to warn that uncooked Dasheen roots are poisonous; and that the ingredients contained in the recipes for Dasheen plant dishes were inadequately tested to insure their safety for human consumption. It was further alleged that Ellie's impliedly warranted that the book was reasonably fit for its intended use, and that it was not, due to inadequate instructions and warning. Finally, it was alleged that Mrs. Cardozo's injuries and Mr. Cardozo's derivative claim were proximately caused by the breach of this warranty."

It appears to us that our answer will be dispositive of the case as to the claim against Ellie's. *See* Fla.App. Rule 4.6(a). Of course, our answers do not bear on the plaintiffs' action against the defendant, True.

Plaintiffs argue that the first question is controlled by the Uniform Commercial Code (U.C.C.), Section 672.314, Florida Statutes; that the second question is answered by the common law of implied warranties. Section 672.314, Florida Statutes provides:

(1) Unless excluded or modified (§ 672.316), a warranty that the goods shall be merchantable is implied in a contract for their sale if the seller is a merchant with respect to goods of that kind. Under this section the serving for value of food or drink to be consumed either on the premises or elsewhere is a sale.
(2) Goods to be merchantable must be at least such as:
   (a) Pass without objection in the trade under the contract description; and
   (b) In the case of fungible goods, are of fair average quality within the description; and
   (c) Are fit for the ordinary purposes for which such goods are used; and
   (d) Run, within the variations permitted by the agreement, of even kind, quality and quantity within each unit and among all units involved; and
   (e) Are adequately contained, packaged, and labeled as the agreement may require; and
   (f) Conform to the promises or affirmations of fact made on the container or label if any.
(3) Unless excluded or modified (§ 672.316) other implied warranties may arise from the course of dealing or usage of trade.

Plaintiffs see the quoted statute as one of general applicability to all retail dealers in consumer goods. They point out that this section of the U.C.C. creates a statutory implied warranty of merchantability imposed by law on the merchant who regularly sells goods and that defendant Ellie's falls in that category in respect to the sale of books. And, while plaintiffs find no decisional law to directly support their contention that Ellie's is liable, the applicability of the statute, they maintain, is obvious from its plain meaning.

Defendant, while recognizing that Ellie's may be subject to the doctrine of implied warranty now imposed by the U.C.C., claims such warranty is limited to the physical characteristics of the books they sell and cannot be construed to include the thought processes conveyed by the author and produced in writing by the publishers of that book. They urge the practical impossibility of book sellers testing every recipe in the books they sell. Moreover, they contend that if such a burden were to be imposed upon the book seller, then the merchant would have to be an expert or retain an expert in every field embraced by the numerous publications they offer. Ultimately, they argue, this would mean the stores which now disseminate information would be forced to close with the resultant infringement on freedom of speech and expression.

[1] The definition of "goods" under the U.C.C. is sufficiently broad to include books. Section 672.105, Florida Statutes. *Cf. Lake Wales Publishing Co. v. Florida Visitor,* 335 So.2d 335 (Fla.App.2d DCA 1976), holding printed pamphlets as goods under U.C.C. Clearly, the defendant Ellie's qualifies as a merchant with respect to books. Section 672.314(1), Florida Statutes.

Thus, we approach the novel question of not whether Ellie's impliedly warranted the recipe book it sold to Mrs. Cardozo, but rather, the scope of that warranty. From reading Section 672.314(2), the requirement of merchantability most relevant here is (c), which requires goods to be "fit for the ordinary purposes for which such goods are used."

[2] As we have observed, books are goods. As such Ellie's is held to have impliedly warranted the tangible, physical properties; *i.e.,* printing and binding of books. But, at this point it becomes necessary to distinguish between the tangible properties of these goods and the thoughts and ideas conveyed thereby. The principle involved is not directly controlled by any precedent of the decisional law, either under the doctrine of implied warranty under common law or as codified under the U.C.C. It is unthinkable that standards imposed on the quality of goods sold by a merchant would require that merchant, who is a book seller, to evaluate the thought processes of the many authors and publishers of the hundreds and often thousands of books which the merchant offers for sale. One can readily imagine the extent of potential litigation. Is the newsdealer, or for that matter the neighborhood news carrier, liable if the local paper's recipes call for inedible ingredients? We think not.

While not directly in point, it is interesting to note that even publishers have not been held liable where injuries have occurred through use of products advertised in their magazines. Thus, in *Yuhas v. Mudge,* 129 N.J.Super. 207, 322 A.2d 824 (1974), the court said that Popular Mechanics Corp. could not be held liable to a plaintiff injured by fireworks resulting from an allegedly defective product advertised in the corporation's magazine. The court pointed out that the magazine had neither endorsed the product or secured any direct pecuniary benefit from the sale of the fireworks. To impose that legal duty upon the publisher, the court said, would have a staggering adverse effect upon the commercial world and our economic system. More closely in point is pre-U.C.C. case, *Mac Kown v. Ill. Publishing & Printing Co.,* 289 Ill.App. 59, 6 N.E.2d 526 (1937), where the court refused to hold a newspaper liable for injuries to one of its readers allegedly resulting from the reader's use of a dandruff remedy recommended as one given to the writer of the article by a reputable physician. The principles of law and considerations of public policy which support denial of liability of a publisher in these instances more urgently mandates denial of liability of a newsdealer.

[3] Closely analogous is the principle that distributors of newspapers and periodicals cannot be even held legally responsible for defamatory material con-

tained therein where the dealer did not know and reasonably could not have known that the publication contained defamatory material. *See* 50 Am.Jur.2d, Libel and Slander, Section 342. Thus in *Sexton v. American News Co.,* 133 F.Supp. 591 (N.D.Fla.1955), the court stated that since:

> ". . . no duty rested definitely on defendant to familiarize itself with the contents of the publication in question and thereby learn of the allegedly libelous matter about the plaintiff, there remains nothing for the court to do in this case but grant defendant's motion for summary judgment."

The Supreme Court of Florida has held that even a newspaper publisher is not liable for the mere reproduction of outside press dispatches from generally recognized sources of daily news. *Layne v. Tribune Co.,* 108 Fla. 177, 146 So. 234 (1933).

[4] Thus liability without fault, which may be present in an action for breach of implied warranty, has long been held inappropriate in an action against one passing on printed words without an opportunity to investigate them. The principle against imposing liability without fault on a publisher in a defamation action has recently been given constitutional status. *See Gertz v. Robert Welch, Inc.,* 418 U.S. 323, 94 S.Ct. 2997, 41 L.Ed.2d 789 (1974); *Time Inc. v. Firestone,* 424 U.S. 448, 96 S.Ct. 958, 47 L.Ed.2d 154 (1976).

The common theme running through these decisions is that ideas hold a privileged position in our society. They are not equivalent to commercial products. Those who are in the business of distributing the ideas of other people perform a unique and essential function. To hold those who perform this essential function liable, regardless of fault, when an injury results would severely restrict the flow of the ideas they distribute. We think that holding Ellie's liable under the doctrine of implied warranty would, based upon the facts as certified to us, have the effect of imposing a liability without fault not intended by the Uniform Commercial Code.

[5] The reasoning applicable to our response to the first question must also conclude the answer to the second. The U.C.C. in codifying the law of sales did nothing to restrict the common law doctrine of implied warranty under Florida law. To the contrary, the code raised the dignity of the doctrine to statute and made it a certainty that warranties would be implied in accordance with the statutory design where the seller is a merchant with respect to goods of that particular kind being sold.

[6] We make no statements concerning the liability of an author or publisher under the facts as certified to us. Nor do we pass upon the question of whether Ellie's could be held liable if it actually knew the book it sold contained recipes with poisonous ingredients. Rather, we hold that absent allegations that a book seller knew that there was reason to warn the public as to contents of a book, the implied warranty in respect to sale of books by a merchant who regularly sells them is limited to a warranty of the physical properties of such books and does not extend to the material communicated by the book's author or publisher.

Accordingly, we answer each of the questions certified in the negative and remand this cause for further proceedings consistent with this opinion.

BOARDMAN, C. J., and HOBSON, J., concur.

449 N.Y.Supp.2d 822
113 Misc.2d 748

CITIBANK, N.A., Plaintiff,

v.

Jannis Ann WARNER, Defendant.

Supreme Court, Special Term,
New York County, Part I.

May 6, 1981.

Bank sued one of its depositors for willful conversion and for money had and received as a result of sum which was mistakenly credited to defendant's checking account. The Supreme Court, Special Term, New York County, Edward J. Greenfield, J., held that: (1) absence of "contributory negligence" is no defense to conversion action or to claim for money had and received, and (2) assertion of "windfall by estoppel" could not be sustained, notwithstanding that bank did not discover error for four months, as bank did not attempt to mislead depositor and she did not change her position to her irreparable damage.

Summary judgment for bank.

1. Trover and Conversion ⬤⛌22

Absence of "contributory negligence" by a defendant is no defense in an action for conversion.

2. Trover and Conversion ⬤⛌22

Although bank may have made a mistake and through its negligence mistakenly credited defendant depositor's account the fact that defendant, who withdrew part of the proceeds, acted deliberately rather than negligence was not a defense to bank's conversion claim.

3. Implied and Constructive Contracts ⬤⛌22

Considerations of negligence have no application in an action for money had and received, based on a payment made under a mistake of fact and, hence, negligence principles were not applicable to bank's action to recover from depositor sum which it mistakenly credited to depositor's account and although bank, which brought action for money had and received, may have been careless it was entitled to be relieved from the consequences of its mistake.

4. Estoppel ⬤⛌56

Although bank did not become aware of its mistaken credit to defendant's checking account for four months, defendant was not entitled to avail herself of doctrine of "windfall by estoppel" on ground that she relied to her detriment in writing checks on the account, some of which she was able to distribute to her relatives, as bank did not attempt to mislead her and she had not changed her position to her irreparable damage and bank made no knowing misrepresentations.

5. Estoppel ⊶87
Fraud ⊶20

Reliance to one's detriment may be the basis for an action for fraud or the predicate for a defense of estoppel.

Zalkin, Rodin & Goodman by William Linden, New York City, for plaintiff.

Jacoby & Meyers, Brooklyn, for defendant.

EDWARD J. GREENFIELD, Justice:

Our patron saint of frugality, Benjamin Franklin, commented in Poor Richard's Almanac that "A penny saved is a penny earned." How much more delightful it is to save your pennies on someone else's earnings!

Plaintiff bank sues the defendant, one of its depositors, for willful conversion and for money had and received as a result of sums mistakenly credited to the defendant's account. Defendant interposes as affirmative defenses "absence of contributory negligence" and reliance on the bank's negligent acts to her detriment. Evidently, the law firm which represents defendant, which has embarked upon unprecedented widespread television solicitation of clients, seeks here to create the novel and innovative doctrine of "windfall by estoppel." Plaintiff bank moves to dismiss the affirmative defenses and for summary judgment.

Defendant is an unemployed woman on public assistance. She receives a payment of $92.00 every two weeks. She maintained a checking account with the plaintiff bank and on December 11, 1979 had a balance of $30.95. On December 13, 1979, the bank which was supposed to credit the account of another of its depositors, the Banco de Chile, mistakenly credited the account of the defendant in the sum of $23,715.00. The mistake evidently arose when during the course of processing the credit, the bank inadvertently microencoded the defendant's account number 010 22666 thereon, instead of the account number of the Banco de Chile 109 22666. The defendant asserts that she truly believed that the money had been deposited in her account by the sponsor of one of the contests she regularly entered. No details are supplied as to what contest, and what sponsor, nor is explanation given as to how the sponsor would know the name of her bank and her account number. Nothing is set forth to indicate that she had ever been notified by anyone of such an actual or potential windfall.

The pattern of the account appears to belie defendant's pretensions of innocence. Against her $30.95 balance, she had written check #123 which was debited to her account in the sum of $30.70 on December 17, 1979, which would have left her with a balance of $0.15. Three other checks were presented on her account thereafter in the sums of $10.00, $20.00 and $30.00 respectively, which, but for the mistaken credit given on December 13, 1979 would have left her account overdrawn in the sum of $63.59. On January 2, 1980, the bank issued its monthly statement which showed that she had $5.41 in her savings account and $23,655.15 in her checking account. Acting on that delightful bit of information, defendant proceeded to write $6,323.60 in checks in the next few days. Then she tried for substantially larger stakes. She wrote check #163 for $75,000.00, check #165 for $4,000.00, check #166 for $20,000.00 and check #169 for another

$20.000.00. Since, at this time, her account showed a balance of $17,331.55, only the $4,000.00 check was debited and the other $115,000 in checks were returned. Even this did not alert the bank however. Check #163 for $75,000.00 evidently was redeposited in February and bounced again, but it was not until March 4, 1980 that the bank became aware of its mistake and transferred the defendant's remaining balance of $13,269.55 to its rightful owner. The bank now is attempting to recover the $10,445.45 for checks which were improperly paid out.

[1, 2] The absence of "contributory negligence" by a defendant is no defense in an action for conversion. It is of no moment that plaintiff may have made a mistake, and through its negligence gave access to sums which defendant was able to convert to her benefit. Conversion is a willful tort, and the fact that defendant acted deliberately rather than negligently is not a defense.

[3] Considerations of negligence likewise have no applicability in an action for money had and received, based upon a payment made under a mistake of fact.

> "An action for money had and received as well as an action to recover money paid under a mistake of fact, although actions at law, are based on equitable principles, requiring those who receive money under certain circumstances to repay the moneys on the ground that to permit the retention of such moneys would be against equity and good conscience (*Schank v. Schuchman*, 212 N.Y. 352 [106 N.E. 127]; *Rothrock Syosset v. Kreutzer*, 2 A.D.2d 777 [154 N.Y.S.2d 816]; *New York Life Ins. Co. v. Guttenplan*, 30 N.Y.S.2d 430, aff'd. 259 App.Div. 1004 [20 N.Y.S.2d 724], aff'd. 284 N.Y. 805 [31 N.E.2d 925])." *Cukierski v. Standard Milling Co.,* 60 Misc.2d 690, 303 N.Y.S.2d 586.

While the bank may have been careless, it is nonetheless entitled to be relieved from the consequences of its mistake. *Ball v. Shepard,* 202 N.Y. 247, 253, 95 N.E. 719; *Hathaway v. County of Delaware,* 185 N.Y. 368, 370, 78 N.E. 153; *Kingston Bank v. Eltinge,* 40 N.Y. 391, 396.

> " . . . the law will compel restitution from a person who obtains money or property from another . . . unjustly, or without authority." *Pink v. Title Guarantee & Trust Co.,* 274 N.Y. 167, 173 [8 N.E.2d 321]; *MacMurray v. City of Long Beach,* 292 N.Y. 286 [54 N.E.2d 828].

[4, 5] Defendant asserts that she "relied to her detriment" upon the negligent acts of plaintiff. That reliance consisted of writing checks in excess of $125,000.00, some of which she was able to distribute to her relatives—how much for them and how much for herself is not stated. Some detriment! The bank did not attempt to mislead her and she has not changed her position to her irreparable damage. Reliance to one's detriment may be the basis of an action for fraud, or the predicate for a defense of estoppel. Here the bank neither defrauded the defendant, nor did it make knowing misrepresentations. Hence, assertion of "windfall by estoppel" cannot be sustained.

There being no valid legal or factual defense to this action, the court cannot condone the unjust enrichment of the defendant and must grant plaintiff's motion for summary judgment.

128 N.Y. Supp. 2d 119
SCHUMER v. SCHUMER.

Supreme Court, Special Term, Kings County, Part V.

Feb. 25, 1954.

Wife's action for annulment of marriage on ground that husband had fraudulently promised to try to have children and to provide her with a nice home in which to raise their family. The Supreme Court, Kings County, Special Term, McDonald, J., held that facts testified to by wife and her mother and stipulated by husband, who withdrew verified answer denying allegation of such facts, were insufficient to establish wife's right to annulment.

Complaint dismissed.

1. Marriage ⬤58(7)
A natural and expected end of marriage being the procreation of children, intention of parties to marriage to try to have children need not be expressed but will be presumed, and, although not expressed, can still serve as basis for annulment for fraudulent promise to try to have children. Civil Practice Act, § 1143.

2. Marriage ⬤60(7)
Fraudulent intent, to be ground for annulment, must be clearly proved before decree will be granted. Civil Practice Act, § 1143.

3. Evidence ⬤590
The principle that the court must accept the positive testimony of unimpeached and uncontradicted witness and that such testimony cannot be disregarded by the court or jury arbitrarily or capriciously does not apply with equal force where witnesses are interested.

4. Marriage ⬤60(3)
Supreme Court has equity jurisdiction to annul marriage contract based upon fraud. Civil Practice Act, § 1143.

5. Marriage ⬤58(7)
The fraud which will induce court to set aside contract of marriage is something different from the fraud which will induce the court to set aside an ordinary contract. Civil Practice Act, § 1143.

6. Marriage ⬤60(7)
In wife's action for annulment of marriage on ground that husband had fraudulently promised to try to have children and to provide her with a nice home in which to raise their family, facts, testified to by wife and her mother and stipu-

lated by husband, who withdrew verified answer denying allegation of such facts, were insufficient to establish wife's right to annulment.

Harold J. Robbins, New York City, for plaintiff.

J. Murray Harris, New York City, for defendant.

McDONALD, Justice.

This is an action to annul a marriage pursuant to Section 1143 of the Civil Practice Act. A verified answer denying the essential allegations of the complaint was interposed. However, at the time of the trial, the answer was withdrawn and a stipulation, not a part of the record but made with the knowledge of the court, was entered into between the parties. No alimony or counsel fee is sought by the plaintiff wife. It is within the atmosphere of this mutually satisfactory arrangement that this litigation was tried.

The only witnesses called were the plaintiff and her mother. The former testified that she and the defendant became engaged to marry in the Christmas season of 1951, after a three month courtship while she and the defendant were still college students, the plaintiff being then in her junior year. Shortly prior to the engagement, while both were examining a photograph album in the plaintiff's home and in the presence of the plaintiff's parents, the defendant is alleged to have said "we would have a large family and that we would even do the family album one better. We would have six children." To which the plaintiff replied that "that was just what she wanted and she was glad he would *try*." While similar conversations were had at other times, they were substantially the same, and it is upon this conversation that the plaintiff principally relies to establish the defendant's false and fraudulent representations. To put it most euphemistically this testimony taxes the credulity of the court. It is difficult to believe that well bred college students, not yet formally engaged, would so seriously and frankly discuss *"trying"* to have children, particularly while within ear-shot of the parents of one of them, or that if there was a discussion of having "six children," it was of a serious nature and not merely facetious banter. It is even more difficult to believe that this was the inducing cause of the marriage of these young people just out of their teens rather than the mutual attractions of young love.

[1] The natural and expected end of marriage being the procreation of children, such intention need not be expressed and would be presumed and, although not expressed, could still serve as a basis for an action of this type. Eldredge v. Eldredge, Sup., 43 N.Y.S.2d 796; Schulman v. Schulman, 180 Misc. 904, 46 N.Y.S.2d 158; Mirizio v. Mirizio, 242 N.Y. 74, 150 N.E. 605, 44 A.L.R. 714; Miller v. Miller, 132 Misc. 121, 228 N.Y.S. 657.

Shortly after the engagement was announced a party was given in honor of the young people at the newly acquired home of relatives at Spring Valley, New York. While returning to New York the defendant is alleged to have said that he would obtain and furnish a similar home where they could raise their family. This is the second of the alleged false and fraudulent representations upon which plaintiff relies. Such a promise must, we believe, be viewed in the light of common sense and experience. It is common knowledge that every young swain builds a castle in Spain, but few ever reach the brick and mortar stage. And, were they held accountable therefor, no marriage would be safe, and the hopes and dreams to which young lovers are prone would have to be scrutinized by a polygraph or other lie detecting instrument rather than the traditional rose-colored glasses.

To establish the falsity of these promises we must again rely solely upon the testimony of the plaintiff and her mother. The plaintiff testified that on their nuptial night, April 6, 1952, the defendant insisted upon using a contraceptive over her protestations and she recalled to his mind that if they were to have six children they would have to start soon. Apparently, the usual bashful approach of the newly married bride was completely lacking in this twenty year old college student who was bent upon immediately getting on with the work of procreating six children. At the risk of being accused of naiveté, the court is most incredulous. Similar conduct on the part of the defendant is alleged to have continued throughout the married life of the parties, always, of course, over the objections of the plaintiff.

The plaintiff also alleges that the defendant never provided her with the home he had promised and that although they leased an apartment and resided in it together for some months, it was furnished only with kitchen furniture supplied by the plaintiff's parents and a couch which opened into a bed. During this period both the plaintiff and the defendant continued to be students although the defendant was at least nominally a partner in his father's business and derived his principal income therefrom. He also acted at times as a substitute teacher in the public school system.

The alleged practices of the defendant and his failure to provide an adequate home led to the separation of the parties in January of 1953.

Shortly after the separation the defendant visited the plaintiff at her parents' home, at which time the following conversation took place:

"'What happened to the children that you said you would try to have with me, and what happened to the home that you said you would give to me; where are those things that you promised me before we were married,' and Alvin said that the only reason he promised that to me was because he knew I wouldn't marry him unless he would give me those things."

When the plaintiff's counsel asked for further elaboration the following colloquy took place:

"Q. Can you address yourself again, for the purpose of the Court hearing your testimony in greater detail, to that final conversation that took place with Alvin Schumer in the latter part of January, 1953? What did Alvin Schumer say to you regarding his intentions? A. That night?

"Q. Yes. A. He said that his intentions were not—he did not—he said he would not have married me—I am confused. May I start again? He said that I would not have married him if he would not have promised to have given me—given me those promises."

One would almost be convinced that these young people have familiarized themselves with the decision in Coppo v. Coppo, 163 Misc. 249, 297 N.Y.S. 744, and other similar cases before their engagement was formally announced or at least before this conversation took place. The plaintiff's mother in substance repeats the testimony of the plaintiff as to the incidents of the picture album and Spring Valley trip as well as the alleged admissions of the defendant that his representations were false when made and were only made to induce the plaintiff to marry him. Does such a record comply with the requirements of Section 1143 of the Civil Practice Act, and what is the responsibility of the court in determining not only the quantity of the proof, but also the quality and weight to be given it?

In the instant case there is a dearth of evidence from any source other than the statements of the plaintiff and her mother and the admissions of the defendant. The fact that the defendant's admissions were testified to by both the plaintiff and her mother gives them no added weight. They still remain the defendant's admissions and they do not satisfy the conscience of the court as the trier of the facts. The legislature, in adopting Section 1143 of the Civil Practice Act, must have intended the court to act as a sieve and screen out the true from the false, the credible from the incredible, rather than to act as a sponge to absorb all the testimony offered without rejecting any of it. If the court were to act otherwise, an electronic recorder would serve as well as a judge.

[2] Fraudulent intent must be clearly proved before a decree will be granted. Bentz v. Bentz, 188 Misc. 86, 87, 67 N.Y.S.2d 345, was a case wherein the plaintiff sought to annul a marriage on the ground that the defendant made a fraudulent promise to have children. At page 87 of 188 Misc., at page 346 of 67 N.Y.S.2d, the court stated as follows:

"Claims of this character are being presented to the Courts of this State in ever-increasing numbers, largely by those who cannot or will not, for various reasons, resort to the statutory ground for divorce. This subterfuge, so apparent in many recent cases, if permitted to persist, will inevitably tend to belittle the institution of marriage and bring discredit upon the Courts. The least the Court can do is scrutinize such claims with great care to the end that no marriage shall be annulled except upon clear and convincing proof of all the essential elements."

[3] While there are decisions enunciating the principle that the court must accept the positive testimony of an unimpeached and uncontradicted witness and that such testimony cannot be disregarded by the court or jury arbitrarily or capriciously, yet the rule does not apply with equal force where the witnesses are interested. In the Matter of Sebring, 238 App.Div. 281, 289, 264 N.Y.S. 379, 389, the Court stated:

"The court is never bound to give full faith and credit to the evidence of an interested witness, even though he is not directly impeached, or his testimony is uncontradicted. The credibility of such a witness must be determined as a question of fact. Gildersleeve v. Landon, 73 N.Y. 609; Brooklyn Crosstown R. R. Co. v. Strong, 75 N.Y. 591; Wohlfahrt v. Beckert, 92 N.Y. 490, 497–498."

In this case the court is called upon to determine whether "other satisfactory evidence of the facts" has been established which would compel the court to grant the plaintiff the relief sought.

[4, 5] We are not dealing here with an ordinary civil contract. What we are dealing with here is a contract of marriage which has been and still is regarded by our present-day civilization as being sacred. While it is true that the court has equity jurisdiction to annul a marriage contract based upon fraud, the fraud which will induce a court to set aside a contract of marriage is something different from the fraud which will induce the court to set aside an ordinary contract. In Butler v. Butler, 204 App.Div. 602, 605, 198 N.Y.S. 391, 394, the court stated as follows:

> "The contract of marriage is something more than a mere civil agreement between the parties, the existence of which affects only themselves. It is the basis of the family, and its dissolution, as well as its formation, is matter of public policy, in which the body of the community is deeply interested, and it is to be governed by other considerations than those which obtain with regard to any ordinary civil contract *inter partes*. For that reason the courts have been strict in laying down and in maintaining rules as to the annulment of this contract, and in requiring a somewhat higher degree of proof before permitting it to be set aside for fraud, than is requisite for the annulment of ordinary contracts."

The crux of the matter in this case is whether or not the court which had the opportunity to observe the demeanor of the witnesses is compelled as a matter of law to accept their testimony because the same is unimpeached and uncontradicted and that besides such testimony is there other satisfactory evidence of the facts required by Section 1143 of the Civil Practice Act. In Boyd v. Boyd, 252 N.Y. 422, 429, 169 N.E. 632, 634, the court, in speaking about the sufficiency of evidence in an annulment action, and the weight to be attached to the testimony of a witness, stated as follows:

> "The judge heard the sound of his voice, and gazed upon his countenance, and tells us that he believes the witness spoke the truth. * * * How can we say the judge is wrong? We never saw the witnesses. No worldling could read the printed lines before us without pausing to reflect that such things as they recount do often happen. * * * To the sophistication and sagacity of the trial judge the law confides the duty of appraisal. If these witnesses imposed upon the credulity of an experienced fact finder, this court cannot correct him. His was the opportunity, the responsibility, and the power to decide."

In De Baillet-Latour v. De Baillet-Latour, 301 N.Y. 428, 434, 94 N.E.2d 715, 717, the Court, in construing Section 1143 of the Civil Practice Act, stated:

> "However, it seems to us, that it was, in the meaning of section 1143 'other satisfactory evidence of the facts'. That language must be construed according to its purpose and, so construed, it requires only that there be in the record, in addition to 'declarations' or 'confessions' of the parties, other material from other sources, substantial and reliable enough to satisfy the conscience of the trier of the facts. See Winston v. Winston, 165 N.Y. 553, 556, 557, 59 N.E. 273, 274."

This was again repeated in Woronzoff-Daschkoff v. Woronzoff-Daschkoff, 303 N.Y. 506, 104 N.E.2d 877.

It thus appears that the other satisfactory evidence of the facts as required by Section 1143 of the Civil Practice Act has by judicial interpretation been construed to be not a rule of evidence but a rule for the guidance of judicial conscience. This principle of law with reference to a marital action was enunciated in the case of Winston v. Winston, 165 N.Y. 553, 59 N.E. 273, affirmed 189 U.S. 506, 23 S.Ct. 852, 47 L.Ed. 922, and has been referred to in the most recent cases in the Court of Appeals concerning the subject matter.

In Hochman v. Hochman, Sup., 68 N.Y.S.2d 886, 894, the rights and duties of the Court were stated as follows:

"Of course, it is true that 'The positive testimony on an unimpeached, uncontradicted witness cannot be disregarded by court or jury arbitrarily or capriciously.' Lomer v. Meeker, 25 N.Y. 361, 363, which was an action on a note where the defense was usury but which has been followed in annulment actions. But this does not mean that an Official Referee or any judicial officer is compelled by law, as a mechanical robot, to sit hermetically sealed, impervious to all light of truth from surrounding circumstances, the documentary evidence, the interest of witnesses and their demeanor, the probabilities, and the whole record. If he does not act capriciously or arbitrarily, he may reject what he reasonably believes to be false testimony."

[6] Having observed witnesses and their manner of testifying, and being aware of the adjustments made between the parties which resulted in the withdrawal of the verified answer on the day of trial, which answer had categorically denied the essential allegations of the complaint upon which it is now asked to act, the court is satisfied that the plaintiff has failed to establish her right to the relief prayed for and accordingly the complaint is dismissed.

54 F.R.D. 282

UNITED STATES ex rel. Gerald MAYO

v.

SATAN AND HIS STAFF.

Misc. No. 5357.

United States District Court,
W. D. Pennsylvania.

Dec. 3, 1971.

Civil rights action against Satan and his servants who allegedly placed deliberate obstacles in plaintiff's path and caused his downfall, wherein plaintiff prayed for leave to proceed in forma pauperis. The District Court, Weber, J., held that plaintiff would not be granted leave to proceed in forma pauperis who in view of questions of personal jurisdiction over defendant, propriety of class action, and plaintiff's failure to include instructions for directions as to service of process.

Prayer denied.

Federal Civil Procedure ⊶2734

Plaintiff would not be granted leave to proceed in forma pauperis in civil rights action against Satan and his servants, who allegedly placed deliberate obstacles in plaintiff's path and caused his downfall, in view of questions of personal jurisdiction over defendant, propriety of class action, and plaintiff's failure to include instructions for directions as to service of process. Fed.Rules Civ.Proc. rule 23, 28 U.S.C.A.; 18 U.S.C.A. § 241; 28 U.S.C.A. § 1343; 42 U.S.C.A. § 1983.

Gerald Mayo, pro se.

MEMORANDUM ORDER

WEBER, District Judge.

Plaintiff, alleging jurisdiction under 18 U.S.C. § 241, 28 U.S.C. § 1343, and 42 U.S.C. § 1983 prays for leave to file a complaint for violation of his civil rights in forma pauperis. He alleges that Satan has on numerous occasions caused plaintiff misery and unwarranted threats, against the will of plaintiff, that Satan has placed deliberate obstacles in his path and has caused plaintiff's downfall.

Plaintiff alleges that by reason of these acts Satan has deprived him of his constitutional rights.

We feel that the application to file and proceed in forma pauperis must be denied. Even if plaintiff's complaint reveals a prima facie recital of the infringement of the civil rights of a citizen of the United States, the Court has serious doubts that the complaint reveals a cause of action upon which relief can be granted by the court. We question whether plaintiff may obtain personal jurisdiction over the defendant in this judicial district. The complaint contains no allegation of residence in this district. While the official reports disclose no case where this defendant has appeared as defendant there is an unofficial account of a trial in New Hampshire where this defendant filed an action of mortgage foreclosure as plaintiff. The defendant in that action was represented by the preeminent advocate of that day, and raised the defense that the plaintiff was a foreign prince with no standing to sue in an American Court. This defense was overcome by overwhelming evidence to the contrary. Whether or not this would raise an estoppel in the present case we are unable to determine at this time.

If such action were to be allowed we would also face the question of whether it may be maintained as a class action. It appears to meet the requirements of Fed.R. of Civ.P. 23 that the class is so numerous that joinder of all members is practicable, there are questions of law and fact common to the class, and the claims of the representative party is typical of the claims of the class. We cannot now determine if the representative party will fairly protect the interests of the class.

We note that the plaintiff has failed to include with his complaint the required form of instructions for the United States Marshal for directions as to service of process.

For the foregoing reasons we must exercise our discretion to refuse the prayer of plaintiff to proceed in forma pauperis.

It is ordered that the complaint be given a miscellaneous docket number and leave to proceed in forma pauperis be denied.

394 F. Supp. 677

Mary ROE, on behalf of herself and all other persons similarly situated, Plaintiff,

v.

Honorable Calvin L. RAMPTON, individually and in his capacity as Governor of the State of Utah, Honorable Vernon B. Romney, individually and in his capacity as Attorney General of the State of Utah, Defendants.

No. C 74–344.

United States District Court,
D. Utah,
Central Division.
Jan. 17, 1975.
Dissenting Opinion March 18, 1975.

Woman who was pregnant by man who was not her husband and who wanted an abortion sought to enjoin operation of state statute requiring physician to notify the husband or parents of a woman on whom an abortion is to be performed. A Three-judge Court, Aldon J. Anderson, J., held that there was no showing of irreparable injury; and that abstention was proper.

Injunctive relief denied and order of abstention and dismissal entered.

Lewis, Chief Judge, concurred in the result and filed an opinion.

Ritter, Chief District Judge, dissented and filed an opinion.

1. Injunction ☞85(1)
Married woman who sought injunction against operation of statute which requires physicians to inform woman's husband before performing abortion did not demonstrate irreparable harm by fact that, in the circumstances of the instant case, her husband would be informed that she was pregnant by another man, on theory that she was being required to incriminate herself. U.C.A. 1953, 76–7–304(2).

2. Abortion ☞1
It cannot be said that husband has no interest in his wife's abortion. U.C.A. 1953, 76–7–304(2)

3. Courts ☞260.4
Abstention is generally proper with respect to construction of a state

statute which is susceptible of a construction by state court which might avoid federal constitutional question.

4. Courts ⬦260.4

Abstention was proper with respect to request of woman, who was pregnant by a man other than her husband, for injunctive relief against operation of state statute which requires husband or parents of woman to be notified by physician that the woman is going to have an abortion. U.C.A.1953, 76–7–304(2).

5. Abortion ⬦1

There is no rational connection between statutory requirement that doctor notify husband of wife's impending abortion and the doctor's duty to exercise his considered medical judgment as to whether to perform the abortion. U.C.A.1953,76–7–304.

David S. Dolowitz, Salt Lake City, Utah, for plaintiff.

William T. Evans, Salt Lake City, Utah, for defendants.

Before LEWIS, Chief Judge, RITTER, Chief District Judge, and ANDERSON, District Judge.

ORDER DENYING INJUNCTIVE RELIEF AND ORDER OF ABSTENTION AND DISMISSAL WITH ACCOMPANYING OPINIONS

For the reasons set forth in the separate opinions which follow, this court, on November 22, 1974, denied temporary injunctive relief and now enters its order abstaining and dismissing the above-entitled action to allow the state courts to decide the questions, including the determination of a class action, presented by this case.

It is therefore ordered that this case be and it is herewith dismissed.

ALDON J. ANDERSON, District Judge

On November 4, 1974, plaintiff in the above-entitled matter filed a class action for injunctive and declaratory relief seeking a ruling that Utah Code Ann. § 76–7–304(2) (1974) contravenes the Fifth and Fourteenth Amendments to the United States Constitution in that it is overbroad in its regulation of abortions in the State of Utah, constitutes an invasion of her privacy, invalidly regulates her relationship with her physician, and, if complied with, would force her to incriminate herself under provisions of the Utah adultery or fornication statutes.

On November 7, 1974, plaintiff filed a motion for a temporary restraining order with an accompanying memorandum. On November 8, 1974, the trial court signed an order to show cause for temporary restraining order. On November 12, 1974, at 9 a. m., oral arguments were heard and the trial court denied the motion for a temporary restraining order. At 3:30 p. m., on November 12, 1974, the trial court heard plaintiff's motion for a reconsideration of the court's earlier ruling denying the temporary restraining order. After evidence and testimony were received and oral argument was heard, the trial court reserved the question of injunctive relief for determination by the three-judge court.

The parties stipulated to the facts in the case and agreed that the matter be finally submitted, together with the request for temporary injunctive relief, to the three-judge court on November 21, 1974. The three-judge court composed of Honorable David T. Lewis, Chief Judge of the United States Court of Appeals for the Tenth Circuit, Honorable Willis W. Ritter, Chief Judge of the United States District Court for the District of Utah, and Honorable Aldon J. Anderson, Associate Judge of the United States District Court for the District of Utah, was duly convened on November 21, 1974, and the matter was presented. On November 22, 1974, pursuant to an order agreed upon by Chief Judge Lewis and Judge Anderson, with Chief Judge Ritter dissenting, a minute entry was entered denying preliminary injunctive relief, reserving for subsequent determination the other issues raised by the pleadings.

FACTS

Plaintiff Mary Roe is seventeen years of age. At the time this action was filed and at the time of the hearing she was in her first trimester of pregnancy. Preliminary injunctive relief was denied on the last day of her first trimester and she has now passed into the second trimester. She desires to have an abortion but has been advised by her physician that under the provisions of Utah Code Ann. § 76–7–304(2) (1974) he is obligated to notify her husband prior to performing an abortion upon her. Plaintiff is married but separated and estranged from her husband and a divorce is pending. Since the date of their initial separation plaintiff states she has had no sexual relationship of any kind with her husband. She claims the child she is bearing is not the child of her estranged husband. Plaintiff is unwilling to allow the doctor to inform her estranged husband of the abortion she seeks, and without complying with the notice provision of the Utah statute the physician is unwilling to perform the abortion. I agreed with Chief Judge Lewis that preliminary injunctive relief should be denied. My reasons are set forth herein. I also find that these facts make this an appropriate case for the federal court to abstain and allow the state courts an opportunity to construe or limit the scope of the statute under question.

PRELIMINARY INJUNCTION

Under the circumstances of this case, plaintiff had the burden to make a prima facie case showing (1) a resonable likelihood of prevailing on the merits, that is, a resonable probability that she would ultimately be entitled to the relief sought, and (2) irreparable injury if the specific injunctive relief sought was not granted. Crowther v. Seaborg, 415 F.2d 437, 439 (10th Cir. 1969).

IRREPARABLE INJURY

The prime requisite for temporary injunctive relief is a showing by the applicant that irreparable injury of a substantial nature is threatened by the conduct against which the restraint is sought. *See* Capital City Gas Co. v. Phillips Petroleum Co., 373 F.2d 128, 131 (2nd Cir. 1967); 7 Moore, Federal Practice ¶ 65.04 (2d ed. 1974). Plaintiff argues that irreparable injury is found in the instant case by the increasing physical risks inherent in having an abortion in the second trimester of pregancy as compared to the physical risks in the first trimester, or in not being able to secure an abortion at all. The facts, however, show that this is not the measure of irreparable injury in this case. Plaintiff is not deprived from obtaining the abortion she seeks, in either the first or second trimester of pregnancy, except by her own decision. She wants a secret abortion and has directed the physician not to notify her husband of her desire. Her physician is willing to perform the abortion, but will not do so without giving her husband notice in conformity with the provisions of the Utah statute herein cited. Irreparable injury, therefore, is measured, not by any increased physical risks or even the likelihood of not being able to have an abortion, but by the injury to plaintiff of having her husband know of the abortion. Under these circumstances notification to a husband of a desired abortion does not justify a conclusion of irreparable injury.

The dissent's statement: "I see nothing in Roe v. Wade or Doe v. Bolton that permits the woman's right to an abortion in the first trimester to be conditioned upon a showing of 'irreparable injury'" is an inaccurate characterization of the denial of preliminary injunctive relief and this discussion of irreparable injury. While it is correct that irreparable injury is not a condition precedent to obtaining an abortion in the first trimester of pregnancy, it is also a fact that the Supreme Court decisions, referred to by the dissent, do not provide a woman with an unconditional right to a "secret" abortion during any trimester of pregnancy. Irreparable injury, therefore, is discussed only to help determine whether or not preliminary injunctive relief should issue pending a determination of whether plaintiff is entitled to a "secret" abortion.

[1] The only other matter discussed by the dissent which bears upon irreparable injury is the observation that the provision of the Utah abortion statute in question requires the plaintiff, under the circumstances of this case, to incriminate herself. This argument suggests that plaintiff could be subject to prosecution under the Utah statues making adultery or fornication misdemeanors if she requested an abortion from her physician, her physician notified her husband, and her husband could convince a prosecutor to file an adultery suit. This case should not be decided by such a remote, hypothetical causal chain. The dissent has overlooked Rule 27 of the Utah Rules of Evidence, adopted by the Supreme Court of Utah effective July 1, 1971, which provides a physician-patient privilege in prosecutions of misdemeanors. The infrequent prosecution under the adultery and fornication statutes, the fact that a physician's testimony concerning plaintiff's pregnancy in such a trial would be privileged under Rule 27 of the Utah Rules of Evidence, the privilege against self incrimination which would protect plaintiff from testifying against herself, and the unknown identity of the plaintiff's unlawful impregnator eliminate any resonable likelihood of prosection for adultery.

SUBSTANTIAL LIKELIHOOD OF PREVAILING ON THE MERITS

The Supreme Court in Roe v. Wade, 410 U.S. 113, 154–55, 93 S.Ct. 705, 35 L.Ed.2d 147 (1973) held that a right to an abortion is fundamental and can therefore be regulated only on the basis of a compelling state interest. In this regard, the Court found that a state has two important and legitimate interests: (1) in protecting maternal health and (2) in protecting the life or potential life of the fetus. However, neither of these interests can be "compelling" throughout the entire pregnancy. During the first trimester of pregacy, the Supreme Court has held that neither interest is sufficiently compelling to justify an interference with an abortion decision of the woman and her physician. During the second trimester, the interest in maternal health increases and the state may regulate the abortion procedure to the extent that the regulation reasonably relates to the preservation and protection of maternal health. During the third trimester, the fetus becomes viable and the interest in protecting it increases, which allows the state to reasonably regulate abortion, taking into account both interests.

In the first trimester of pregancy "the attending physician, in consultation with his patient, is free to determine, without regulation by the State, that, in his medical judgment, the patient's pregnancy should be terminated." Roe v. Wade, *supra* at 163, 93 S.Ct. at 732. The Supreme Court's observations on "medical judgment" from Doe v. Bolton, 410 U.S. 179, 192, 93 S.Ct. 739, 747, 35 L.Ed.2d 201 (1973) are also relevant:

> We agree with the District Court, 319 F.Supp. [1048] at 1058, that the medical judgment may be exercised in the light of all factors—physical, emotional, psychological, familial, and the woman's age—relevant to the well-being of the patient. All these factors may relate to health. This allows the attending physician the room he needs to make his best medical judgment. And it is room that operates for the benefit, not the disadvantage, of the pregnant woman.

With this constitutional backdrop, the statute in question, Utah Code Ann. § 76–7–304 (1974), provides:

> Considerations by physician—Notice to minor's parents or guardian or married woman's husband.—To enable the physician to exercise his best medical judgment, he shall:

(1) Consider all factors relevant to the well-being of the woman upon whom the abortion is to be performed including, but not limited to,

(a) Her physical, emotional and psychological health and safety,

(b) Her age,

(c) Her familial situation.

(2) Notify, if possible, the parents or guardian of the woman upon whom the abortion is to be performed, if she is a minor or the husband of the woman, if she is married.

Weighing the constitutional considerations provided by the Supreme Court decisions cited above against the Utah statute in question, I am unable to conclude that there is a substantial likelihood that plaintiff will prevail on the merits of this suit. This conclusion is based upon an appraisal of the merits of the case and several theories that would allow a construction of the questioned statute in a manner that would avoid a constitutional confrontation.

First, the challenged subsection 2 of the Utah statute which provides for notice to be given, if possible, to the husband of a woman securing an abortion might be sustained as a valid provision intended to provide the physician with relevant information concerning the woman's physical, emotional, psychological or familial situation in order for him to exercise his best medical judgment. The statute, admittedly, is awkwardly drafted as a provision to supply relevant medical data to the physician since it does not require the doctor to receive or even seek any information apart from merely notifying the husband of the abortion decision. It was acknowledged at the hearing by plaintiff's cousel that "in all probability" a consultation with the husband would have some medical significance in determining the psychological profile of the woman. (Transcript at 21.) I am unable to say that this provision does not contemplate that in the notification process that some relevant information, albeit minimal, would be exchanged. Even if no relevant information were exchanged in the notification process, the mere observation by the doctor of the reaction of the husband or parents to the abortion decision would provide insight into the psychological or familial setting into which the woman would return following the abortion. The requirement "to notify, if possible" is minimal. No spousal or parental consent is required. The abortion decision is left to the woman and her physician, as is constitutionally required. A reasonable construction of the provision would allow it to be sustained as providing at least some relevant insight into the woman's present or future health.

Second, the notification provision of the Utah statute could be justified since a husband or parents have a recognized interest in the abortion decision being contemplated. The nature of the husband's interest has been recognized and explained by commentators and courts alike.

In Brodie, Marital Procreation, 37 Oregon L.Rev. 245, 246 (1972) it states:

> One of the rights of marriage is the right to procreate. In Meyer v. Nebraska, the Supreme Court spoke of the due process "right of the individual . . . to marry, establish a home and bring up children. . ." In Skinner v. Oklahoma, the Court stated that "[m]arriage and procreation are fundamental to the very existence and survival of the race," and proceeded to use an equal-protection argument as the basis for striking down legislation authorizing the sterilization of certain criminals. An equally positive description is found in the approval of a legislative divorce in the 1888 case of Maynard v. Hill where marriage was called "the foundation of the family and of society, without which there would be neither civilization nor progress."

The case of Doe v. Doe, Mass., 314 N. E.2d 128 (1974) decided by the Supreme Court of Massachusetts states:

> We are deeply conscious of the husband's interest in the abortion decision, at least while the parties are living together in harmony. Surely that interest is legitimate. Surely, if the family life is to prosper, he should participate with his wife in the decision. But it does not follow that he must have an absolute veto, or that his veto, reasoned or unreasoned, can be enforced by the Commonwealth.

The United States District Court for the Southern District of Florida in the case of Coe v. Gerstein, 376 F.Supp. 695, decided April 17, 1974, sitting as a three-judge court, observed:

> We recognize that the interest of the husband in the embryo or fetus carried by his wife, especially if he is the father, is qualitatively different from the interest which the mother may have in her health and the interest of the viable fetus in its potential life. The interest which a husband has in seeing his procreation carried full term is, perhaps, at least equal to that of the mother. The biological bifurcation of the sexes, which dictates that the female alone carry the procreation of the two sexes, should not necessarily foreclose the active participation of the male in decisions relating to whether their mutual procreation should be aborted or allowed to prosper. It may be that the husband's interest in this mutual procreation attaches at the moment of conception.

The Supreme Court expressly recognized in footnote 67 in Roe v. Wade, *supra,* that an interest in the father was not ruled out by its decision:

> Neither in this opinion nor in Doe v. Bolton, 410 U.S. 179 [93 S.Ct. 739, 35 L.Ed.2d 201], do we discuss the father's rights, if any exist in the constitutional context, in the abortion decision.

The nature of the interest in the family of a minor is also well established and stated concisely by the Court in Prince v. Massachusetts, 321 U.S. 158, 166, 64 S.Ct. 438, 442, 88 L.Ed. 645 (1943):

> It is cardinal with us that the custody, care and nurture of the child reside first in the parents, whose primary function and freedom include preparation for obligations the state can neither supply nor hinder.

[2] An abortion operation is different and easily distinguished from other operations in which an absolute right to the control of one's body might be argued. A husband is a partner to his wife's pregnancy and has an interest in the future posterity and fruits of the marriage relationship. The marriage contract contemplates the making of a home and the raising of a family—basic goals of tremendous importance to society. The Supreme Court has not yet considered whether or not a husband's consent may be required before an abortion may be performed on his wife. This question is also not before this court. The Utah statute in question would merely provide the husband with notification of the abortion decision. I believe that the husband should have the right to be advised concerning any significant action affecting the family life. Even though not presently given a right to determine with his wife whether an abortion should be had, the husband being apprised of a contemplated abortion should have an opportunity to consult with her. It is socially and constitutionally naive to consider the abortion decision as solely a woman's concern.

That the Utah Legislature recognized an interest in the husband or parents of a minor in the area of abortion is evidenced in several ways. First, the Legislature included the abortion statute in part 3 of Chapter 7 of the Utah Criminal Code entitled, "Offenses Against the Family." A family contemplates a husband if the woman is married, or parents if the woman is an unmarried minor. Second, § 76–7–304's predecessor (§ 76–7–304 in the 1973 Utah Abortion Statute) showed a strong concern for such an interest in these words: "Inasmuch as various persons have an interest in through an unborn child . . .." The new § 76–7–304 bearing the title, "Considerations by physician—Notice to minor's parents or guardian or married woman's husband" provides notice to the same persons recognized by the old statute to have an interest in the unborn child. Although it is arguable that the purpose of the notice provision under question is limited by the introductory phrase regarding the best medical judgment of the physician, it is more likely that the Legislature was concerned not only with the health and well-being of the mother, but also with providing at least some protection to the interest of the husband or parents under appropriate circumstances. Further, the 1974 statute retains a majority of the provisions of the 1973 statute. The Legislature modified only those portions thought necessary to render the statute constitutional after this court struck it down last year. Third, it may be argued that the Legislature did not require notice to be given in the case of a pregnant, unmarried 18-year-old woman because technically she has reached her majority.

In defending a constitutional attack on a statute under the strict scrutiny analysis, a state must show an interest of a "compelling" nature. In asserting state interests, states are not limited to only those interests or purposes described in the title, preamble, or text of the statute, but may raise any interests which plausibly and logically are also purposes implicit in the statute. It is deemed sufficient if the attorney general raises such interests in defending the constitutionality of the statute. *See* Gunther, Foreword: In Search of Evolving Doctrine on a Changing Court: A Model for a Newer Equal Protection, 86 Harv.L.Rev. 1, 47 (1972). The state argued the husband's interest in its case before this court. We are therefore not precluded from seriously weighing the husband's interest in the "compelling state interest" computation despite any contrary argument raised in connection with the limiting introductory phrase in the text of the statute. I am unable to say at this time that the husband's interest is not a "compelling state interest" which would sustain the notification provision under attack.

Considering only the facts presented by plaintiff's case, it might be argued that the husband here has no interest because he is not the father, and with a divorce pending there may be no future familial relationship to consider. We must consider the husband's interest in this case, however, because the attack on the statute is made in the form of a class action—the plaintiff purporting to represent "a class made up of women having unwanted pregnancies who desire to abort and terminate said pregnancies. . . ." Our considerations must be broader than plaintiff's specific facts as long as there are possible class action implications respecting all women with unwanted pregnancies.[1]

The plaintiff has failed to meet the dual requirement for the preliminary injunction in this case. Plaintiff has shown neither irreparable injury nor a substantial likelihoood of success on the merits. For these reasons, I joined in the order denying preliminary injunctive relief.

ABSTENTION

[3] Abstention is permissible only in narrowly limited special circumstances, but one of the special circumstances is when the challenged state statute is susceptible of a construction by the state courts that would avoid or modify the federal constitutional question. Harrison v. NAACP, 360 U.S. 167, 176–77, 79 S.Ct. 1025, 3 L.Ed.2d 1152 (1959). In Lake Carriers' Ass'n v. MacMullan, 406 U.S. 498, 511 92 S.Ct. 1749, 1757, 32 L. Ed.2d 257 (1972), a case involving a constitutional challenge to Michigan's Watercraft Polution Control Act of 1970 in which the Supreme Court sanctioned abstention, the Court quoted Harman v. Forssenius, 380 U.S. 528, 534, 85 S.Ct. 1177, 14 L.Ed.2d 50 (1965) as follows:

---

[1]Even if only plaintiff's facts were being considered, the court is concerned about the precedent that might be set if it were to rule that a woman who was pregnant by one other than her husband was not factually under the Utah statute and would therefore secure an abortion without notification being given to her husband. Would this allow a woman to circumvent the requisites of the Utah abortion statute merely by secretly alleging to her physician that the pregnancy was conceived by one other than her husband? If a valid interest in the husband exists, it should not be defeated by an *ex parte* representation of spousal infidelity.

> Where resolution of the federal constitutional question is dependent upon, or may be materially altered by, the determination of an uncertain issue of state law, abstention may be proper in order to avoid unnecessary friction in federal-state relations, interference with important state functions, tentative decisions on questions of state law, and premature constitutional adjudication. . . . The doctrine . . . contemplates that deference to state court adjudication only be made where the issue of state law is uncertain.

Following this rationale, a three-judge court in our circuit abstained last year in an abortion case. Judges Holloway, Barrow and Eubanks considered the constitutionality of the Oklahoma criminal abortion statutes and related laws in Henrie et al. v. Derryberry et al., D.C., 358 F.Supp. 719 (1973). They found several of the abortion provisions unconstitutional; however, regarding the Oklahoma statute prohibiting the destruction of a quick child, that court said:

> We must, however, recognize the right of the State courts to construe or limit the statute so as to save its constitutionality. *Id.* at 726.

* * * * *

> Abstention by the Federal courts is most appropriate where, as here, the State law is uncertain and susceptible of a construction that would avoid or modify the federal constitutional issue. *Id.*

[4] It is apparent that there are possible constructions of the provision in question which would avoid a constitutional confrontation. I, therefore, would abstain for the state courts to decide the questions, including the determination of a class action, presented by this case.

LEWIS, Chief Judge (concurring).

[3,4] Each of my fellow judges has chosen to write at some length in this case and has arrived at a different conclusion from reasoning bound to the extreme and opposite ends of the spectrum concerning the emotional and agonizing subject of abortion. Judge Anderson has earlier joined with me in an order denying temporary injunctive relief to plaintiff and I now agree with and join Judge Anderson in holding that the court should abstain from entering a declaratory judgment. The basic problem here is the interpretation of a state statute which, absent exceptional circumstances, should be left to and is the responsibility of the state courts. So, too, it is not desirable to issue declaratory or advisory comments and views of an anticipatory nature as a fore-guess on matters presently pending before the Supreme Court of the United States. However, in deciding to deny injunctive relief and thereafter abstain, the members of the court have necessarily had to consider some unsettled areas in the field of abortion and I consider it necessary to express, largely by summary, the areas in which I agree and disagree with my Brothers where the particular posture of this case requires it.

[5] 1. I do not accept the claim that there is a rational connection between the statutory requirement that the doctor notify the husband of the wife's impending abortion and the doctor's duty to exercise his considered medical judgment as to whether to perform the abortion. If it is necessary or even desirable for the doctor to consult with the husband that fact is not apparent on the statute's face nor is there any evidence in this record to establish it. Nor do I accept in any way as desirable that it should be the statutory duty of the doctor to notify the hus-

band of his wife's condition. This duty, if such it be, lies with the wife and when imposed upon the doctor would seem to project him very personally into a family situation unrelated to his professional commitment to his patient. Such a burden might well act as a deterrent to his willingness to perform the operation, and were this "chilling effect" established by expert testimony it might well invalidate the statute. Thus I consider the subject statute to be faulty in this regard. However, I do not deem this factor determinative of the case. Here, it was stipulated that the doctor was *willing* to notify the husband, absent the wife's objection. To me, the doctor's *willingness* was a prime factor leading to my vote to deny injunctive relief.

[1] 2. I reject entirely the premise that any legal significance attaches to the claim of plaintiff that she became pregnant by someone other than her husband. She volunteered this information to her doctor who, in turn, had no statutory obligation to reveal that information to anyone. I see no violation of the confidential doctor-patient relationship in this regard nor any side effect of criminal prosecution under state law. Every *unmarried* woman who recieves an abortion must admit to her doctor an earlier act in violation of state law. Here, the revelation of adultery is no different. The more basic question is whether the woman has to reveal the fact of her marriage at all and the Supreme Court has settled this matter. In Doe v. Bolton, 410 U.S. 179, 93 S.Ct. 739, 35 L.Ed.2d 201, it was specifically held that the woman's familial situation was a proper medical consideration in the formation of a considered medical judgment.

[2] 3. Finally, I find nothing in any Supreme Court decision that in any way negatives a husband's legal interest in the abortion of his wife. To the contrary, this question has been recognized by the High Court and pending cases have submitted that issue for consideration. The Utah statute does not require the husband to *consent* to the operation. It requires only that he be *notified* of her intent to have an abortion. If the husband has any legal interest in the abortion of his wife, such interest must begin with knowledge of the situation. The Utah statute requires no more and, to me, it would be a constitutional anomaly to hold that such a requirement is patently unconstitutional so as to invalidate the statute as plaintiff here seeks and to grant immediate relief as requested. I am certainly not prepared to say that a husband has no interest, actual, legal or otherwise, in his wife's abortion.

RITTER, Chief District Judge (dissenting).

The plaintiff is a child under the age of 18, separated from her husband against whom she has filed for divorce. She has had no sexual relationship with her husband since the initial separation, and he is not the father.

She is in the first trimester of her pregnancy, desires an abortion, has requested her physician to perform it, and he, in his best medical judgment, believes the abortion should be performed in the interest of her physical and mental health. He is willing to perform it, but unwilling to risk prosecution as a felon[1] for

---

[1]"Any person who performs, procures or supplies the means for an abortion other than authorized by this chapter is guilty of a felony of the second degree", and subject to a prison term of up to fifteen years or a fine of up to $10,000. Utah Code Ann. § 76–7–314 (Laws of Utah 1974), and §§ 76–3–203, 76–3–301 (Laws of Utah 1973). The violation by a physician may also be basis for disciplinary action for unprofessional conduct. See Utah Code Ann. (1953) §§ 58–12–35 and 58–1–25.

violation of section 76–7–304(2), Utah Code Annotated (1974), and has told plaintiff he will not perform the abortion without informing her husband of her intent to obtain it. She has directed her doctor not to inform her husband.

The Utah Legislature first requires that "No abortion may be performed in this state without the concurrence of the attending physician, based on his best medical judgment." Section 76–7–303 Utah Code Annotated (1974).

And now, the Legislature has added another requirement, "To enable the physician to exercise his best medical judgment, he shall . . . Notify, if possible, the parents or guardian of the woman upon whom the abortion is to be performed, if she is a minor or the husband of the woman, if she is married." Section 76–7–304(2).

Note the phrase: "To enable the physician to exercise his best medical judgment, he shall . . . Notify," etc. No evidence was offered remotely tending to show anything at all the husband could supply to assist the physician. On the contrary, as we shall see.

Two of the judges of this court have denied plaintiff injunctive relief on the ground: " It appears that the plaintiff is not deprived from obtaining the abortion she seeks except by her own decision. . . . The plaintiff has directed the physician not to inform her husband of the desired abortion. Under these circumstances the court does not believe a conclusion of irreparable injury is justified."

From this "Order" I dissent for the reasons hereinafter set out, including the reason that the statement of the facts stipulated to is incomplete, misleading, and legally insufficient.

These judges say, the girl has the "key" to obtain an abortion. She has a key all right—a key to her own special brand of hell, which the legislature has cunningly contrived for her.

It is clear as the bright sunlight on a summer's day what the husband in such a situation as the present will do. The girl is suing him for divorce, presumably making the usual demands: support money, property settlement, and findings that he wronged her. He will fight back, and the families, friends and acquaintances will choose up sides.

Into this fray, with an atmosphere already highly charged, the girl's physician drops news, not less explosive than TNT: "Your wife is pregnant by another man and wants an abortion."

The result is inevitable, immediate, catastrophic, and terribly destructive. Common knowledge tells us, and the woman, such news is published in the court proceedings, and is ferreted out and spread far and wide through the sensational newspapers and broadcasters.

She will feel in her heart, as did Hester Prynne,[2] the

"whole dismal severity of the puritanic code of law." She "underwent an agony * * * as if her heart had been flung into the street for them all to *spurn and trample* upon." (pp. 60 and 63–64. Emphasis added.)

[2]Nathaniel Hawthorne, *The Scarlet Letter*, New York: Random House, Inc. (1950).

"The grim beadle now made a gesture with his staff. 'Make way, good people, make way, in the King's name!' cried he. 'Open a passage, and, I promise ye, Mistress Prynne shall be set where man, woman, and child may have a fair sight of her * * * from this time till an hour past meridian. A blessing on the righteous Colony of the Massachusetts, where iniquity is dragged out into the sunshine! Come along Madam Hester, and show your scarlet letter in the market place!" (p. 63.)

"'Truly, friend; and methinks it must gladden your heart, after your troubles and sojourn in the wilderness,' said the townsman, 'to find yourself, at length, in a land where iniquity is searched out, and punished in the sight of rulers and people; as here in our godly New England.'" (p. 71.)

"'Now, good Sir, our Massachusetts magistracy * * * in their great mercy and tenderness of heart, they have doomed Mistress Prynne to stand only a space of three hours on the platform of the pillory, and then and thereafter, for the remainder of her natural life, to wear a mark of shame upon her bosom.'" (p. 72.)

"There can be no outrage, methinks, against our common nature—whatever be the delinquencies of the individual—no outrage more flagrant than to forbid the culprit to hide his face for shame: as it was the essence of this punishment to do." (p. 64.)

It is "wronging the very nature of woman to force her to lay open her heart's secrets in such broad daylight and in the presence of such a multitude." (p. 75.)

"The voice which had called her attention was that of the reverend and famous John Wilson, the eldest clergyman of Boston, a great scholar like most of his contemporaries in the profession, and withal a man of kind and genial spirit. This last attribute, however, had been less carefully developed than his intellectual gifts, and was, in truth, rather a matter of shame than self-congratulation with him. There he stood, with a border of grizzled locks beneath his skullcap, while his gray eyes, accustomed to the shaded light of his study, were winking, like those of Hester's infant, in the unadulterated sunshine. He looked like the darkly engraved portraits which we see prefixed to old volumes of sermons; and had no more right than one of those portraits would have, to step forth, as he now did, and meddle with a question of human guilt, passion and anguish." (pp. 74–75.)

"The other eminent characters by whom the chief ruler was surrounded were distinguished by a dignity of mien belonging to a period when the forms of authority were felt to posess the sacredness of Divine institutions. They were, doubtless, good men, just, and sage. But, out of the whole human family, it would not have been easy to select the same number of wise and virtuous persons who should be less capable of sitting in judgment of an erring woman's heart, and disentagling its mesh of good and evil, than the sages of rigid aspect towards whom Hester Prynne now turned her face." (p. 74.)

This is the price the plaintif has to pay for her abortion. The Utah statute exacts it. She must give up her right of privacy.

This is the right of privacy which the United States Supreme Court held was "founded in the Fourteenth Amendment's concept of *personal liberty* and restriction upon state action", and which the Court held "is broad enough to encompass a woman's decision whether or not to terminate her pregnancy." Roe v. Wade, 410 U.S. 113, at page 153, 93 S. Ct. 705, at page 727, 35 L.Ed.2d 147 (1973). (Emphasis added.)

This is the right of privacy of which the Court said in Eisenstadt v. Baird, 405 U.S. 438, at page 453, 92 S.Ct. 1029, at page 1038, 31 L.Ed.2d 349 (1972):

"If the right of privacy means anything, it is the right of the individual, married or single, to be free from unwarranted governmental intrusion into matters so fundamentally affecting a person as the decision whether to bear or beget a child."

And, this is the right of privacy which was held constitutionally protected by the United States Court for the District of Utah in Doe v. Rampton, 366 F.Supp. 189 (D.Utah, 1973). We there declared the predecessors to this statute Sections 76–7–303, 76–7–304, and 76–7–305 Utah Code Ann. (1973), which required the consent of the husband or parents to an abortion, "unconstitutional and totally void."[3]

The decision of the three-judge federal district court should have been followed here on the principle of *stare decisis.*

[5] The state legislature has attempted, in the section under consideration, to inform a physician that he must, to exercise his best clinical judgment, notify the parents or husband of a woman who seeks an abortion. On the face of this statute it is clear that this notification requirement is without any rational basis and is not in any sense connected with the exercise by a physician of his best medical judgment. It is really an attempt to inform the physician by law what shall be his medical judgment based on factors which are non-medical in nature. It applies to all abortions, at all stages of pregnancy.

This is clearly unconstitutional and void in the first two trimesters of pregnancy under the decision of the Supreme Court in Roe v. Wade, 410 U.S. 113, 93 S.Ct. 705, 35 L.Ed.2d 147 (1973).

Section 76–7–304(2), Utah Code Annotated (1974), creates an overbroad regulation of a constitutionally protected right, that is, the right of privacy which encompasses both the right of the privacy of the woman to decide to have an abortion on her own without regulation by the State and her right to a doctor-patient relationship free of regulation by the State in the exercise of this constitutionally protected right. Doe v. Bolton, 410 U.S. 179, 183, 191–200, 93 S.Ct. 739, 35 L.Ed.2d 201 (1973).

The Supreme Court of the United States held that in regulating the exercise of a constitutionally protected right which is fundamental in nature such as is true in the instant case, the regulation must be on the basis of a "compelling state interest," 410 U.S. at 155, 93 S.Ct. at 728. Any regulation of this fundamental interest must be "narrowly drawn to express only the legitimate state interests at stake," 410 U.S. at 155, 93 S.Ct. at 728. There is no compelling state interest at stake in requiring notification of any person in regard to the decision to perform an abortion. This statute is an attempt to effectuate indirectly what could not be done directly. The attempt by the Legislature of the State of Utah to require the

---

[3]Lewis, Chief Judge: "Accordingly, and for the reasons stated by my brothers, I agree that sections *303, 304, 305,* 307, 308, 311, 314, and 316 are unconstitutional and totally invalid." 366 F.Supp. at 199.

Ritter, Judge: "Section 76–7–304 is invalid because it subjects exercise of the individual right of privacy of the mother, in all abortions at all stages of pregnancy, to the consent of others." 366 F.Supp. at 193.

Anderson, Judge: "I concur with the majority in striking the following sections: part of *303,* and *all of 304,* 305, 307, 308, 309, 311, 314 and 316." 366 F. Supp. at 200.

consent of persons other than the doctor and his patient to the abortion was struck down as being constitutionally invalid. Doe v. Rampton, 366 F.Supp. 189 (D.Utah, 1973). The challenged statute is an attempt to do indirectly what was declared could not be done directly.

The Supreme Court held in regard to the first trimester:

". . . for the period of pregnancy prior to this 'compellng' point, the attending physician in consultation with his patient, is free to determine, *without regulation by the State,* that in his medical judgment, the patient's pregnancy should be terminated. If that decision is reached, the judgment may be effectuated by an abortion *free of interference by the State.*" (emphasis added) 410 U.S. at 163, 93 S.Ct. at 732.

The Court stated in regard to the second trimester:

"With respect to the State's important and legitimate interest in the health of the mother, the 'compelling' point, in the light of present medical knowledge, is at approximately the end of the first trimester . . . It follows that, from and after this point, a State may regulate the abortion procedure to the extent that the regulation reasonably relates to the preservation and protection of maternal health. Examples of permissible state regulation in this area are requirements as to the qualifications of the person who is to perform the abortion; as to the licensure of that person; as to the facility in which the procedure is to be performed, that is, whether it must be a hospital, or may be a clinic or some other place of less-than-hospital status; as to the licensing of the facility and the like." 410 U.S. at 163, 93 S.Ct. at 732.

The provisions of Section 76–7–304(2), Utah Code Annotated (1974), require the plaintiff to incriminate herself. If her physician carries out the directives of that statute and informs her estranged husband that she desires an abortion, he will then be in a position to bring charges against her by her own admission, pursuant to the provisions of Section 76–7–103 or Section 76–7–104, Utah Code Annotated (1974). He would be made aware of the fact that the child she was expecting would not be his own. This is clearly contrary to the provisions of the Fifth and Fourteenth Amendments to the Constitution of the United States of America.

Among the other vices of this statute are that in all abortions and all stages of pregnancy the woman, in order to obtain an abortion, must surrender her doctor-patient privilege of confidentiality, and as well her privilege against self-incrimination protected by the Fifth and Fourteenth Amendments to the Constitution of the United States. Nothing could be more clearly unconstitutional and utterly void.

Plaintiff has been most grievously injured, and not at all of her own choosing. I am afraid my brothers, on this court, have gone the legislature one better. I see nothing in Roe v. Wade or Doe v. Bolton that permits the woman's right to an abortion in the first trimester to be conditioned upon a showing of "irreparable injury". All that the Supreme Court requires is that she, with her physician, decides should have an abortion.

Let us see clearly what the United States Supreme Court is telling us: This is a free country in which people can make their own decisions. There is nothing in what the Supreme Court said that forces a woman to have an abortion and there is nothing that forces a doctor to perform an abortion.

All the Supreme Court held is that the woman and her doctor, in the first trimester, are permitted to follow their consciences in this matter without having their consciences dictated by the state legislature.

What the Justices are saying is: We think in this situation neither side has the right to force its position on the other side.

The Supreme Court protects the right of the woman; and what the Justices say is quite clear: There is a fundamental basic right, personal to the woman, to decide whether and when to have a child.

The Court relies upon the integrity of the doctor and the natural solicitude of the mother for her babe.

The old abortion law was a drastic constitutional invasion of the rights of human beings, namely, women, who were compelled to go through with a pregnancy, which is a form of involuntary servitude.

And there is something terribly wrong about compulsory pregnancy in a society where men and women are supposed to have freedom of choice, and a right of privacy, constitutionally guaranteed.

The Supreme Court in these decisions is not forcing anything on anybody. The decision is a declaration of freedom of choice—a declaration of independence for women. And that seems to me to be a mighty good point of view this year, being the 355th since the landing of the Puritans in Massachusetts, and the eve of the 200th anniversary of the signing of the Declaration of Independence.

It is high time we learned the lessons from Salem Village and the Massachusetts Bay Colony. They have more than antiquarian interest for us today. Three hundred years is long enough.

The court should find the provisions of Section 76–7–304(2), Utah Code Annotated (1974) unconstitutional and void and their enforcement should be restrained.

DISSENTING FROM THE COURT'S ABSTENTION IN C 74–344

This is an action for injunctive and declaratory relief as authorized by 42 U.S.C. § 1983 to secure rights, privileges and immunities established by the Fifth and Fourteenth Amendments to the United States Constitution. The plaintiff seeks an injunction to restrain the defendants, their agents, employees, and successors in office from applying, enforcing and implementing Utah Code Ann. §76–7–304(2) (1974), hereinafter called the notice-requirement provision of Utah's anti-abortion statutes. For the reasons discussed above, I believe that the notice-requirement provision constitutes an invalid and overreaching interference with the right of privacy, attempts unlawfully to regulate the relationship between the plaintiff and her physician in violation of the Supreme Court's holdings in Roe v. Wade, supra, and Doe v. Bolton, supra, and forces the plaintiff to take actions which may tend to incriminate her in violation of the Fifth and Fourteenth Amendments.

My two associates earlier joined in an order denying temporary injunctive relief to the plaintiff and now join in holding that the Court should abstain from entering a declaratory judgment. My reasons for dissenting from the denial of injunctive relief are set forth above. I shall now set forth my reasons for dissenting from the order of abstention.

Although a number of opinions of the United States Supreme Court, the Courts of Appeals and federal district courts approve the so-called "abstention doctrine" whereby federal courts refuse to adjudicate the constitutionality of state statutes until state courts have been afforded an opportunity to pass upon them, I believe that this case does not present a proper context for abstention.

In 1821 in the famous case of Cohens v. Virginia, 6 Wheat. 264, 403, 5 L.Ed. 257, Chief Justice Marshall stated, with singular force:

> It is most true, that this court will not take jurisdiction if it should not: but it is equally true, that it must take jurisdiction, if it should. The judiciary cannot, as the legislature may, avoid a measure, because it approaches the confines of the constitution. We cannot pass it by, because it is doubtful. With whatever doubts, with whatever difficulties, a case may be attended, we must decide it, if it be brought before us. We have no more right to decline the exercise of jurisdiction which is given, than to usurp that which is not given. The one or the other would be treason to the constitution. Questions may occur, which we would gladly avoid; but we cannot avoid them. All we can do is, to exercise our best judgment, and conscientiously to perform our duty.

In the present case the plaintiff and an Assistant Attorney General of the State of Utah were properly before the Court, prepared to litigate the constitutionality of the notice-requirement provision. However, each of my fellow judges chose to "decline the exercise of jurisdiction which is given" and, in effect, invited the plaintiff, who was entering the second trimester of her pregnancy, to pursue her constitutional claim in state courts. In this regard I am persuaded that Justice Douglas has stated the better view:

> I think the federal courts, created by the First Congress, are today a haven where rights can sometimes be adjudicated even more dispassionately than in state tribunals. At least Congress in its wisdom has provided since 1875 (18 Stat. 470) that the lower federal courts should be the guardian of federal rights. . . . And in my view there is no more appropriate tribunal for an adjudication of that issue than the Federal District Court . . . This is not intermeddling in state affairs nor creating needless friction. It is an authoritative pronouncement at the beginning of a controversy which saves countless days in the slow, painful, and costly litigation of separate individual lawsuits . . . Martin v. Creasy, 360 U.S. 219, 79 S. Ct. 1034, 3 L.Ed.2d 1186 (Douglas, J., dissenting in part), 228–29, 79 S.Ct. 1039 (1959).]

In the present case my associates seem to believe that because a state law has been challenged in federal court, the state courts should first be called upon to give the law some construction which might save it. However, they disagree about why the abstention should be invoked, as well as about which construction the state courts might give to the notice-requirement provision in order to save it.

Judge Anderson believes that the notice-requirement provision may have a valid medical justification and also may protect the father's and parents' interest in the fetus. Judge Lewis explicitly rejects the alleged medical justification, but not the alleged protection of the husband's interest. In this case, however, the estranged husband against whom a divorce action was pending was not the father of the plaintiff's child. It is difficult to see what interest he may have in the fetus, except perhaps to raise its existence as a shield or as a sword in the divorce proceedings.

Judge Anderson believes that "Abstention is permissible *only* in narrowly limited special circumstances . . .", whereas Judge Lewis believes that "a state statute . . ., *absent* exceptional circumstances, should be left to and is the responsibility of the state courts." (Emphasis is added.) However, Justice Frankfurter, concurring in the result but dissenting from the abstention rationale in Alabama Public Service Commission v. Southern Railway, 341 U.S. 341, 360–61, 71 S.Ct. 762, 774, 95 L.Ed. 1002, stated:

> Equity by its very nature denies relief if, on balance of considerations relevant to equity, it would be inequitable to grant the extraordinary remedy of an injunction. Federal courts of equity have always acted on this equitable doctrine. But it was never a doctrine of equity that a federal court should exercise its judicial discretion to dismiss a suit merely because a State court could entertain it.

> This is so because discretion based solely on the availability of a remedy in State courts would for all practical purposes repeal the Act of 1875. This Act gave to the federal courts a jurisdiction not theretofore possessed so that a State could not tie up a litigant making such a claim by requiring that he bring suit for redress in its own courts. That jurisdiction was precisely the jurisdiction to hear constitutional challenge to local action on the basis of the vast limitations placed upon state action by the Civil War amendments . . .

> I regret my inability to make clear to the majority of this Court that its opinion is in flagrant contradiction with the unbroken course of decisions in this Court for seventy-five years.

Justice Douglas in his dissenting opinion in Harrison v. N.A.A.C.P., 360 U.S. 167, 179–81 and 184, 79 S.Ct. 1025, 1031, 3 L.Ed.2d 11523, criticises the use of the abstention doctrine in cases which arise under the Civil Rights Act. His criticism is clearly applicable to my associates' abstention in the present case:

> The rule invoked by the Court to require the Federal District Court to keep hands off this litigation until the state court has construed these laws is a judge-made rule. It was fashioned in 1941 in the decision of Railroad Commission of Texas v. Pullman Co., 312 U.S. 496 [61 S.Ct. 643, 85 L.Ed. 971], as a device to avoid needless friction under the Federal Constitution where a resolution of state law questions might make those adjudications unnecessary. Since that time, the rule of the Pullman case has been greatly expanded. It has indeed been extended so far as to make the presence in federal court litigation of a state law question a convenient excuse for requiring the federal court to hold its hand while a second litigation is undertaken in state court. This is a delaying tactic that may involve years of time and that inevitably doubles the cost of litigation. When used widespread, it dilutes the stature of the Federal District Courts, making them secondary tribunals in the administration of justice under the Federal Constitution.

> With all due resepct, this case seems to me to be the most inappropriate one of all in which to withhold the hand of the Federal District Court. Congress has ordained in the Civil Rights Act that . . . "Every person who, under color of any statute . . . subjects, or causes to be subjected, any citizen of the United States or other person . . . to the deprivation of any rights . . . secured by the Constitution and laws (is subjected to suit) . . ." 42 U.S.C. § 1983; and has given the District Courts "original jurisdiction" of actions "to redress the deprivation, under color of any State law, . . . of any right . . . secured by the Constitution of the United States or by any Act of Congress providing for equal rights of

citizens . . ." 28 U.S.C. § 1343. The latter section was invoked here. From the time when Congress first implemented the Fourteenth Amendment by the comprehensive Civil Rights Act of 1871 the thought has prevailed that the federal courts are the unique tribunals which are to be utilized to preserve the civil rights of the people. Representative Dawes, in the debate on the 1871 bill, asked "what is the proper method of thus securing the free and undisturbed enjoyment of these rights?" Looking to the Act which eventually became law he answered, "The first remedy proposed by this bill is a resort to the courts of the United States. Is that a proper place in which to find redress for any such wrongs? If there be power to call into the courts of the United States an offender against these rights, privileges and immunities; and hold him to account there, I submit . . . that there is no tribunal so fitted, where equal and exact justice would be more likely to be meted out in temper, in moderation, in severity, if need be, but always according to the law and fact, as that great tribunal of the Constitution." Cong. Globe, 42d Cong., 1st Sess. 476 (1871).

It seems plain to me that it was the District Court's duty to provide this remedy, if the appellees, who invoked that court's jurisdiction under the Civil Rights Act, proved their charge that the appellants, under the color of the Virginia statutes, had deprived them of civil rights secured by the Federal Constitution.

＊　＊　＊　＊　＊　＊

We need not—we should not—give deference to a state policy that seeks to undermine paramount federal law. We fail to perform the duty expressly enjoined by Congress on the federal judiciary in the Civil Rights Acts when we do so.

In the present case my associates join in abstaining from deciding what they believe to be solely a matter of state law. Without retaining any jurisdiction whatsoever, they dismiss the case and invite the plaintiff to litigate her constitutional claim in state courts, but give her no assurance that she can get expeditious determination of her claim in state courts. They ignore the facts that the plaintiff was beginning her second trimester of pregnancy and that any state court litigation would take time—perhaps a great deal of time. In the present case we are not called upon to decide anything like "a constitutional challenge to Michigan's Watercraft Pollution Control Act of 1970", discussed by Judge Anderson in his opinion. In such a case a delay in obtaining a decision on the merits is not especially crucial. Here, however, we were called upon to decide whether a particular woman can have an abortion in Utah during the first trimester of pregnancy without state interference. In this case a delay in obtaining a decision on the merits will have extraordinary consequences. It may be good policy to abstain in the Watercraft Pollution Control Act case, but it is unconscionable to abstain in the case before this Court.

One of the principal costs of the abstention doctrine is the prolonged delay it often brings in its wake. For example, the use of the doctrine kept the Spector case in the federal courts for almost a decade. See Spector Motor Service v. McLaughlin, 323 U.S. 101, 65 S.Ct. 152, 89 L.Ed. 101 (1944) (decision requiring abstention), and Spector Motor Service v. O'Connor, 340 U.S. 602, 71 S. Ct. 508, 95 L.Ed. 573 (1951) (decision on the merits.) In United States v. Leiter Minerals, Inc., 381 U.S. 413, 85 S.Ct. 1575, 14 L.Ed.2d 692 (1965), the case was dismissed as moot eight years after abstention was ordered.

Justice Douglas' experience with abstention caused him to reexamine completely the doctrine in England v. Louisiana State Board of Medical Examiners, 375 U.S. 411, 423, 84 S.Ct. 461, 11 L.Ed.2d 440 (1964) (concurring opinion). He would scrap the doctrine on the grounds that it necessitates multiple law suits, increases the costs and time period of litigation, undermines federal jurisdiction especially in civil rights cases, and creates procedural traps for the unwary.

In the recent case of Harris County Commissioners Court et al. Moore, 420 U.S. 77, 95 S.Ct. 870 , 875, 43 L.Ed.2d 32 (1975), in which the Supreme Court reviewed and applied the abstention doctrine, the Court said:

> We have repeatedly warned, however, that because of the delays inherent in the abstention process and the danger that valuable federal rights might be lost in the absence of expeditious adjudication in the federal court, abstention must be invoked only in "special circumstances", see Zwicker v. Koota, 389 U.S. 241, 248 [88 S.Ct. 391, 395, 19 L.Ed.2d 444] (1967), and only upon careful consideration of the facts of each case. Baggett v. Bullitt, 377 U.S. 360, 375–379, 84 S.Ct. 1316, 1324–1327, 12 L.Ed.2d 377 (1964); Raiload Comm'n v. Pullman Co., *supra*, 312 U.S. [496] at 500 [61 S.Ct. 643, at 645, 85 L.Ed. 971].

In the present case, "because of the delays inherent in the abstention process and the danger that valuable federal rights might be lost in the absence of expeditious adjudication in the federal court", there should have been no abstention. Here, at the time of the hearing on whether temporary injunctive relief should be issued, the plaintiff was beginning her second trimester of pregnancy. Because the interests of the plaintiff and of the State substantially change during the second and third thrimesters of pregnancy, and because of the delay necessitated by requiring the plaintiff to initiate proceedings in state courts, there was no feasible alternative to the adjudication of her constitutional claim in this Court. Even a minimal delay in state court adjudication of her claim would create "the danger that valuable federal rights might be lost in the absence of expeditious adjudication in the federal court." Thus, this Court should have proceeded to decide the plaintiff's claim on the merits.

For the reasons stated above, I believe that abstention in this case was an improper exercise of discretion from which I dissent.

Index